THE IMAGE-MAKERS

THE IMAGE-MAKERS

POWER AND PERSUASION ON MADISON AVENUE

WILLIAM MEYERS

NYT
Times
BOOKS

Published by TIMES BOOKS,
The New York Times Book Co., Inc.
130 Fifth Avenue, New York, N.Y. 10011

Published simultaneously in Canada by
Fitzhenry & Whiteside, Ltd., Toronto

Library of Congress Cataloging in Publication Data

Meyers, William.
  The image-makers.

  Bibliography: p.223
  Includes index.
  1. Advertising—Psychological aspects. I. Title.
HF5822.M42 1984   659.1   84-40106
ISBN 0-8129-1135-0

Manufactured in the United States of America

84 85 86 87 88 5 4 3 2 1

For Deborah

ACKNOWLEDGMENTS

I began this book with the idea of explaining America's post–World War II consumer culture, which has helped mold our values, attitudes, and beliefs over the past three decades. Once I immersed myself in the project, however, I discovered what a challenging—and often daunting—undertaking this really was. Fortunately, I received guidance, assistance, and encouragement from others over the past two years—and for that I am grateful. *The Image-Makers* could not have been written without the support of many bright, generous, and sensitive people.

First, I'd like to thank Edward M. Meyers and Betty Gardner-Meyers, advertising executives with thirty years of experience on Madison Avenue, who also happen to be my parents. Their marketing acumen has been instrumental in stimulating my interest in the agency business.

My agent, Rollene W. Saal, bolstered me throughout the writing of this book, providing as much attention as any author ever received.

At Times Books, I owe a great deal to Joseph Consolino, Jonathan Segal, and Roger Straus, who initially endorsed this project, and to Kathleen Moloney, my editor, who helped shape *The Image-Makers* from the very beginning with her creative suggestions and close reading of the manuscript.

I could not have penetrated the complex and often obscure world of modern advertising without the help of more than 200 marketing executives and analysts around the country, who provided me with the insights and information on which this book is primarily based. Many of these men and women agreed to assist me on the condition that their names and companies not be mentioned in print. I have respected these confidential agreements in the belief that this was the only way to find out what really goes on behind Madison Avenue's closed doors.

Several Ad Alley veterans went out of their way for me, and their kindness must be mentioned here. Mark Stroock of Young & Rubicam helped steer me through difficult straits on numerous occasions by pointing me in the right direction and introducing me to people who always turned out to have interesting and provocative things to say. Celestine Frankenberg, also of Young & Rubicam, assisted me with hours of research. Norman Goluskin, the president of Smith/Greenland advertising in New York, understands the science of marketing as well as anyone on Madison Avenue today, and my many conversations with him over the years have proved invaluable.

Advertising people weren't the only ones who helped me to complete this manuscript. At *The New York Times,* my former employer, Max Frankel, and Charlotte Curtis encouraged me and gave me a sense of positive achievement. In Houston, Mack and Cece Fowler offered the warmth and comfort of friendship. And in Santa Fe, Diane Jergins was a never-failing source of optimism. Linda and George Austin-Martin of Santa Fe's Computer School provided the word processor on which I wrote this book.

Finally, I want to thank Deborah C. Phillips, my wife and a fellow journalist, who kept me on track with her support and wise editorial input.

October 1984

In our factory, we make lipstick;
In our advertising, we sell hope.

—Charles Revson
  Founder of Revlon Cosmetics

CONTENTS

THE IMAGE-MAKERS

INTRODUCTION

The "Hidden Persuaders" Get Down to Business

In the late 1950s, sociologist Vance Packard shocked the nation with a searing exposé of the advertising industry called *The Hidden Persuaders*. As the title of his book makes clear, Packard believed that slick executives on Madison Avenue were manipulating consumers and, in essence, hoodwinking them into purchasing specific goods and services. The author's indictment revealed many of Ad Alley's darkest secrets—bringing to light its trickiest sales techniques as well as its contempt for the American public. After dragging agency copywriters and art directors over the coals, Packard concluded his controversial study on a cautionary note. If the advertising business was left unchecked, he warned, it would eventually run our lives.

Today, almost three decades after *The Hidden Persuaders* was first published, Vance Packard's stinging prophecy has, for the most part, come true. Madison Avenue's power and presence in contemporary America are more directly felt than ever before, and Ad Alley's wizards have firmly established themselves as both the creators and the controllers of our consumer culture.

Marketers have had to refine their sales pitches, exploit the electronic media, and channel enormous sums of money into commercial campaigns in order to achieve their current position of dominance in this country. But as a result of their long-term efforts—which were only just beginning when Packard's hard-hitting book appeared—they are now able virtually to dictate the foods we eat, the soda or beer we drink, the cigarettes we smoke, the clothes we wear, the cars we drive, even the Presidents we elect.

Madison Avenue contributes little of tangible value to our society; its primary objective is to reap the financial rewards of the manic—and often unnecessary—public purchasing it induces. To keep us spending, spending, spending, Ad Alley has thoroughly blanketed our environment with its handiwork. From highway billboards to mass-transit displays, from newspaper or magazine ads to 30-second television commercials, advertising is everywhere. It is just as much a fact of life today as, say, paying taxes—and there's no escaping it.

The American marketing community bombarded consumers in this country with approximately $80 billion worth of sales messages last year, a promotional expenditure that exceeded the entire gross national product of oil-rich Saudi Arabia. This sum also represented more money than the United States government allocated for domestic health or education programs in 1983. During the past twelve months, America spent approximately $350 per person on commercials and ads, while Japan, the second-largest advertiser among nations, with total media billings of $12 billion, spent just $95 per citizen.

Perhaps the most significant indication of Ad Alley's overall strength and importance, however, is the crucial role it plays in the grand economic scheme of things. John Kenneth Galbraith—the venerable economist—once estimated during the late 1960s that if Madison Avenue's television commercials were to vanish suddenly from the screen, the gross national product of the United States would shrink by over 50 percent.

Television's dynamic technology, more than any other factor, has been responsible for the advertising industry's rise to prominence in this nation over the past few decades.

In recent years, Ad Alley has consistently capitalized on the knowledge that the American public's favorite leisure-time activity is watching the tube. Consumers in nearly 84 million households from coast to coast currently flip on their television sets whenever they're not working or sleeping, and, as a result, they end up sitting in front of the magic box for an average of seven hours each day. This video audience has proved to be irresistible for Madison Avenue executives, who spent approximately $20 billion on television commercials last year—a twentyfold increase over their electronic expenditures in 1957, when *The Hidden Persuaders* was published. Thirty seconds of prime time on one of the three major television networks today costs almost $100,000—an exorbitant price, but one that many marketers say they don't mind paying, because broadcast advertising reaches millions of viewers across the country at one time.

Ad Alley's leaders believe that television commercials are an effective form of salesmanship. The half-minute spot—with its mesmerizing combination of sight, sound, and motion—is revered on Madison Avenue for its unique ability to drum a marketing message into a consumer's head. Apart from a wide range of sit-coms, soaps, and shoot-'em-ups, the average television viewer is exposed to approximately 700 commercials a week—as many as 3,000 a month. Today's typical television watcher knows as much about how Colonel Sanders makes his Kentucky Fried Chicken as he does about how J. R. Ewing makes his "Dallas" millions. By the time a youngster graduates from high school in this country, he's probably seen over half a million of these hypnotic 30-second sales pitches; in addition to the three Rs, he can probably recite a litany of familiar jingles—from the McDonald's chain's "You Deserve a Break Today" to Ma Bell's "Reach Out and Touch Someone" to Anheuser-Busch's "This Bud's for You."

To ensure that its commercials are persuasive and memorable, Madison Avenue constantly updates its sales techniques.

The 30-second spot—video haiku—has to be continuously fine-tuned if Ad Alley is to remain one step ahead of the public.

During the late 1950s, when Vance Packard reported on the state of the American marketing establishment, television advertising was pretty primitive. Most agency creative people functioned like individual artists in those days, and their quirky, eccentric commercials reflected an intensely personal vision. Instead of using complex consumer research and incorporating the potential purchaser's feelings, tastes, or attitudes in their ads, Madison Avenue's electronic pioneers seemed to pull their sales messages out of thin air. After scribbling their ideas down, Ad Alley's veterans gauged their commercials' chances for success by "running them up the flagpole"; if enough people in the office thought the spots made sense, they were filmed and broadcast to the entire nation.

Madison Avenue has come a long way since then. Each year, it has honed its creative strategy in order to persuade an increasingly astute and cynical citizenry to purchase its clients' products. As a result of all this tinkering, Ad Alley's new and improved salesmanship is smoother, more subtle, and more sophisticated today than it has ever been.

Unlike the impulsive, intuitive agency people of thirty years ago, the advertising executive of the 1980s is a buttoned-down technician, more of a scientist than an artist. The contemporary ad man relies on reams of cold, hard research data rather than individual imagination to induce people to buy. He doesn't conjure up commercials; he builds them, as if they were complex pieces of computer hardware.

At the heart of Madison Avenue's new, elaborately engineered system of persuasion lies one fundamental premise: Each group in our society has its weaknesses and deep-seated emotional needs. If Ad Alley can uncover these psychological problems in the course of its lengthy interviews with citizens and then devise 30-second television spots that make it seem as if ordinary, everyday products are part of the soothing solution, grateful and relieved consumers will purchase the advertised goods. Agencies can make big profits by isolating and identifying each population segment's vulnerabilities, transforming average run-of-the-mill items into magic panaceas, and then targeting their newly designed therapeutic sales pitches at the right cluster of people.

The American marketing community's exploitive brand of psychoanalysis is perhaps best described by one of its most prosperous—and candid—practitioners, Jerry Della Femina, author of *From Those Wonderful Folks Who Gave You Pearl Harbor*. In a 1981 magazine interview, the outspoken ad executive said: "Advertising deals in open sores. . . . Fear. Greed. Anger. Hostility. You name the dwarfs and we play on every one. We play on all the emotions and on all the problems, from not getting ahead . . . to the desire to be one of the crowd. Everyone has a button. If enough people have the same button, you have a successful ad and a successful product."

Some of America's largest and most profitable corporations fattened up their bottom lines during the past decade by employing the psycho-sell. Pushing the right buttons in their television campaigns enabled these companies to "solve" millions of needy consumers' personal problems. As a reward for restoring ailing citizens to emotional health, the firms received their appreciative "patients' " loyal patronage.

McDonald's, Coke, Pepsi, and Ma Bell, for example, helped to fill the gap in lonely people's lives by running warm, family-oriented commercials that stressed togetherness. Once these advertisers were associated with belonging in the public's mind, they gained the support of many in this country who yearned for a sense of community and human connection. On the other hand, cigarette brands such as Marlboro, Camel, and Winston linked themselves with macho self-reliance and toughness in their ads, and this helped them to win over impressionable young consumers in search of an identity. Johnnie Walker Black positioned itself as a deluxe scotch, emphasizing status, affluence, and elegance in order to attract insecure social climbers. And Japanese automobile manufacturers beat Detroit at its own game by communicating practicality and simplicity in their sales pitches aimed at rebellious antiestablishment individualists.

The erosion of the powerful middle class—which had dominated the consumer culture of the United States since the end of World War II—first began with the economic hardships and political upheavals of the Johnson and Nixon years. Gradually, the nation was transformed from one vast homogeneous community bound by shared materialistic goals into a mosaic of smaller, more diverse markets that revealed an eclecticism previously unknown in this country. The birth of fragmented America—and the death of the mass audience—was confirmed during the early 1970s, when such venerable general-circulation magazines as *Life, Look,* and *The Saturday Evening Post* went out of business. These general-interest magazines were replaced by a host of special-interest publications that catered to every conceivable group in the marketplace—from body-building enthusiasts to science-fiction buffs to gourmet-food fans.

The recent development and growth of cable television, with its individualized programming designed to appeal to special audiences, is another solid indication of how diffused our society has become. As the "narrowcasting" revolution has taken hold in cities and towns across the country over the last ten years, the centralized broadcast networks have lost large numbers of thoughtful viewers, who feel that the mass-oriented shows on ABC, CBS, and NBC aren't nourishing or interesting enough. The segmentation of the United States has even permeated the governmental process. Washington is run today by fervent, fire-breathing single-issue groups—not by broad-based coalitions, as in the past. Environmentalists, tax-cutters, right-to-lifers, and antinukers all want to be heard by Congress, and they are prepared to put their votes—and dollars—where their causes are.

One group of citizens is rapidly emerging as the most important and influential element in America's new social, cultural, and political mosaic. Baby-boomers—those people born in the affluent post–World War II era—have come of age, and they are beginning to make their presence felt. After experiencing an adolescence filled with protest, drugs, free love, and rock music, they have brought an entirely new set of values and attitudes to mainstream American society. Unlike their outer-directed, upwardly mobile parents, members of the Woodstock Generation—or, as journalist Landon Y. Jones has dubbed them, the superclass—place a premium on the Five I's: innovation, introspection, individuality, intellect, and integrity. They care as much about preserving the wilderness and world peace as they do about achieving material comfort or success.

By 1990, the superclass will account for approximately one-third of the nation's total population. Obviously, reaching this enormous segment of consumers represents a major challenge for marketers in this country; if Ad Alley and its clients wish to remain profitable over the next ten years, they must find a way to sell their goods to these inner-directed baby-boomers. Unfortunately, however, most of Madison Avenue's executives have thus far failed to communicate effectively with this difficult and demanding group. A large number of the advertising industry's commercials targeted at the Woodstock Generation today continue to stress prestige, status, or professional fulfillment; and many 30-second spots intended for the counterculture are filled with traditional—and outdated—Middle American clichés.

Despite Ad Alley's general inability to talk the baby-boomers' language, there are a handful of shrewd marketers on Madison Avenue who have successfully captured the loyalty of this lucrative consumer audience. Apple Computers, for example, has been able to win over inner-directed citizens by positioning its machines as friendly mind-expanders, not corporate accouterments; and Clinique cosmetics has gained a strong following among Woodstock women by promoting its products as understated natural health aids rather than flashy artificial beauty-inducers.

The future on Madison Avenue belongs to those agencies that can unlock the pocketbooks of counterculture consumers throughout America. Although very few advertising enterprises have yet to come to grips with the growing inner-directed realities that now confront them, the opportunities for profit in this marketplace are too great to be ignored. Undoubtedly, Ad Alley's polished and persuasive executives—with their vast arsenal of scientific weaponry—will soon come up with a scheme that persuades skeptical baby-boomers to purchase enthusiastically and without cynicism.

After all, the psycho-salesmen always seem to get their way.

1 PSYCHOGRAPHICS
Advertising Discovers the World According to VALS

Madison Avenue was in deep trouble a decade ago. After almost twenty-five years of unparalleled prosperity and growth —due in large part to the emergence of television as a powerful sales tool—it was no longer able to persuade the American public to purchase its clients' goods and services. Like a star pitcher who mysteriously loses the control of his fastball, the advertising industry's deft marketing touch had vanished.

The sudden disappearance of Ad Alley's consumer clout during the early 1970s shocked and alarmed advertisers across the country. Once-prosperous companies, realizing that their commercials were having little or no impact on potential customers, watched in dismay as their sales dropped, inventories grew, and bottom lines shrank.

The Age of Affluence, begun in the afterglow of World War II, was over. Buffeted by repeated bouts of inflation and recession, the average citizen was more concerned with coping and surviving than consuming and shopping. Even when marketers pushed America's BUY button—as they did frequently—it was

11

often difficult for people to pay for advertised products and still make the monthly mortgage payments.

Between 1970 and 1981, stagflation slashed the purchasing power of a dollar by nearly 60 percent; productivity plummeted, and foreign competition took more than 2 million industrial jobs away from American workers, more and more of whom went on unemployment. And, naturally, debt deepened—from 35 percent of after-tax income in 1955 to 85 percent in 1975—as consumers tried to keep up with both the Joneses and the Consumer Price Index.

The Age of Leisure ended, too, as an increasing number of American women began making the daily trek to the office or factory. Stay-at-home females had traditionally been the advertising executive's favorite audience—chauvinists in the business called them "sitting ducks"—easy to reach on the tube via morning game shows or afternoon soap operas. These ladies, who had once welcomed visits from the Man from Glad and other Madison Avenue sales surrogates, were suddenly unavailable to advertisers during most of the day. They had exchanged the coffee klatch for the executive lunch, and the cleansing power of suds didn't matter so much anymore.

The Age of Innocence also came to a close, and the Age of Cynicism dawned. Skeptical and hostile consumers, wounded by Vietnam and wary after Watergate, turned against Madison Avenue and its version of the American Dream. Ralph Nader led the revolt against advertising's hidden persuaders and hucksters by pointing out their propensity for half-truth, exaggeration, and misrepresentation. He wasn't all wrong.

During the 1950s, executives up and down Ad Alley had created commercials that played fast and loose with the public. They put marbles in a bowl of soup so the few vegetables it contained would float to the top; they sprayed shaving cream, rather than real whipped cream, on a dessert to make it look richer; and they dressed actors as doctors and let them endorse drugs.

The advertising industry wasn't above using scare tactics to move goods thirty years ago either. One commercial warned of the "dangers" of heartburn and the "benefits" of an antacid tablet by pouring "stomach acid" over a handkerchief until it burned a hole in the cloth. Other phony demonstrations were common, too. One razor blade manufacturer had a piece of sandpaper "shaved" as smooth as silk on television to con men into buying its product.

The ads of the 1960s were equally hollow, although they were a bit more sophisticated. Consumers were still taken for granted and treated like ten-year-olds by Madison Avenue, which now relied on the gimmick instead of the trick as its primary tool of persuasion. Braniff Airlines painted its planes in bold, colorful patterns designed by the artist Alexander Calder and dressed its stewardesses in uniforms by Emilio Pucci. The advertising campaign crowed that this marked "The End of the Plain Plane," but it never mentioned what was in it for passengers. Hathaway threw a black eyepatch on a model to help make its shirts seem more stylish, and a bearded Commander Whitehead from Britain was recruited to make the drinking of tonic water appear cosmopolitan.

The 1960s were also the days when Tony the Tiger roared loudly to kids that Kellogg's Frosted Flakes were *G-r-r-reat,* even if they did contain an overdose of sugar, and the Pillsbury Doughboy waddled about on behalf of frozen rolls that were kept alive with chemicals and preservatives. And a rugged, healthy-looking cowboy became Marlboro's enduring symbol, riding off into the sunset inhaling the clean, fresh air of the Wild West between puffs on cancer-causing cigarettes. With a track record like this, it's no wonder that by the 1970s advertising executives regularly appeared at the bottom of the public's "most respected profession" list—below insurance salesmen and pawnshop proprietors.

Madison Avenue received its lowest marks from the members of the Woodstock Generation, who in the 1970s were dropping out of the consumer culture that Ad Alley had taken such pains to create. This group, of about 50 million disillusioned people between the ages of twenty-five and forty, constitutes approximately 20 percent of the total United States population today. Advertisers had been counting on these post–World War II baby-boomers to follow in the footsteps of their upwardly mobile parents, to become the strivers of tomorrow. But the stress and strain required for success made no sense to the children of the counterculture. They refused to accept the burden of ambition, and they rejected materialism. They sought inner growth rather than goods, meaning instead of money, personal fulfillment over power, and liberty over luxury. And this drove advertising executives crazy.

With their backs to the wall, advertising agency people were forced to examine where they had gone wrong and why consumers had begun to resist their sales pitches. After intensive study and research, the executives finally concluded that America was undergoing fundamental changes that were dramatically altering our society's values, attitudes, and beliefs. It became clear that Madison Avenue's old-fashioned gimmicks and stunts were no longer relevant to the average citizen. In short, we were living in a new age.

To get the rebellious public purchasing again, Ad Alley devised a new marketing technique: image transformation. This approach, known along Madison Avenue as the "face lift," sought to increase the value and worth of mundane mass products in the consumer's mind. By performing "plastic surgery" on various items and making them seem more appealing, advertising executives believed they could recycle and sell a host of goods and services that people said—or thought—they didn't want. Based on sophisticated psychological principles, this subtle form of manipulation linked products to people's most pressing vulnerabilities while offering them easy remedies for their anxieties and insecurities. A campaign that offered people an emotional reward improved their perception of an item. By associating blue jeans with sex appeal or cigarettes with peer approval, for example, Ad Alley was able to cajole recalcitrant citizens into buying. What's important to a potential customer on the verge of purchasing is how he feels about a product—not how, or whether, it works. Brand personality triumphs over brand performance.

To implement this innovative and insightful marketing strategy, Madison Avenue began dividing up Americans according to their innermost needs—their fears, desires, and prejudices. It adopted *psychographics,* as opposed to the Census Bureau's traditional demographics, to ensure that its sales pitches were aimed at the most susceptible consumer targets. Ad executives no longer relied exclusively on mere statistics to assess their audience. Instead, they developed detailed profiles of each population segment's attitudes and beliefs.

Agency-employed psychologists and sociologists refined this art of emotional exploitation by using a variety of psychographic research systems. For example, several shops conducted extensive interviews with consumers and partitioned the public into Resistant, Successful, and Traditional adapters— people who were either open to change and new ideas or tied to conventional standards. One firm broke the country down into Easy Streeters, Service Seekers, Environmentally Concerned, and The Resigned. Another company labeled post– World War II baby-boomers the "Sensation Generation," because its findings revealed that these consumers yearned for a rich and varied life-style.

One of the most widely used psychographic approaches on Ad Alley today, however, is VALS (Values and Life-Styles), designed by SRI International (formerly known as Stanford Research Institute) in Northern California. The world according to VALS is simple. There are essentially five basic groups of citizens in this nation—Belongers, Emulators, Emulator-Achievers, Societally Conscious Achievers, and the Need-Directed. Each segment of VALSociety is driven by its own special demons, demons that the advertising industry seeks to exorcise with its 30-second television commercials and print ads.

Whether today's marketers use the actual VALS terminology or another psychographic system, SRI's research approach accurately represents the way Madison Avenue divides America's consuming public into easily defined segments. The VALS labels are used throughout this book.

VALS tells us that almost one out of three citizens in the United States today is a *Belonger*—the typical traditionalist, the cautious and conforming conservative. Archie Bunker is a Belonger; he believes in God, country, and family. The lifeblood of the Belonger's world is a strong community consciousness. Change is his archenemy. Without a secure, stable, and structured society, this staunch defender of the status quo is unable to cope.

The Belonger's consumer profile reflects his old-fashioned view of things. He usually drives a Dodge or a Plymouth; he drinks Coke, Pepsi, or Budweiser; he eats at McDonald's with the family; he loves Jell-O; and his wife scrubs the bathroom tiles with Lestoil or Spic and Span.

In the 1970s, Belongers were caught by surprise as their sheltered environment, so carefully constructed through the years, was dismantled bit by bit. The cherished concept of a happy home and hearth withered over the decade as nonfamilial living in America increased by 75 percent, largely because of divorce and the flight of young adults from the nest at an earlier age. By 1980, one out of four American households was headed by a single man or woman. The spirit of community camaraderie faded away as approximately 50 percent of all Americans hit the road, often moving from the densely populated inner-city neighborhoods of the Northeast and Midwest to the sprawling suburbs and rural ranges of the Sunbelt. A sense of self-sufficiency also evaporated during these ten years; paychecks from industrial jobs and hard manual labor, which had once fueled the Belonger's faith in the American Dream, were gradually lost as the industrial economy shriveled and a service economy took its place.

Madison Avenue rescues Belongers and helps bind their psychic wounds with commercials that offer a world of idealized images. McDonald's, for example, uses the Big Mac in its ad campaigns to lure the shattered family back together. Pepsi and Coke have traditionally featured picnics and Frisbee flings. Ma Bell eases the loneliness of long-distance relationships with its "Reach Out and Touch Someone" campaign. And Miller Beer's advertising reinforces the warm glow of fraternity to help lessen the pressures of the workplace.

Emulators are not so set in their ways. They are a small but impressionable group of young people in desperate search of an identity and a place in the adult working world. These kids, who represent about 15 percent of the American population, will do almost anything to fit in. Most of them lack self-confidence and are discouraged about their prospects. They envision little future for themselves in our society. They compensate for this pessimism with unabashed personal hedonism. Confused and vulnerable, Emulators will purchase products from advertisers who offer solutions to their postadolescent dilemmas. In dealing with Emulators, advertisers prey on their insecurity.

Chevrolet, for example, has sold hundreds of thousands of Camaros to these uncertain youngsters by positioning the vehicle as the coolest car on the market. Dr. Pepper became a major soft drink in this country with its "Be a Pepper" campaign, which offered teenagers the reassurance of group acceptance and friendship. The tobacco business also capitalized on this segment's precarious sense of self-worth.

During the 1970s, the cigarette industry became a tough-but-tender authority figure for Emulators. With most adult smokers already hooked on their favorite brands, the growth of individual tobacco companies depends on the uninitiated. That's why cigarette manufacturers spend almost $2 billion a year trying to get youngsters to light up. By law, these corporations can't harness the power of television to advertise, so instead they have created a striking iconography in newspapers and magazines.

Tobacco ads featuring heroes and heroines, Madison Avenue's idea of role models, help unsure Emulators to find themselves. The solitary cowboy's message for young men is to smoke Marlboro if they want to be independent and strong. The macho outdoorsmen from Camel and Winston seem to say, "Take a puff of this and you'll be tough like us." The Kool campaign, associating that brand with a hip jazz ensemble, lets young blacks know that it's cool to smoke Kools.

Fashionable ladies symbolizing Virginia Slims inject young women with the positive spirit of accomplishment. If this is your cigarette, they seem to be saying, all good things are possible—especially a glamorous and profitable career. The message must be getting through. Despite medical studies linking tobacco to cancer, the number of female teenage smokers in this country has increased by 40 percent since 1975.

Emulator-Achievers, America's materialists, have already made it. These acquisitive consumers often own a Mercedes; they feel most comfortable with such "uptown" brand names as Dom Pérignon, Tiffany, or Gucci; and they have to have the latest in high-tech toys—Sony's Betamax or Casio's wristwatch television.

Although they have reached a prosperous plateau of middle-class success and status, Emulator-Achievers still want to derive even greater financial rewards from the system. But the new era of limits has cramped their hard-driving style, making additional monetary gains next to impossible. Emulator-Achievers, approximately 20 percent of the population, are in a funk. Once they believed the sky was the limit; today they feel frustrated, perhaps a bit cheated, stuck just below the top rung of the economic ladder. Despite their relative affluence, three-quarters of these striving citizens said they were dissatisfied with the quality of their lives in the early 1980s. Over 50 percent of them feared they wouldn't be able to attain their fiscal goals during the coming decade.

Madison Avenue cheers up Emulator-Achievers with commercials that transform everyday items into accouterments of accomplishment, success, and taste. Advertisers convince these compulsive consumers that by purchasing certain products they will be seen as the modern aristocrats they seek to be.

Clothing manufacturers such as Ralph Lauren and Izod, who put little polo players and alligators on the breast pockets of cotton shirts, offer simple togs with fancy prices that give consumers a sense of upper-crust respectability. And one recent ad for Johnnie Walker Black showed a picture of a mansion with a lawn stretching as far as the eye could see. The caption informed covetous Emulator-Achievers, "On the way up, the work may not get easier, but the rewards get better." The message was clear: Serve this scotch to your friends, and you'll be just like the landed gentry—even if you do live on half an acre in the suburbs. Ad executives know that to get Emulator-

Achievers into the stores, you've got to offer them the opportunity to be king or queen for a day.

Societally Conscious Achievers are the flower children of America's consumer culture. They are members of the post–World War II baby-boom generation who care more about inner peace and environmental safety than about financial success and elegant surroundings. Personal, not professional, fulfillment matters most to these individualists. Societally Conscious Achievers, constituting approximately 20 percent of the U.S. population, are experimental—they will try anything from acupuncture to Zen, as long as it fits into their uncomplicated life-style. Unlike the Emulator-Achievers, whose materialistic drives are constrained by the economy, these gradually graying hippies are self-constrained in their purchasing behavior. Many of them are dropouts from the world of commerce—reformed strivers who no longer see the need for conspicuous consumption.

A typical Societally Conscious Achiever might be an antiques dealer living in a nineteenth-century barn he restored himself. Instead of spending his weekends carousing at the country club with doctors, lawyers, or stockbrokers, he's busy tending to his organic garden. A lover of the outdoors, he wants to share this experience with his kids, who spend their free time hiking through the woods rather than playing video games.

Societally Conscious Achievers often shop for their clothing by mail, choosing L. L. Bean moccasins over Gucci loafers, and they usually drive small foreign cars—Mazda, Honda, Volvo, or Subaru. Lighter wines or such wholesome beverages as herbal tea, fruit juice, or bottled water are preferred by these inner-directed citizens to the scotch, vodka, or gin that their parents drink. If they smoke at all, counterculturalists generally puff on "healthy" low-tar Merits. These fitness-oriented citizens also take their exercise seriously; Nike and New Balance running shoes are essential parts of their athletic wardrobe.

Societally Conscious Achievers are the ad industry's toughest challenge. They turn a deaf ear to advertising unless it whispers softly. They need to be told in their own iconoclastic language that their low-key values and attitudes make sense. Several imported car manufacturers have won the confidence of Societally Conscious Achievers by emphasizing such counterculture buzzwords as "simplicity" and "integrity." Volvo calls itself "a car you can believe in." Subaru says it's "inexpensive, and built to stay that way."

Societally Conscious Achievers are elusive, but they are the fastest-growing and most influential group of citizens in the country. It is estimated that by 1990 almost one-third of the United States will share their practical world view. As a result, an increasing number of marketers are quickly learning the new vocabulary and switching from high-tech to high-touch commercials.

Need-Directed Americans are the survivors, the people struggling to sustain themselves on subsistence incomes. Mostly welfare recipients, Social Security beneficiaries, and minimum-wage earners, these citizens, who represent close to 15 percent of the country, aren't consumers in the true sense of the word. They're so busy trying to make ends meet that they really don't have time to worry about the type of beer they drink or the image projected by the cigarettes they smoke. The Need-Directed aren't driving new cars or acquiring state-of-the-art personal computers, and they rarely have enough money to take the family out for even a fast-food meal.

As far as Ad Alley is concerned, the Need-Directed don't exist. They are the people who are least affected by television commercials in this country. When you're dirt-poor, a dollar will stretch only so far, and you buy what you can afford. Even the wizards of Madison Avenue can't find a cure for poverty.

2 PIONEERS OF PERSUASION
The Wheel Is Invented

Madison Avenue as we know it today began thirty years ago, in 1954. That year several ad executives, led by the late Rosser Reeves, then head of Ted Bates & Company, met for a three-martini lunch at the Baroque, a French restaurant on Manhattan's East 53rd Street. It was there that Reeves dazzled his underlings by sketching the world's first real television commercial.

The 60-second sales message he created was for Anacin, a headache remedy marketed by American Home Products. In quick, broad strokes, before the group ordered its meal, Reeves drew the outline of a man's skull on a linen napkin. Inside it, he put three boxes. One contained a crackling lightning bolt, another a creaky spring, and the last a pounding hammer. The idea was to illustrate the symptoms of a throbbing headache. Toward the end of the finished commercial, Reeves planned to have an announcer calmly ask viewers: "Are you looking for fast, fast, *fast* relief? Then take Anacin. Anacin stops headache pain fast, relieves tension fast, and calms jittery nerves fast. Anacin—for fast, fast, *fast* relief." Once this pitch was made, the cacophony of lightning bolts, coiled springs, and hammers would mercifully cease.

As the luncheon drew to a close, Reeves, the son of a fiery fundamentalist preacher from Virginia, offered a rousing benediction, telling his slightly inebriated colleagues that the Anacin commercial would prove to be one of the most lucrative pieces of mass communication ever produced. He was right. Seven years after the doodles on the napkin were transferred to television, the noisy sales message was still going strong, and the mighty pill had made more money for American Home Products than *Gone With the Wind* had grossed for MGM in a quarter of a century.

With his ability to harness the immense power of television, Rosser Reeves transformed advertising almost overnight from low-keyed salesmanship into high-powered persuasion. Known along Madison Avenue as "the blacksmith," he believed that commercials should be mind-pulverizing. To be effective, they had to bludgeon people into buying.

Reeves's aggressive assault on American consumers was a radical departure from the way the advertising industry had traditionally conducted business. The first ad executives, who appeared on the scene just over a century ago, were content to buy space from magazines and then sell it to clients—at a hefty profit, of course. From 1870 to 1900, advertising was in the dark ages. The object was simply to keep the advertiser's name in front of the public. Ads were pedestrian, like the ones you find in high school yearbooks today; unimaginative copy such as "Compliments of Prudential Insurance" or "Cameras by Eastman Kodak" prevailed.

In the early 1900s, advertisers woke up, however, and began giving people *reasons* to purchase products. Reeves would have sneered at some of his predecessors' soft promises. Palmolive Soap offered women "a schoolgirl complexion"; Steinway pianos were called "the instrument of immortals"; and Squibb said its vitamins were made with the "priceless ingredient of integrity." In those days, nobody boasted or bragged, shouted or screamed. During the first half of the twentieth century, advertising remained demure, devoid of hype and

hucksterism—even after the birth of radio, the first mass me-
dium, in the 1920s. A retailer's recommendation used to mean
much more to the average citizen than a page in *The Saturday
Evening Post* or sponsorship of "The Lucky Strike Hit Parade."
The public wasn't motivated—or manipulated—by Madison
Avenue until television came into the picture.

It was then that Rosser Reeves and other bold ad men first
barged into the living rooms of millions of Americans. And
once inside, the intruders from Ad Alley refused to leave. They
spent exorbitant amounts of money making their presence felt,
tattooing their sales messages onto people's consciousness. In
1954, American Home Products, for example, backed Anacin
with the previously unheard-of sum of $20 million. That figure
was about forty times more than the nation's leading advertiser
in 1940, American Tobacco Company, had allocated for media
fourteen years earlier. And it dwarfed the $350 that Eastman
Kodak, one of the largest clients of the nineteenth century, paid
for magazine ads in 1873.

Anacin's $20 million campaign wouldn't raise many eye-
brows today, though. Business pressures have forced many
major marketers to expend as much as $50 million for commer-
cials and ads annually—just to stay competitive. Procter &
Gamble, which currently buys more advertising than any other
United States corporation, provided networks, magazines, and
newspapers with close to $1 billion last year.

Rosser Reeves's "go for the jugular" style of advertising and
his willingness to promote products with large amounts of
money revolutionized Madison Avenue and helped build a cottage industry into a global communications power. For example, Ted Bates & Company, the agency he helped launch in the
early 1940s on a shoestring budget, is today a $3 billion con-
glomerate with offices in more than fifty countries all over the
world.

Recognized as the founder of modern Madison Avenue,
Reeves was just one of the many audacious characters who has
populated Ad Alley over the years. James Walter Thompson,
who began the first advertising agency in 1867, also had a flair
for the dramatic. A twenty-year-old Civil War veteran who had

helped the Union cause by shoveling coal on a steamboat, Thompson secured a line of credit for his fledgling business by presenting the bank with documents that claimed he had been a commodore—and war hero—in the Navy. Despite this bit of chicanery, however, Thompson was worth backing. He understood earlier than anyone else that magazines and corporations needed one another if they were to grow. Before Thompson came along, periodicals did not solicit advertising, relying instead on subscription revenue alone. Manufacturers during the nineteenth century depended almost entirely on positive word of mouth for their sales. Thompson recognized the mutual advantages of bringing these two parties together: Companies could use magazines as a vehicle to promote their goods and services, and publications could increase their income by selling ads.

Sensing an opportunity to cash in as a matchmaker, Thompson went to several journals and, serving as agent for aspiring advertisers, offered to buy pages from them each week. The magazines turned him down cold, saying that advertising would tarnish their image and alienate readers. But the young entrepreneur wouldn't take no for an answer, and he began to play rough. With borrowed capital, he bought large interests in several major periodicals, eventually forcing the magazines to accept ads. In only a short time, publications got used to the idea of making more money, and advertising became a widely accepted practice.

During the 1880s, Thompson made close to $5 million by purchasing cheap space in journals and selling it at almost twice the price to such companies as Eastman Kodak, Prudential Insurance, and Pabst Brewing. Keeping his overhead low, he ran a pipe-rack outfit out of a small, dank office in Manhattan. Clients got only what they paid for—pages in magazines. There were no copywriters or art directors to create ads; that was a job for the advertiser, not the advertising agent.

Thompson's penny-pinching ways made him a millionaire many times over, and his new moneyed status enabled him to hobnob with Cornelius Vanderbilt, Jim Fisk, and other affluent robber barons of the Gilded Age. His empire soon extended overseas with the establishment of a London office in 1900. By 1916, however, the executive sensed that the ad game had crested. Seeing little financial gain left in it, he sold his business for $20 million and turned to a life of yachting until his death, twelve years later. For all his genius, Thompson did not envision Madison Avenue's lucrative future. Today, the agency that still bears his name is the third-largest advertising enterprise in America, a $3 billion worldwide concern with a long list of blue-chip clients, including Ford Motor Company, Lever Brothers, Burger King, and, 117 years later, Eastman Kodak.

Albert Lasker, who dominated the advertising scene from 1900 to 1940, was Madison Avenue's greatest tycoon. He brought flash and flamboyance to Ad Alley the way David O. Selznick and Louis B. Mayer brought glitz and glamour to Hollywood. In 1898, Lasker left his home in Galveston, Texas, and joined Lord & Thomas, a Chicago agency. He was just eighteen years old. In only eight years, this brilliant and driven young man rose from the mailroom to the presidency of the company. His greatest strength was spotting, hiring, and then nurturing talent. He believed in the star system, and for a generation he surrounded himself with the best and brightest ad men money could buy.

Lasker's first coup took place in a smoky Chicago saloon in 1906. Late one afternoon, a messenger came to his office at Lord & Thomas and handed him a note that read: "I am in the bar downstairs and can tell you what advertising is. A meeting with me will mean much to you." It was signed "John E. Kennedy."

Intrigued, the busy ad executive took the elevator down to find Kennedy. The two men hit it off right away, talking and drinking together until midnight. Kennedy, a former Royal Canadian Mountie, believed that an ad should be salesmanship in print, not just news or publicity. Advertisers had to do more than merely inform people about their products, he said. They had to persuade the public to purchase. Lasker, impressed by this thinking, hired Kennedy for a staggering $50,000 a year—much more than the $2,000 yearly salary that most copywriters received at the time (many of today's creative heavyweights command only $100,000 a year).

Two years after Kennedy joined Lord & Thomas, Lasker discovered a forty-one-year-old ad man named C. C. Hopkins. Hopkins had come to Lasker's attention because of campaigns he had created for Bissell Carpet Sweepers, Swift Packaged Meats, and Dr. Shoop's Restorative, a highly regarded patent medicine of the early 1900s. His carefully crafted ads stressed the unique qualities of a product and listed specific reasons why it should be bought. People in the industry called this "scientific selling." During his fifteen-year tenure at Lord & Thomas, Hopkins produced many advertising classics that would influence consumers for generations to come: Schlitz was "the beer that made Milwaukee famous"; Quaker puffed oats were "shot from guns"; Goodyear made an "all-weather tire"; and Pepsodent was labeled "the film-removing toothpaste."

Despite his brass-knuckled copy, Hopkins was a shy, soft-spoken man who had really wanted to follow in his father's footsteps and become a minister. His family was so poor, however, that he was forced to turn to advertising, a better-paying profession. Lasker, a big-spending impresario, a flamboyant, George Steinbrenner type, brandished his large checkbook and tried to erase any regrets Hopkins might have had about not entering the church. He allowed his employee to set his own salary each year and approved it regularly without uttering a word. In 1912, Hopkins's astounding compensation package included $65,000 in base pay, a $30,000 cash bonus, and a car for his wife. Although Lasker made him a rich man, Hopkins remained frugal. Throughout his life, he refused to spend more than $6.50 on a pair of shoes.

Another Lasker advertising all-star rose to fame and fortune when the radio era began in the mid-1920s. Frank Hummert, a programming whiz, made Lord & Thomas millions of dollars by developing such soap operas as the Kleenex-sponsored "Story of Mary Marlowe." Back then, before there was a Federal Communications Commission, advertising agencies often wrote and produced radio shows as vehicles for their clients. Today, in

most cases, networks create televised entertainment independently, seeking Madison Avenue's ad dollars only after the fact.

Hummert and several of his colleagues also came up with the
idea of using celebrities to endorse products, a practice advertising executives—not to mention Bill Cosby, John Houseman,
James Garner, and Lauren Bacall, among others—still heartily
believe in. The Lord & Thomas men put Bob Hope to work on
behalf of Pepsodent; hired Bing Crosby to sing about MJB Coffee; signed Hedda Hopper, the Hollywood gossip columnist, to
represent Sunkist lemons and Armour canned meats; and recruited Frank Sinatra and Jack Benny to promote Lucky Strikes
and Pall Malls. By the time Hummert left Lasker's lair, in the late
1930s, to start his own agency, Lord & Thomas clients controlled the airwaves and sponsored close to three-quarters of all
radio shows.

Like Hummert, many of Lasker's ambitious protégés eventually departed from the successful shop. Several looked beyond
Madison Avenue for their careers. Alan Jay Lerner, for example,
gave up writing Lucky Strike radio commercials for the Broad-
way stage, and Jimmy Cannon traded his job as Lord & Thomas's public relations man for a life in sports journalism.

Employee turnover at Lord & Thomas was high because of
one man—George Washington Hill, the mercurial chairman of
American Tobacco Company and the most demanding client in
Madison Avenue history. To agency people working on his account, the cigarette marketer resembled the mad emperor
Nero. Hill—all 300 pounds of him—used to sit sprawled behind
a massive desk wearing a trout fisherman's hat, and from this
throne he spewed forth a steady stream of orders in a high-
pitched whine. The hard-driving tobacco merchant thought
nothing of waking copywriters at two in the morning to criti-
cize their ads, and he was known to scream in the middle of
crowded restaurants at account executives who didn't agree
with him.

Hill was totally obsessed with selling cigarettes. He refused to
deal with anyone who didn't smoke his company's products
(Lucky Strikes and Pall Malls were the main brands). The aggressive marketer pasted used cigarette packages in the windows of

his Rolls-Royce to get extra publicity, and he belittled his major competition, Camels, at every available opportunity. L.S./M.F.T. (Lucky Strike Means Fine Tobacco), the rhythmic chant that reverberated in the heads of smokers from the 1930s through the 1950s, was his own personal creation. To get women to light up, he devised the "Reach for a Lucky Instead of a Sweet" campaign. When the United States Army told him he couldn't continue to print the familiar green Lucky Strike package because a chemical contained in the ink was needed for the war effort against the Nazis, Hill changed to a white pack with a red bull's-eye and capitalized on this potentially disastrous loss by running patriotic ads that announced: "Lucky Strike Green Has Gone to War."

Working with the maniacal Hill finally became too much, even for Albert Lasker. The experience was filled with so much tumult and tension that he decided to leave the advertising business for good. Lasker certainly didn't need the money. During his forty-three years on Madison Avenue, he had amassed a fortune of almost $75 million. He owned a luxurious town-house on Manhattan's Beekman Place and had an art collection that included some superb Renoirs and Monets. And he didn't need the aggravation. He had a large coterie of friends with whom to spend time, including Walter Lippmann, the political pundit; David Sarnoff, head of RCA; Bill Paley, founder of CBS; and Robert Hutchins, president of the University of Chicago. And so, in December 1941, the ad man closed the doors of Lord & Thomas.

Lasker's spirit still lives on, however. One month after his retirement, a group of former colleagues reopened the agency under a new name—Foote, Cone & Belding—which it still retains today.

Luck, perhaps as much as any other factor, contributed to the great advertising boom of the 1950s. Although the invention of television provided Madison Avenue with the most powerful sales tool ever known, the tube probably would have had less impact on the buying public if the postwar economy had not been so bountiful. This was a golden age for advertisers, an idyllic time when everything went right and marketers had the world on a string, when big sales rolled in day after day with almost boring regularity.

After two decades of deprivation, during the Depression and World War II, there was enormous demand for products. People were hungry to purchase, and they had money to spend. Unemployment was virtually nonexistent, inflation was a cool 1 percent, and cheap energy was plentiful. The average citizen in the United States had six times as many discretionary dollars in his pocket in 1955 as he had had in 1940.

This rich and revitalized society was led by a mushrooming middle class of growing families, a large mass of upwardly mobile consumers who spent as much time in supermarkets as they did in their newly purchased suburban tract houses. Americans were busy making up for lost time.

Nobody on Ad Alley understood the consumer's midcentury cravings better than Rosser Reeves. He believed that every person's mind was divided into a series of purchasing receptacles marked "soap," "headache remedies," "toothpaste," "cigarettes," and so on. There is only so much room in each container, he said, so the advertiser must be certain that his sales message is crammed into the right space. To help ensure this, Reeves created commercials with a USP—a Unique Selling Proposition.

USP advertising singled out—and remorselessly pounded away at—the differences between his client's product and the competition's. Reeves spent huge sums of money on television time during which he drummed USPs into people's heads. Once the appropriate cranial container had been filled and the opposition's ads had been squeezed out, consumers would be conditioned to select the item that Reeves was pushing. Critics called the ad man a huckster and referred to his hard-hitting campaigns as brainwashing, and there was more than a little truth in these accusations. Nonetheless, during the 1950s his dramatic sales techniques succeeded in promoting everything from orange juice to ballpoint pens.

When Mars candy started losing business to Hershey's, it came to Reeves for assistance. The ad executive quickly real-

ized that M&M's— the bite-sized, sugar-coated nuggets produced by Mars—had a built-in advantage over Hershey chocolate bars. This superiority was exploited in commercials that
ran for over a decade. As every mother knows, "M&M's milk
chocolate melts in your mouth—not in your hand."

Reeves was also instrumental in helping Bic pens to get
started in this country. Thirty years ago, most ballpoints didn't
have much staying power. Recognizing this problem, Reeves
produced a campaign in which Bics were shot from rifles and
crossbows and then used as bits in electric drills. Following
these torture tests, the USP appeared on the screen. "Bic writes
the first time, every time" reminded consumers that Scripto
and other pen manufacturers made an inferior product.

The bloodiest marketing war of the 1950s was between Crest
and Colgate toothpastes, and Reeves was right in the center of
the conflict. Each brand tried to persuade the public that it
fought tooth decay more effectively than the other, but their
claims were slightly suspect in consumers' minds.

Reeves's masterstroke was the creation of GARDOL, an "invisible protective shield" that convinced millions of Americans
that Colgate was the better toothpaste. In the ad man's commercials, Ed Herlihy, then a sports announcer, hurled a baseball
at viewers sitting in their living rooms. As it approached, the
ball looked as though it would shatter the TV screen. Suddenly
the projectile slammed against a clear plastic wall. Herlihy
walked over, confidently rapped his knuckles on the hard surface, and began describing Colgate's similar "invisible protection." Crest protested that this ad was misleading, but the
Federal Trade Commission—much more lenient in those days
—upheld Reeves's side of the argument and permitted it to remain on the air.

The Colgate campaign wasn't the only instance in which
Rosser Reeves may have tiptoed around the truth in his advertising. Several years later, he created the controversial "optical
cure" for Rolaids antacid tablets. Rolaids was being defeated in
drugstores because of upbeat commercials that featured sexy
young men and women getting rid of their indigestion after eating Tums. Reeves called these competitive ads puffery and win-

dow dressing and began to work on a more realistic campaign for Rolaids.

The finished commercials featured a glass beaker filled with a dark-colored liquid that Reeves claimed was gastric juice. Rolaids were dropped into the glass, and almost immediately, before the viewers' eyes, the fluid turned crystal-clear. The USP then trumpeted the fact that "Rolaids absorbs forty-seven times its weight in stomach acid." Consumers were obviously convinced by the demonstration: Over the next six months, Tums sales dropped 35 percent, and Rolaids became the leading antacid on the market. Despite this success, many observers on Madison Avenue today still believe that Reeves hoodwinked the public and an easygoing FTC by using food coloring and water in the container.

The first studies warning that cigarettes were a health hazard appeared during the early 1950s. Ted Bates & Company, whose largest client at the time was Brown & Williamson Tobacco, stood to lose a lot of money if the public took this research seriously and cut down on its smoking. Reeves, determined not to let this happen, countered the medical profession's bad news by developing a "reassurance campaign" for Viceroy cigarettes. His commercials calmed smokers' fears by asserting that "the nicotine and tars trapped by the exclusive Viceroy filter cannot reach your nose, throat, or lungs." The copywriter's sales pitch sounded so authoritative that it convinced millions of people to continue puffing away. Over the next six years, Brown & Williamson sold 22 billion Viceroys while revenue from the brand reached $200 million.

Reeves's ads for Kool cigarettes were equally duplicitous. "Break the chain of the hot cigarette habit—with Kools," he wrote. Customers misconstrued this deceptive message. It wasn't the cigarette's refreshing menthol taste that attracted them to the brand; they were attracted by the implicit suggestion in the campaign that they would eventually be able to quit smoking by switching to Kool.

Reeves went over to the other side and joined forces with the doctors in his effort to sell America on frozen orange juice during the early 1950s. Most people squeezed their own oranges back then, believing that fresh OJ was healthier than the frozen variety. This prejudice threatened to destroy Minute Maid, a company attempting to introduce a line of reconstituted citrus juices.

Reeves visited orange groves in Florida, went to processing plants, and hung around in supermarkets looking for an answer to Minute Maid's problem. Finally, he spoke with several nutritionists, who mentioned in passing that despite high levels of vitamin C, fresh oranges sometimes contained small amounts of bacteria or toxic material from their peels. This was more than enough ammunition for Reeves. He devised a campaign with a USP that stated: "Doctors prove Minute Maid is better for your health than oranges squeezed at home." The millions of mothers who saw these commercials came away feeling that fresh orange juice would endanger their children's health. Naturally, they decided to stock their freezers with Minute Maid.

Madison Avenue entered the political arena for the first time during the 1952 Presidential election, when Reeves produced television commercials for the Republican candidate, Dwight D. Eisenhower. Ike had been a victorious military commander during World War II and a success as president of Columbia University, but he was seen by many Americans as less brainy than his professorial Democratic opponent, Adlai Stevenson. Reeves sought to alter the public's perception of the general as a lesser intellect with what came to be known as his "Ask Mr. Wizard" campaign.

The ad executive assembled a large crowd in New York's Radio City Music Hall, giving various members of the audience cards with questions on them about national or foreign affairs. When called, they stood up and read their lines into a camera, as if they were talking directly to General Eisenhower, who was actually out on the campaign trail somewhere. Several weeks later, Reeves brought Eisenhower into a TV studio and filmed him as he recited prepared answers to the people's questions. A deft editor spliced the appropriate questions and responses together for the finished commercials.

Very few people knew about Reeves's Machiavellian advertising techniques until after the election, when he was loudly censured for selling a President like a tube of toothpaste. Reeves, victorious once again, just smiled.

Over the past three decades, television advertising has become an indispensable tool for politicians seeking public office. You can't get elected today without effective commercials. It was Rosser Reeves's innovative work on behalf of Eisenhower over thirty years ago that opened the way for the electronic politics of the 1980s.

Reeves's chief rival on Madison Avenue during the 1950s was a delightfully dotty Englishman named David Ogilvy. Once married to Reeves's sister-in-law, Ogilvy entered the American advertising business late in life, at the age of thirty-seven. Before landing on Ad Alley, he had spent the better part of two decades roaming through Europe and the United States. After flunking out of Oxford in the early 1930s, he served as an apprentice chef in the kitchens of the elegant Hotel Majestic in Paris. From there, he moved north and sold stoves door to door in Scotland.

When he tired of this sales job, Ogilvy turned to his older brother, who helped him secure an entry-level position at Mather & Crowther, a London advertising agency. Four years later, the itinerant young man came to the United States, where he landed a post with pollster George Gallup. During World War II, Ogilvy assisted Sir William Stephenson—better known by the code name "Intrepid"—in gathering intelligence for the Allies.

Once the Nazis were defeated, the vagabond retreated to a tobacco farm in the Amish countryside of Pennsylvania. He emerged from this reclusive life several years later with a desire to reenter the advertising business. But instead of seeking employment at an established agency in London or New York, the maverick chose to start his own shop. With $6,000 he had inherited from an aunt and another $90,000 raised from two British ad agencies—Mather & Crowther and S. H. Benson—Ogilvy moved to Manhattan and in 1948 launched Hewitt, Ogilvy, Benson & Mather (after several years, Anderson Hewitt left the firm, S. H. Benson's loan was repaid, and the fledgling company was renamed Ogilvy & Mather).

Ogilvy took a more genteel approach to advertising than Reeves. He once described the perfect ad executive as combining "the tenacity of a bulldog with the charm of a spaniel." He didn't believe in pistol-whipping people into purchasing or in abusing the public's trust. But he was far from soft when it came to persuading consumers to buy certain products. Ogilvy was a rigid rule-maker. Like an old-fashioned schoolmaster at Eton or Harrow, he attempted to codify the fundamentals of the ad game in little pamphlets called "Magic Lanterns," which were distributed to help enlighten O&M employees about their craft. One of these primers stated unequivocally that "factual advertising outsells flatulent puffery."

Ogilvy, a fact fanatic, claimed that the more he told, the more he sold, and he always loaded up his copy with detail in order to persuade readers or viewers that his client had built a better mousetrap. In the mid-1950s, for example, he wrote 719 long words on behalf of Rolls-Royce. This magazine ad contained an exhaustive eighteen-word headline—"At 60 miles per hour, the loudest noise in this new Rolls-Royce comes from the electric clock"—and twenty obscure nuggets of information about the expensive car. Ogilvy told his audience that when Rolls-Royce engineers tested their autos, they used stethoscopes to listen to the motor. He also noted that each engine had to run perfectly for seven hours on its own prior to installation, and he took great pains to describe how every Rolls was given five coats of primer paint before fourteen coats of finishing paint were added. The car's rear-window defrosting system, with its 1,500 invisible wires, was emphasized, along with the fact that Rolls-Royce seats were upholstered with eight hides of leather, enough to make 128 pairs of shoes.

This overwhelming display of data more than impressed affluent citizens in the market for a luxury automobile. Ogilvy's impeccable presentation provided people with everything they ever wanted to know about Rolls-Royce but hadn't even thought of asking. After assessing his authoritative argument, potential buyers could have little doubt that the car was worth its expensive $60,000 price tag.

Ogilvy's pedagogy, his "know-it-all" style of advertising, helped build his company into a $2 billion conglomerate, making it the fourth-largest ad agency in America today. Ogilvy & Mather's high-powered client list currently includes American Express, General Foods, and Trans World Airlines.

David Ogilvy, now almost seventy-five, is in semiretirement, spending most of his days exploring France's Loire Valley near his sixty-room medieval chateau. Despite this life of leisure, he still sends executives in New York urgent telexes each day. His messages usually offer sales statistics about a specific product or criticism of a current O&M commercial that he feels lacks sufficient facts. When D.O., as he's called along Ad Alley, visits his Manhattan offices—which he does several times a year—he is a familiar figure. Wearing bright-red suspenders and a broad smile, he is regarded by his Madison Avenue colleagues as the warm, ebullient fellow who created the coldly rational sales pitch.

If David Ogilvy tried to reduce advertising to a precise science, Bill Bernbach attempted to raise it to an art. Known as the Picasso of Madison Avenue, Bernbach led a creative rebellion during the 1960s against the heavy-handed hucksters of the previous decade. He refused to dupe consumers or to steamroll them with facts. Instead, he brought humor, honesty, and humanity to Ad Alley, for the first time in its history. Bernbach's campaigns had a light touch; they sold softly, persuaded politely. He was convinced that the public would buy more if the sales pitch was less intense.

But despite its understated style, his agency's work got people involved. Viewers almost never got up to go to the refrigerator when a Doyle Dane Bernbach commercial came on the screen. Instead, they usually remained glued to the tube so that they could watch a gorilla manhandle American Tourister luggage or listen to James Garner and Mariette Hartley trade quips about Polaroid cameras. These typical Bernbach spots were always funny and amusing. Apart from generating smiles, however, they also sent customers scurrying into stores to purchase clients' products.

In addition to being a gentle, witty, and effective communicator, Bernbach was a reserved salesman. Unlike his competitors, who would do almost anything to land an account, he never directly solicited new clients. The executive believed that his ads spoke for themselves and that his portfolio made the definitive statement about the quality of his agency. While other shops spent time and money wining and dining prospective advertisers, Bernbach's staff kept churning out commercials for current clients.

This iconoclastic approach to advertising didn't inhibit Doyle Dane's early success. A decade after opening the company, in 1949, Bernbach and his two partners—Maxwell Dane, who had previously run his own small shop in New York, and Ned Doyle, who had worked alongside the creative rebel as an account executive at Grey Advertising after World War II—had a stable of superstar clients that included Volkswagen, Avis Rent-a-Car, and Seagram Distillers. Their agency grew rapidly during the 1960s, even though it broke most of the advertising industry's conventional rules. Taking its cue from the counterculture mood of the times, Doyle Dane emphasized creative freedom over Madison Avenue's predictable hard sell. Bernbach liked to compare his shop to Summerhill, an experimental school in England where open classrooms and individual expression prevailed. He reveled in constructive chaos and fostered a minimally structured environment that encouraged fresh advertising ideas.

Art directors and copywriters, the philosopher kings and queens of Bernbach's offbeat domain, were pampered. They created their own hours and set their own deadlines. There was no dress code at DDB. Shaggy hair, T-shirts, beads, and sandals replaced Ad Alley's traditional uniform—the gray flannel suit. The single crime in Bernbach's book was lack of originality. He spent much of his time urging his charges on to new creative heights, demanding that they produce the most inventive ads possible. Whenever one of his underlings was stuck in a rut and going stale, he recited his favorite quote, from the jazz pianist

Thelonius Monk: "The only cats worth anything are the cats who take chances. Sometimes I play things I never heard myself."

The most daring campaign Bernbach ever created was for Volkswagen, the unattractive and unassuming little car that was first imported from Germany after World War II. Volkswagens sold poorly in this country during the 1950s, primarily because Americans associated them with Adolf Hitler and the Nazi Holocaust. At the same time, the status-conscious American public was also having a love affair with the big car, so nobody trying to keep up with the Joneses would be caught dead in a VW.

Doyle Dane changed this negative perception dramatically when it got the Volkswagen account in 1960. Rather than bombarding consumers with dry facts in the Ogilvy manner and stressing VW's unappreciated assets, Bernbach capitalized on the car's obvious limitations and liabilities. His tongue-in-cheek copy refused to take Volkswagen seriously; instead, it poked fun at it. The object was to make people feel good, to get them to laugh. Once they did, the ad man believed, their attitude toward Volkswagen would improve and—who knows?—they might even buy one.

One of Bernbach's initial Volkswagen ads showed a simple black-and-white photograph of the car, below which ran the stark two-word headline "Think Small." Another of his early self-effacing sales messages for the vehicle admitted that the "VW engine doesn't have Super Skyrocket Thrust or Dyna-Turbo-Chargers," and went on to acknowledge that "some people even think it's a funny little engine." The humorous copy concluded with a humble bit of self-congratulation, a barely audible sales pitch, noting that "our funny little engine sure can push our funny little car fast." Americans were chuckling coast to coast after reading Doyle Dane's first modest messages for VW.

Within months, thousands of consumers streamed into Volkswagen showrooms across the country to see the "funny little car." Soon after, another basic photo of a VW appeared in magazines. This time, the ad's headline consisted of just one word, "Lemon"—the most dreaded term in an auto buyer's vocabulary. Bernbach did the unthinkable in his copy. He confessed that Volkswagen sometimes produced an inferior car. But he also pointed out that VW had one of the greatest inspection systems in the world at its plant in Wolfsburg, Germany, and he described how inspectors looked at each automobile through a magnifying glass to see if it had any tiny scratches. If a vehicle was even slightly damaged, it was immediately yanked off the assembly line. Bernbach assured readers that "Volkswagen plucks the lemons, you get the plums."

It took time, but people gradually began to think positively about what had once been the Führer's car. Doyle Dane's campaign agreed with Americans that VWs were small and ugly, but it convinced the public that they were also sturdy, dependable automobiles. One ad in the mid-1960s, for example, impishly announced to consumers, "There's finally a beautiful picture of a Volkswagen." Above this headline was a photograph of snow tracks on a desolate country road—no trace of a VW. Another ad showed a tow truck pulling a Volkswagen. "A Rare Photo," said the caption.

In the early 1970s, after the VW mystique had spread to all corners of the United States, Bernbach was still busy at work promoting the car. In 1973, when the Arab oil crisis unexpectedly jolted the country, sending gas prices through the roof, the creative executive devised an ad to emphasize Volkswagen's fuel economy. Rather than merely listing mileage statistics, as all the other advertising agencies had done for their car accounts, Doyle Dane drew a cartoon of a man putting a gas-hose nozzle to his head, as if to shoot himself over the sudden high cost of driving. At the very bottom of the page was Bernbach's masterful footnote: "Or buy a Volkswagen."

Bernbach's sense of humor helped to sell many other products besides the VW. To demonstrate that American Tourister luggage was indestructible, he created a commercial in which an angry gorilla banged and kicked a suitcase around a cage for 30 seconds. If a bag could withstand that kind of abuse, it surely could survive the carelessness of bellhops and airlines. And in his effort to convince the gentile world that there was a tasty alternative to white bread, he put up subway posters that featured blacks, Indians, and Asians enjoying hefty deli-style sand-wiches. The headline read: "You don't have to be Jewish to love Levy's Real Jewish Rye."

For Avis Rent-a-Car, he employed the VW strategy again and told the bitter truth: Avis lagged behind Hertz in the market-place, so it had to do a better job if it wanted to stay afloat. The copy for the campaign, which ran for over a decade, blatantly confessed: "We're #2. We try harder."

There has never been anyone quite like Bill Bernbach on Madison Avenue. More than a brilliant creative mind, he also tried to serve as the conscience of Ad Alley. In one of the last speeches he made before his death, in 1982, he spoke passion-ately about his profession's responsibility to the public. "All of us who use the mass media are the shapers of society," he said. "We can vulgarize that society. We can brutalize it. Or we can elevate it." Throughout his career, which spanned over four decades, this ad man always took the high road.

During the 1960s, in the wake of Bill Bernbach's success, charming the public became the big thing on Madison Avenue. Clients up and down the street wanted their agencies to help them captivate consumers with the kind of enchanting advertis-ing that Doyle Dane had made so famous. Out of this creative renaissance emerged a diverse handful of bright ad people whose own individualistic sensibilities resulted in a series of memorable campaigns.

Leo Burnett of Chicago, for example, a seventy-five-year-old executive who had been writing copy since 1916, finally achieved long overdue national recognition. His agency is re-sponsible for giving us such unforgettable all-American icons as Morris the Cat, Tony the Tiger, the Jolly Green Giant, and the Pillsbury Doughboy. Unlike Bernbach, whose humorous ads were characterized by sophisticated irony, Burnett produced commercials based on a down-home fantasy and innocence that Walt Disney would have been proud of.

By contrast, Mary Wells, another Ad Alley success story, was—and still is—as chic as the late Leo Burnett was folksy. The first woman to flourish as a Madison Avenue agency head—

she opened her own shop, Wells Rich Greene, in 1966—the former copywriter from Doyle Dane created a slick brand of advertising for such clients as Philip Morris, Braniff Airlines, and American Motors. Like Bernbach, once her mentor, Wells stressed humor in her campaigns; she also brought her own special sense of style and good taste to each of her creative efforts. This sophisticated approach to marketing has been handsomely rewarded over the past two decades. Today, Wells Rich Greene is a $600 million agency with considerable clout in the U.S. business community.

Among Wells's more celebrated television commercials are those she and her partners created for Alka-Seltzer two decades ago. Humorously focusing on the mid-sections of people from all walks of life—including a sweaty, paunchy jack-hammer operator—these upbeat spots made fun of stomachaches and cheered up consumers who were suffering from indigestion.

Another of her campaigns—for Benson & Hedges 100s—took an equally witty approach. Following Bernbach's Volkswagen strategy of turning a product's potential disadvantages into positive attributes, Wells merrily bemoaned the special problems of enjoying an extra-long cigarette. Benson & Hedges devotees were shown getting their deluxe-length smokes caught in elevator doors and car windows—the small price they paid for lighting up such a long-lasting tobacco treat. By poking fun at B&H's size, the ad woman also brought home the important fact that serious smokers could savor three or four extra puffs per cigarette.

While Wells's campaigns for Benson & Hedges and Alka-Seltzer were ingenious, they were also closely modeled after Bill Bernbach's earlier ads. The astute protégé didn't really come into her own until she developed "designer" commercials for both American Motors and Braniff Airlines. Recruiting Emilio Gucci and Pierre Cardin to create swanky signature interiors for AMC's automobiles, she generated enormous publicity for her client. This high-fashion tactic was also employed when Wells had Braniff commission Calder to decorate the exterior of its airplanes.

The high-powered executive's trendy approach to advertising is reflected in her life-style. Wells and her husband—Harding Lawrence, former Braniff chairman—jet back and forth between homes in New York, Texas, and the French Riviera. Their villa overlooking the Mediterranean, like their posh triplex on Manhattan's East River, boasts interiors designed by society decorator Billy Baldwin. The couple count among their friends such influential people as Philip Caldwell, chairman of Ford Motor Company.

Mary Wells is Ad Alley's fairy princess, and hers is a glittering rags-to-riches story. From her position as a copywriter for McKelvey's department store in Youngstown, Ohio, over thirty years ago, this daughter of a furniture salesman has risen to become the preeminent woman in the male-dominated American advertising industry.

The success of Madison Avenue during its first hundred years—from J. Walter Thompson to Rosser Reeves to Mary Wells—was largely due to the quirky creative vision of several eccentric entrepreneurs. Until recently, advertising was inward-looking, as much a form of personal expression as a tool of persuasion. Ads traditionally reflected the attitudes, tastes, and feelings of such individualistic copywriters as C. C. Hopkins and Bill Bernbach. The public's consciousness was, for the most part, overlooked.

All of this changed, however, when the economy went haywire and consumers revolted in the 1970s. These twin calamities forced agency executives to turn to science for help. During the past ten years, commercial psychoanalysis has gradually replaced imagination as the driving force behind most advertising. Ad Alley's brainy, zany pioneers have given way to a new generation of squeaky-clean image technicians.

3 IMAGE TECHNICIANS

Ad Alley Discovers Freud

The offbeat commercials that were so popular in the 1960s left Ad Alley in the lurch during the early 1970s. Those were the years when the public lost its sense of humor. People were in no laughing mood as they were forced to tighten their belts and confront a new era of limits. This consumer backlash spelled trouble for Madison Avenue. It became obvious to clients that the advertising industry had lost its rapport with Americans and was no longer capable of persuading them to acquire goods and services.

The danger signs were most evident at Young & Rubicam, then the third-largest agency in the country. Led by Stephen O. Frankfurt, a thirty-six-year-old creative whiz, Y&R lost over $50 million in commissions and fees in 1968 and 1969—close to 10 percent of its total billings. The company continued to sink financially, and by 1970 it was drifting aimlessly, with little hope for the future. Such prestigious advertisers as General Electric and Procter & Gamble were abandoning ship, withdrawing important product assignments from the agency, primarily because of Frankfurt's ineffective and self-indulgent commercials. In a depressed economy, he spent clients' money extravagantly without delivering much in the way of sales results.

The executive's lavish "Wings of Man" campaign for struggling Eastern Airlines was typical of this shallow brand of advertising. Ignoring the fact that Eastern was in the transportation business, Frankfurt appeared to be more intent on involving viewers in the beauty of flight than on selling airplane seats. One 60-second spot focused on a young man diving off an Acapulco cliff into the sea; another minute was devoted to birds dipping and soaring over a Brazilian jungle; a third 30-second snippet showed Icarus gliding through the heavens. Each of these ads featured thunderous background music provided by the London Symphony Orchestra. This was undisciplined off-the-wall art, not advertising. Potential customers had no inkling what Eastern stood for or what it was trying to promote, and the airline lost its shirt.

Frankfurt's excesses, which were the accepted norm on Ad Alley in the late 1960s, almost destroyed Young & Rubicam. Fortunately, the agency was rescued before it was too late. One morning in November 1970, Y&R underwent a coup d'état. A group of concerned executives headed by Edward Ney, the forty-five-year-old president of the international division, took charge during a board meeting in the company's conference room. Ney and his comrades had lost confidence in Frankfurt—once Madison Avenue's golden boy—and they demanded the free-spending ad man's resignation. In a cost-cutting move, one-quarter of Y&R's New York staff was also let go.

Once the new regime had disposed of the old guard, it was forced to turn its attention to the pressing matters at hand—getting the public interested in buying its clients' products again. During the next few months, Ney sought the advice of economists, psychologists, sociologists, business consultants, and communications specialists. It gradually became clear to the new agency leader that the only way Y&R could hope to recover its lost business was to produce ads that addressed consumers' psychological needs and helped solve their personal problems.

The wizards of Madison Avenue could no longer afford to create capricious commercials; they had to dwell on their customers' innermost concerns if they wanted to succeed. For Ad Alley, which had traditionally ignored the public and developed campaigns according to its own set of rules, Ney's new approach was revolutionary.

Converting his company from an ad agency into a clinic for psychoanalyzing American consumers was a big gamble for Ed Ney, but his wager paid off handsomely. In the fourteen years since he radicalized Y&R—and Madison Avenue—Young & Rubicam has increased in size almost sevenfold and become the foremost advertising enterprise in the United States, with just over $3 billion in annual billings. Many firms on Ad Alley have since adopted Ney's winning ways, but over the past decade, no one has been so successful in bringing Freud to television.

Young & Rubicam's dramatic turnaround—and the advertising industry's resurgence during the 1970s—helped fulfill Edward Ney's driving ambition to become the most powerful man on Madison Avenue. Known as "the Godfather" because of his raspy whispering voice and silver-gray hair, Y&R's chairman is an odd blend of Cary Grant and General Patton. An immaculate dresser (he wears Turnbull & Asser shirts and Paul Stuart suits) and a classy, courtly man, he lives the good life, vacationing regularly in such posh spots as St. Moritz. At the same time, he is a demanding taskmaster who expects his employees to put in sixteen hours a day. The word among his chief executives is: "Don't come to the office on Monday if you weren't there on Sunday."

Ney himself adheres to a rigorous regimen consisting of hard work and stressful physical exercise. He's at his desk by eight o'clock each morning after a daily three-mile run. Like his father, who sold plumbing supplies during the Depression, the agency head is, first and foremost, a businessman who keeps his eye fixed on the bottom line. Rarely getting involved in the day-to-day artistic affairs of his agency, he prefers to leave such matters to his brilliant protégé, a former copywriter named Alexander Kroll.

Ney, the profit maker, gave birth to the psychological advertising movement, but it was Kroll, the image technician, who developed its creative expression. Plucked from relative obscurity to help run Young & Rubicam's worldwide empire at the tender age of thirty-one, Kroll was born to be an ad man. Reaching the top at Y&R was the logical result of a lifelong fascination with consumer purchasing habits. Kroll had always been obsessed with what people bought and why they selected the products they did.

In many ways, the ad man began preparing for a career on Madison Avenue when he was a small boy growing up in Leechburg, a poor mill and mining town in western Pennsylvania, near Pittsburgh. While his classmates were busy doing their homework, Kroll would sit on his front porch counting the number of Chevrolets and Fords that passed by, trying to figure out why the neighbors didn't drive Chryslers (they couldn't afford them). When he wasn't scrutinizing automobiles, the youngster could be found in a local drugstore inquiring about the town's best-selling cold remedies. Mini-marketing exercises of this kind helped to alleviate the crushing boredom and harshness of life in Leechburg for an imaginative child.

Kroll added to his considerable store of knowledge about consumer behavior when he joined the high school football squad. It was then that he fell under the spell of a crusty old coach named Ellis McCracken, who was a master of motivation. Nobody understood how to manipulate a group of people better than this shrewd athletic mentor. Kroll, who was captain and an all-state center as a senior, was amazed by McCracken's uncanny ability to push the right "action button" for each team member. Leechburg players were regularly outweighed by their opponents, but they were never outhustled or overmuscled. Not surprisingly, McCracken's teams were the scourge of Pennsylvania high school football during the late 1950s.

Kroll went on to become an all-American at Rutgers, a key factor in the university's undefeated 1961 season. He was so good that the New York Titans, who were eventually renamed the Jets, drafted him after graduation. At six feet three and 250 pounds, the hulking athlete seemed to have a bright future ahead of him as a professional football star. But the bumps and bruises were too painful, and after just twelve games in the old American Football League, he quit the gridiron for good.

Kroll is one of the only pro-football players ever to launch a second career on Madison Avenue. After he left the Titans, his fame as a sportsman helped him line up interviews at several ad agencies in New York. Most of the executives he spoke with, however, were put off by his appearance. Here was a monstrous man with a shaved head who looked more like a furniture mover than a copywriter. But despite his imposing physical presence, Y&R's personnel director was immediately impressed by Kroll's solid grasp of marketing and his natural feel for salesmanship. He hired the big guy on the spot.

Kroll's first years at Y&R, during the mid-1960s, weren't always rewarding. After operating in the disciplined world of football for so long, he found it extremely difficult to function amid Frankfurt's creative chaos. The rookie writer, who grew up in austere blue-collar surroundings, couldn't understand —or accept—the razzle-dazzle advertising that his long-haired colleagues produced. Kroll's commercials were different from those of his co-workers. They were less artificial and contrived; they touched people's raw emotions, appealed to their innermost feelings. Instinctively, the up-and-coming marketer always seemed to pull the right psychological lever to make a sale.

Take, for instance, an ad he wrote for Eastern Airlines in 1965. "The farther you travel, the closer you become" read the headline—an emotional pitch for family togetherness that was markedly different from the flashy Frankfurt style but quite similar to the warm McDonald's campaign that would run ten years later. Kroll also sensed the yearnings of Societally Conscious Achievers before anyone on Madison Avenue even knew what a hippie was. His 1966 spot for Eastern empathized with the restless young by inviting them to "See the world, before you change it."

Kroll didn't acquire his perceptive understanding of people from a textbook, of course. His expertise was the result of two decades of observing and studying consumers in action. Keeping in touch with the public was his only formula for success, and he worked hard to maintain his grass-roots contacts. Each weekend, the ad man would go to the supermarket near his house in rural Connecticut to talk with shoppers. Wearing a tag identifying him as an interviewer from the "Bureau of Independent Research," he would listen to what they had to say about the products they were buying. Often he would tape these conversations and then film his subjects. In fact, Kroll even made "home commercials" featuring his own family as the cast. His award-winning spot for Metropolitan Life Insurance, in which a mother puts her small son on a school bus, first took shape this way.

By the time he assumed control of Ney's psychological advertising revolution, Kroll knew that there was much more to research than just going out to the local mall and chatting with shoppers or shooting commercials based on personal experiences at home. Y&R's new creative leader believed that by using the most up-to-date clinical techniques available he could learn what really made consumers tick and dramatically improve the effectiveness of his agency's campaigns.

Kroll began a long talent search, looking for people who could help explain the public's changing attitudes. Interviewing close to one hundred candidates, the former football player eventually hired two brilliant professionals, Joseph Plummer and Susan Gianinno, both of whom worked in Chicago.

Plummer, who had studied mass communication theory while getting his Ph.D. at Ohio State, was toiling at the Leo Burnett Company in the mid-1970s when he first met Kroll. The young researcher, then in his thirties, believed that people were drawn to TV programs that mirrored real-life situations. The best-watched shows, he said, were those that helped viewers deal with their daily dilemmas. In his opinion, the main reason for the popularity of "M*A*S*H" and "All in the Family," for example, was that Hawkeye and Archie Bunker were able to cope with a host of easily recognizable problems each week. Plummer thought that Burnett could improve its commercials if it applied this lesson to advertising. He wanted the agency to

produce campaigns that offered people more relevance and reality than the Jolly Green Giant or the Man from Glad.

Unfortunately, the Burnett executives were set in their ways,
and Plummer's memos, calling for ads that increased consumer
involvement, were filed away. Research at Leo Burnett at this
time was primarily quantitative, and the main task of Plummer
and his colleagues was to measure an audience demographical-
ly—rather than defining what that audience was thinking or
feeling. Kroll heard about Plummer's battles at Burnett and
sought him out. He explained to the rebellious researcher that
at Y&R he would have ample opportunity to put his theories
into practice, a prospect that excited Plummer.

Part of Plummer's effectiveness as an interviewer—one of the
reasons he gets shoppers to talk so candidly—is his disarming
appearance. With his fresh-scrubbed face and close-cropped
blond hair he looks more like an innocent choirboy than an ana-
lyst of human behavior. But beneath the angelic facade lurks a
real manipulator. Plummer is a probing scientist, and he spends
most of his time at Y&R experimenting with the public's emotional chemistry. His soft eyes light up and the halo disappears
with each new discovery of consumer vulnerability; he knows
that this signals big sales for the agency's clients.

Like Plummer, Susan Gianinno also projects a benign image.
A slender and sporty Cheryl Tiegs look-alike in her mid-thirties,
she was working as a researcher for Needham Harper & Steers,
a Chicago agency, when she first interviewed at Y&R. Although
Gianinno—a former psychological counselor at the University
of Chicago—spoke in slow, measured sentences, she asked provocative questions and convinced both Kroll and the recently
hired Plummer that she would be a skilled judge of people,
someone who could dig down into a person's inner world
without ruffling any feathers.

The two male executives were also captivated by Gianinno's
thoughts on purchasing behavior. The researcher believed that
individuals are defined by what they buy—that such products
as beer, cars, cigarettes, and soft drinks are badges that make
bold statements about their users. One of her theories explained how material goods have provided members of the

public with their identities throughout modern history—going all the way back to the Renaissance, when the aristocracy first began to ride around in ornate coaches.

Today this phenomenon, said Gianinno, is more pronounced than ever. The breakdown of family and community in America has created a lonely, impersonal society, and one of the few ways that citizens can express themselves or communicate with one another is through their possessions. It didn't take much to convince Gianinno to leave the Windy City. She was eager to put her hypotheses to the test at Y&R, to see if she could seduce consumers into wearing the badges of her choice.

During their first few months working together, Plummer and Gianinno spent their time establishing the ground rules for Y&R's new psychological advertising. The researchers realized that although Americans during the 1970s seemed bitter and hostile—in no mood to purchase—they could still be won over by Ad Alley. Extensive videotaped interviews with consumers revealed how worried and depressed they were about the direction their lives were taking. After Vietnam, Watergate, the Arab oil crisis, and the youth revolt, people felt their country was falling apart, and government, business, and religious leaders seemed unable to improve matters. Plummer and Gianinno sensed an opportunity. If Madison Avenue could find out what was bothering folks and then create commercials that eased the public's troubles, then the grateful nation would start buying again.

During the late 1970s, Young & Rubicam's dynamic duo worked hard to refine their research methods; consumers were becoming increasingly sophisticated, and it was essential to remain one step ahead of the quarry. More important, perhaps, was the fact that other agencies along Ad Alley had begun to dabble in image transformation. Ney and Kroll, determined to retain the edge over their competitors, knew that Y&R couldn't hope to dominate Madison Avenue unless it won the research race. So they pressed Plummer and Gianinno to come up with even trickier techniques to entice the populace. The researchers devised a new approach to interviewing—one that would subtly psychoanalyze people in their own homes.

Plummer and Gianinno and their associates traveled all over the country to garner fresh insights about consumers. In each city they visited, the researchers would go to the local telephone directory and phone a large number of households at random. Based on responses to a series of prepared questions, the ad people would screen potential candidates for in-depth, at-home interviews. Every evening the agency representatives invaded new households, and there for three or four hours they'd chew the fat with folks, always keeping the conversation unstructured and informal. The hidden agenda for these sessions was to gain an understanding of how the average citizen lived, to see the world through his eyes. These relaxed dialogues usually provided a gold mine of information. They were far more helpful to Y&R than the more structured focus groups that other agencies conducted at their offices. As the name implies, focus groups are restricted to a prearranged topic—beer, for example. Paid participants at these sessions frequently try to outdo each other with boring and meaningless comments as a way of justifying their stipends. Y&R's one-on-one meetings yielded entirely different—and much more productive—results.

A typical evening on the road with Susan Gianinno—in, say, Peoria, Illinois—would go something like this: After dinner, the researcher arrives at the home of Mr. and Mrs. Robert Atwood, a small ranch-style house located in a subdivision several blocks from Main Street. The Atwoods and their three children who still live at home—Tommy, sixteen; Carol, thirteen; and little Bobby, twelve—have been expecting her. Gianinno brings Anne Atwood a bouquet of flowers as a way of saying thank you for the interview. The kids run off, back to "The Dukes of Hazzard," while the adults retire to the den. Coffee and homemade coconut cake are served.

As pleasantries are exchanged, Gianinno scans the room to get a better idea of the Atwoods' life-style. These people are clearly Belongers. Family photos cover the pine-paneled walls, and an American Legion Bowling League trophy sits prominently on the mantelpiece. Back issues of *People* magazine, *Good Housekeeping,* and *Field & Stream* are displayed on a molded plastic coffee table. Shelves containing a Chicago Cubs mascot doll and other bric-a-brac, including a picture of astronaut Neil Armstrong first setting foot on the moon and a framed NRA sharpshooter certificate of merit, also catch the researcher's eye.

Old copies of Norman Vincent Peale's *The Power of Positive Thinking* and Dale Carnegie's *How to Win Friends and Influence People* collect dust on the windowsill. One of the kids has left a plastic *E.T.* drinking mug lying around on the floor, which is partially covered by a shaggy orange throw rug.

Bob Atwood, nearing forty-five and graying at the temples, is a strapping six-footer, pleasantly dressed in a plaid flannel shirt, old chino trousers, and high-cut construction boots. He works on the assembly line at Caterpillar, building heavy-duty farm equipment. Times have recently been tough for the Atwood family. In the past three years, Bob has been laid off four times for a total of eighteen months. Despite Anne's part-time job as a waitress, it has been difficult for them to meet monthly expenses.

Even with their hardship, however, the Atwoods consider themselves fairly fortunate. Several of their best friends, lifelong citizens of Peoria, were forced to move to Texas for employment. The Atwoods' eldest son, nineteen-year-old John, unable to find a job after he graduated from high school two years ago, also had to leave town. He's now a laborer on an oil rig somewhere in the Gulf of Mexico, and Anne misses him terribly.

Having gained an overall picture of the Atwoods, Gianinno is interested in gathering more specific information, such as the kinds of automobiles they're interested in. She noticed a beat-up '73 Chevy in the driveway, so maybe the family is thinking about a new car. The researcher begins with a series of interpretive—rather than descriptive—questions. She doesn't come right out and ask the Atwoods what auto they intend to buy. Instead, she talks with Anne and Bob about the kind of clothing they wear, how they select shirts or blouses, whose opinion they solicit when choosing a new pair of shoes, what their favorite colors are, whom they seek to emulate in their dress.

In this way, Gianinno gains insight into the Atwoods' style, which, as she quickly learns, is very conservative. From this brief conversation, it becomes apparent that these folks are self-conscious about standing out and expressing themselves. Their main need is to conform. They don't want to wear clothes—or drive a car—that will set them apart from their neighbors. They feel comfortable only when they blend in, when they're part of the group. Safety—more than status or individuality—will be the key factor when the Atwoods eventually purchase a new automobile.

The researcher next moves on to the subject of food. Again, she doesn't ask what Anne buys at the supermarket but tries instead to understand the role meals play in the life of the Atwoods. As Anne explains, dinner brings the entire family together, and having her children around the table is the most meaningful event of the day. Bob adds that after a difficult shift at the plant he really enjoys catching up with his wife and kids. From what she's heard, Gianinno can tell that the family unit is the Atwoods' security blanket, their refuge, and that suppertime is an essential respite from the stark reality that otherwise shapes their lives. They will purchase foods that offer good feelings as much as good taste.

It's getting late, and Bob and Anne have been talking for several hours. At this point, Gianinno switches gears and begins to use a technique she calls laddering. The object of this exercise is to get consumers to go beyond mere product description, to articulate what specific brands in a category mean to them. In this case, the researcher asks Bob's opinion of several varieties of beer. His responses naturally focus on each product's unique attributes—Miller is smooth, Heineken is heavy, Coors is foamy, etc. Gianinno next asks Bob what benefits he feels each beer offers him, to which he replies, for example, that Budweiser's softness enables him to drink more than one bottle at a sitting. Finally, the researcher wants him to tell her where beer drinking fits into his life. Bob goes on to describe how having several beers with his buddies after work smooths the edges off a particularly rough day. His revealing comments bring to light for Gianinno the burdens that blue-collar men like Bob face daily and shows how beer can help alleviate these troubles.

Armed with a suitcase full of notes from her interviews with citizens across the country, the researcher returns to her office at Young & Rubicam in New York. She and her colleagues begin sifting through their information and assembling psychographic profiles of specific groups of American consumers, supported by data from SRI International's VALS system.

These collective psychological portraits will provide a scientific frame of reference for Y&R's marketing efforts. From them, the agency's executives can understand exactly which buttons they have to push to make a sale. Once a target audience is selected, the rest is easy. To reach Belongers, such as the Atwoods, they only have to press Self-Esteem or Togetherness; for Emulators, they trigger Self-Confidence. Emulator-Achievers, on the other hand, respond to Status, while Societally Conscious Achievers react to Individualism.

After these keys to consumer motivation are established, Gianinno and her staff turn their attention to various product categories. The researchers use data from their interviews to match up VALS groups with particular brands. Beer, for instance:

Belongers	Emulators
Budweiser	Stroh's
Miller Lite	
Miller High	
Life	

Emulator-Achievers	Societally Conscious Achievers
Heineken	Coors
Löwenbräu	Bud Light

Once they've studied this product breakdown, Y&R's copywriters and art directors just have to insert the right psychological hook into their commercials. Then it's only a matter of time before viewers do what they've been programmed to do.

Over the past decade, Y&R has employed consumer insights unearthed by these slick research techniques to produce the most consistently effective advertising on Madison Avenue. One of the agency's specialties is breathing new life into dying goods and services—reviving humdrum, run-of-the-mill items that the public has grown tired of by transforming them into indispensable products that fill the psychological needs of many people.

Jell-O is the classic born-again brand. This dessert, which is composed mostly of sugar and artificial coloring, first came to America's attention in 1897, when the Jell-O Girl told us how pure and wonderful a treat it was. Her efforts were followed by Jack Benny's now familiar J-E-L-L-O jingle on radio in the 1920s and 1930s. During the next two decades, Y&R, which first got the account in 1928, stressed the product's versatility by running recipe ads. By the time this campaign ended, almost everyone in the country had eaten a fruit-studded Jell-O mold at least once. Convenience, the ease with which housewives could prepare Jell-O, was the watchword of commercials throughout the 1960s. When 1970 rolled around, however, the dessert was in desperate shape, sitting unused on supermarket and pantry shelves. People had realized that the powdery stuff didn't exactly create chocolate mousse. It was filled with nutritionally useless calories, and it took over an hour to set after it was made—far too long for the busy working woman.

Ney and Kroll, now running things at Y&R, sought to revitalize Jell-O; this was a $20 million piece of business they couldn't afford to lose. Having decided to change the product's old-fashioned advertising completely, the executives began to sell Jell-O as a family unifier to bruised Belongers in the mid-1970s. Using upbeat, emotional music, the new commercials helped spread Jell-O joy across the nation.

In one spot, "Cousin's Reunion," Mother comes to the dining-room table, where the entire family—aunts, uncles, cousins, and grandparents included—have just finished off a huge turkey. "I've decided—no dessert," she announces. "No dessert?" groans the group, on the verge of committing matricide. "No," says Mom, "let's have some fun instead." With that, she brings out a shimmering bowl of Jell-O, and the staid meal turns into a love fest.

In these 30 seconds, Y&R elevated a dessert mix into an elixir. Jell-O sales zoomed upward again when anxious people, like the Atwoods, who cherish home and hearth, began to perceive the product as a soothing tonic that would chase their blues away.

John Ferrell, head of the team that created "Cousin's Reunion" and helped to transform Jell-O into an antidepressant, is typical of the new breed of copywriter who appeared on Madison Avenue during the 1970s. Unlike his predecessors, those scrappy individualists who produced ads on the basis of their gut feelings, Ferrell's muse is research. First he digests the psychological strategy that's been selected for a campaign. Then he often looks at videotaped interviews with members of the target audience. Finally he immerses himself in the product he's writing about.

When Ferrell was fashioning the Jell-O commercials, it was rumored throughout Y&R that he bought twenty packages of the stuff, locked himself in a hotel room, and for two whole days did nothing but wolf down serving after serving of the dessert. This obsessive behavior has always been a Ferrell trademark. As a youngster growing up in Moline, Illinois, he channeled much of his energy into developing mock campaigns for cigarettes, detergents, and frozen foods. When it came time to produce a senior thesis at the University of Illinois, where he studied psychology and mass communication, he convinced a local Pontiac dealer to lend him a brand-new car so he could shoot a series of television commercials. Ferrell spent several months in the woods laboring on the project; the finished ads were so impressive that Y&R and thirteen other agencies offered him a job after his graduation.

A short, hyperactive man, the forty-one-year-old Ferrell is a workaholic. He arrives at his office each morning by five o'clock, and usually he doesn't leave until nine in the evening—

sixteen hours later. Ferrell's bizarre dress—wide, pleated pants, an old-fashioned two-color bib shirt, and a microscopic bow tie slightly larger than a thumbnail—makes him look more like a turn-of-the-century haberdasher than a superstar copywriter at America's largest advertising agency.

One shouldn't be fooled by these trappings of nonconformity, though. John Ferrell makes over $200,000 a year altering the public's perception of things, and the image he has worked hardest on is his own. The offbeat clothing is just an updated version of Ad Alley's old gray flannel uniform. Ferrell has an almost religious faith in advertising, and he believes Y&R can link consumers' emotional needs to any product in the marketplace—even dog food.

The rebirth of General Foods's Gainesburgers in the mid-1970s represents one of Y&R's greatest successes. Originally advertised in the early 1960s as the only "dry" dog food that was moist, Gainesburgers sold well at first because each portion was individually wrapped in a neat cellophane package, eliminating the bother of messy cans. People liked that convenience—even if it did cost them more. When the economy collapsed in 1973, however, financially strapped pet owners were forced to give up expensive Gainesburgers and serve their canines canned meals once again. General Foods was hurt badly by this sudden dog food defection, and the agency was called in to fix matters.

Y&R's research showed that Belongers own the majority of pooches in this country and that their pets are usually treated with great affection. The shop's new commercials for Gainesburgers exploited this psychological insight by transforming the product into an expression of love for the dog. Each spot showed Rover doing something adorable—like bringing Dad his slippers after a hard day at work. An announcer told viewers that their dogs did a lot for them and that, in return, the pets deserved all the warmth and tenderness money could buy. A Gainesburger in the shape of a heart then appeared on the screen. Y&R realized that Belongers will pay almost any price to keep their families happy and together. The trick in selling them dog food is to reinforce the fact that a pet is just like a son or daughter, and to make them feel guilty for not giving one of their "children" the best.

In addition to nursing tired old brands back to health, Young & Rubicam has used the potent effects of image transformation to attract some of the largest and most prestigious American companies over the past decade. Since 1970, when the management team led by Ed Ney and Alex Kroll assumed control, such blue-chip corporations as AT&T, Merrill Lynch, Ford Motor Company, Richardson-Vicks, Gillette, Heublein, Dr. Pepper, and Kodak have become the agency's clients. This staggering amount of new business has broken every record on Madison Avenue and added approximately $2 billion to Y&R's coffers.

One of the men responsible for luring new advertisers to the agency is Craig Middleton, a protégé of Charles Revson, who probably knows more about image transformation than anybody in the industry today. With Middleton's help, Y&R has snared three out of every four potential clients it has recently sought. This glittering success hasn't been achieved by using such old Ad Alley traditions as wining and dining prospects at expensive restaurants or dealing on the golf course. The stocky, red-haired Middleton isn't particularly sociable, and he doesn't believe in putting on the extravagant new-business presentations that are such a favorite pastime of his Madison Avenue colleagues.

The independent ad man disdains dog-and-pony shows like the one that reportedly took place in 1981, when Bozell & Jacobs, a New York–based shop, pitched the $50 million American Airlines account. The agency, sources say, spent a considerable sum redecorating American's Dallas conference room for its day-long presentation. The office space, according to several who attended the meeting, was made to resemble the interior of a 747, and women were hired to impersonate stewardesses. As a finishing touch, several of the ad executives apparently dressed up like pilots. This dazzling display helped to convince the airline to choose B&J to do its advertising. J. Walter Thompson wasn't as fortunate, however, when it sought the Kentucky Fried Chicken account in 1967. When members of Thompson's team showed up at their presentation wearing feathery chicken

outfits, the KFC people—who take their business very seriously—walked out of the meeting.

For Middleton, the new-business game is a matter of life or
death—not a costume party. He views himself as a sort of military man, constantly battling other agencies for clients. He and
his small staff operate out of a quiet suite several floors below
Y&R's daily hustle and bustle. One of the offices in this insu-
lated bunker contains a round oak table surrounded by plush
chairs. The walls are lined with blue looseleaf notebooks,
crammed with "top secret" details about American consumers.
A heavy door with several locks guards the entranceway. This
is the "War Room." It remains unoccupied until one of Middleton's intelligence sources, scattered throughout the Fortune
500 companies, reports that a major corporation has decided to
seek a fresh approach to advertising. At this point, the Y&R executive mobilizes the agency's high command. When Kroll,
Plummer, and others join him in this inner sanctum, strategy
for acquiring the new account is developed.

The most critical of these gatherings took place in 1977,
when it was learned that Kentucky Fried Chicken was looking
for a new agency. Y&R had never had a fast-food client, so
Kroll dispatched researchers all over the country to talk to KFC
customers and to learn how the business actually operated. Executives at Ted Bates, Y&R's main competition for the account,
spent much less time outside their New York headquarters
doing similar homework. Y&R's team in the field reaped the rewards of its hard work by bringing back a remarkable set of
videotaped interviews with Belongers, KFC's prime patrons.

It seemed that the chicken chain was losing its clientele to
McDonald's because KFC's franchises were situated in unsafe
inner-city locations. People felt more comfortable stopping at
the brightly lit Golden Arches than at KFC. Late one evening,
during a discussion in the War Room, John McGarry, a senior
executive at Y&R, came up with a way to get the fading fast-
food giant back on its feet.

Kentucky Fried Chicken, like Jell-O, had to become a vehicle
for pulling Belonger families together. The chain's ads had to
show moms and dads and kids sharing wonderful moments at

the dinner table after picking up a friendly old-fashioned meal of fried chicken, mashed potatoes, and biscuits and bringing it back to the house. Let McDonald's woo folks out into the night with its greasy burger snacks and plastic ambience. Kentucky Fried Chicken would promote such wholesome virtues as home, hearth, and nutrition.

Young & Rubicam created a speculative campaign featuring warm country music and an uplifting theme: "It's so nice to feel so good about a meal, feel so good about Kentucky Fried Chicken." Kroll believed that this approach would help to erase the harsh opinion people had about KFC and to create a new, cozier image. Bates, on the other hand, offered advertising of the hard-hitting Rosser Reeves type that hammered away at the hamburger while doing very little to alter the public's negative perception of KFC. After two weeks of deliberation, Y&R was awarded the account. In the seven years since the agency first began to work with KFC, the chain has regained its financial health and registered double-digit sales increases on a regular basis.

Young & Rubicam has gained many new clients over the past few years, but none has benefited from the agency's Freudian advertising as much as Dr. Pepper. The shop landed the soft-drink account a little over a decade ago, when W. W. "Foots" Clements, Dr. Pepper's feisty president, flew up to New York from Texas in search of marketing help. At that time, the beverage was sold primarily in the South and Southwest, but Clements wanted to distribute it nationally, to compete against the big boys at Pepsi and Coke.

This seemed like an audacious dream—even to the brazen executives on Madison Avenue. Nonetheless, almost every agency in town made a pitch for the $20 million piece of business. Most of the ads presented to the company's chief imitated the commercials produced by Pepsi or Coke: pretty people, wet bottles, volleyball games, surfing parties—Clements saw every cliché in the book. Then he visited Young & Rubicam.

The agency had spent several months interviewing postadolescents, some of America's biggest soda guzzlers, and it had learned many refreshing things about young consumers' tastes in carbonated beverages. These Emulators felt uncertain about their prospects for success in adult society. They were nervous, uptight, and eager to make their mark in the world. The research showed that they would be receptive to a unique kind of soda, a brash, outrageous drink that would set them apart as they began to make their way through life. The Y&R campaign that won Clements over positioned Dr. Pepper as a confidence-building beverage, not just sweet, fizzy pop. The advertising empathized with kids struggling to find themselves by portraying Dr. Pepper as an underdog, too—"America's most misunderstood soft drink." Several years later, the agency began to reinforce youngsters' sense of individuality by calling the beverage "The most original soft drink." And by the late 1970s, when Dr. Pepper was well established among the young, commercials featured a charismatic pied piper who pushed the peer approval button and informed all the stragglers that it was cool to join the crowd, to "be a Pepper."

Young & Rubicam's advertising strategy, which helped Dr. Pepper become a reassuring friend for confused and uncertain Emulators, has boosted the soft drink into the big leagues. It's now the fifth-largest-selling soda in the United States, behind Coke, Pepsi, diet Coke, and Seven-Up.

One of Y&R's most satisfying moments came in 1979, when it snatched the Merrill Lynch account away from Ogilvy & Mather, its archrival. The brokerage house had severed relations with O&M when David Ogilvy chose its competitor, First Boston Corporation, to offer additional stock in his agency. Donald Regan, currently Secretary of the Treasury, then Merrill Lynch's chairman, took this as a personal affront and immediately began searching for a new advertising partner. Regan fired O&M as a matter of principle, not because it lacked creative spark. He knew that the agency's powerful campaign—"Merrill Lynch Is Bullish on America"—had helped his firm flourish on Wall Street during the early 1970s, despite a depressed economy.

Y&R was one of the many suitors from Madison Avenue to go after the $20 million Merrill Lynch business. But once again, Plummer's research separated it from the pack. Interviews with consumers revealed that the "Bullish on America" ads, which featured a herd of cattle, appealed primarily to group-oriented Belongers. The message these viewers took away from the commercials was that Merrill Lynch offered people safety, security, and an opportunity to share in America's economic growth. Young & Rubicam told Regan that Merrill Lynch could increase its business if it focused attention on the more affluent Emulator-Achievers, the heaviest investors in the country. This was music to the Wall Street baron's ears. He wanted to transform his company from a simple securities specialist into a vast financial supermarket that would sell an entire line of such high-priced goodies as precious metals and deluxe real estate properties. Merrill Lynch would have to attract well-heeled customers if his plan was to work.

Plummer's profile of the Emulator-Achievers indicated that these are success-driven citizens who have personal—not collective—monetary goals. They don't want to share their wealth with anybody. People like these are elitists who reject any attempt to lump them in with the rest of society. Young & Rubicam believed that if a herd of cattle continued to star in Merrill Lynch's commercials, the firm would lose its opportunity to appeal to these big-spending cowboy capitalists.

The agency unveiled a subtle variation on Ogilvy's old theme. In the new campaign, a solitary bull strutted across the television screen. This animal—and, by association, the target audience—was labeled "A Breed Apart." One spot showed the arrogant bull searching for, and finding, a golden needle in a haystack. Clearly, investors who did business with Merrill Lynch were savvy, resourceful moneymakers. Regan, impressed by Young & Rubicam's perceptions, handed the responsibility for his company's advertising over to Ney's people—a decision that helped turn Merrill Lynch into one of the dominant financial institutions in America.

Young & Rubicam's second major new-business win over Ogilvy & Mather followed on the heels of its Merrill Lynch victory. During the spring of 1979, both agencies fought for the $75 million Lincoln-Mercury account. It was a close contest, but Y&R won because it presented advertising that promised to alter the automobile manufacturer's image radically. For years, Mercury had been seen as an overpriced and poorly made American family car. Ferrell believed that a dramatic television campaign could help erase this perception and convince consumers that Mercury was a high-tech engineering marvel, equal to any import on the market.

He wanted his commercials to attract Societally Conscious Achievers, who had deserted Detroit in droves during the 1970s. The copywriter sensed that these inner-directed people were driving Toyotas, Datsuns, Saabs, and Volvos because domestic automobile ads no longer reached them. The typical 30-second spot from Detroit was as American as Mom and apple pie. Folksy families, who lived in houses bordered by white picket fences, boasted about Chevrolet or Oldsmobile as they slowly cruised through town in their new cars. Often they would include confusing mileage statistics or some nuts-and-bolts information about legroom in their sales pitches. This archaic approach captivated old-fashioned Belongers, but you couldn't expect experimental Societally Conscious Achievers to be impressed—especially when they had the option of choosing sleek and durable Japanese and German "driving machines."

With his "Genesis" campaign for Mercury, Ferrell hoped to regain the attention of Societally Conscious Achievers. These were mysterious and eerie commercials. During one half-minute, the camera simply focused on a new Lynx sitting alone on a mountain of volcanic rock somewhere in the middle of a barren desert. In another spot, the car rose from the sea (attached to the top of a hidden submarine) and floated into shore on foaming surf.

Each of these science-fiction ads, dubbed "new wave" by Madison Avenue observers, had pulsating electronic background music by Vangelis, who wrote the score for the movie *Chariots of Fire*. The entire effort cost more than $2 million to produce, making it one of the most expensive creative endeavors in Ad Alley's history.

The money was well spent, however; Societally Conscious Achievers soon began trickling back into Mercury showrooms to look at the new cars. And after a year, sales for the once distressed auto manufacturer had increased by almost 100 percent.

The next part of Ferrell's plan for transforming Mercury was more down-to-earth than "Genesis." Y&R's shrewd wordsmith realized from Plummer's research that Societally Conscious Achievers, the best-educated people in our society, still didn't believe that American cars were well made. So to help Mercury appear more like Volvo than like General Motors, he developed a series of insightful commercials appealing to the intellect of these skeptics. His copy for a Cougar ad, for example, used introspective language: "Even from a coldly rational, strictly analytical perspective, Cougar is beautiful. A car that's designed to please the eye is no longer enough. It must also please the mind. The shape of the American automobile just became more intelligent. Mercury. The substance shows."

Ferrell's psychological campaigns for Mercury—so different from David Ogilvy's factual descriptions of Rolls-Royce in the 1950s and Bill Bernbach's low-key humor on behalf of VW in the 1960s—brought a new breed of customer to the ailing Detroit company and helped set it on the road to recovery.

Young & Rubicam's pioneering use of image transformation in the 1970s had even more impact on Madison Avenue and American society than Rosser Reeves's first television commercials had two decades earlier. Y&R's adoption of psychoanalysis taught Ad Alley executives how to exploit consumers' emotional vulnerabilities. By stamping the cachet of indispensability on the most ordinary products and persuading the public to purchase at will, these image technicians ushered in a new and improved era of materialism.

4 GIANT-KILLER

Philip Morris Takes On the Marketing Establishment

One of the corporations that benefited most dramatically from the psychographic advertising revolution of the 1970s was Philip Morris. The perceptive company produced a steady stream of marketing breakthroughs during the past decade, for such products as Miller Beer, Merit Cigarettes, and the Seven-Up line of soft drinks. These innovations have helped to increase the firm's annual revenue from $1 billion in 1970 to approximately $12 billion in 1983.

Philip Morris's strength—what really sets it apart from the competition—is its unique ability to sense shifts in consumer attitudes and capitalize on them before anyone else. This valuable skill isn't the result of gazing at a crystal ball; rather, the company has one of the largest and most talented in-house research departments in the business. Philip Morris researchers—unlike those employed by many other corporations—are renowned for the long hours they spend in the field as well as their vigilant surveillance of the American public's changing tastes and values. Time and time again over the last fourteen years, this kind of legwork has enabled the company to contend with—

and often defeat—larger, more affluent opponents in the marketplace. For Philip Morris, knowledge is power.

The firm's first major success came in the early 1970s at the expense of Anheuser-Busch, the St. Louis beer baron. Sensing an opportunity for profit in the world of suds and lager, Philip Morris spent $130 million to purchase Miller Brewing, a small, fading enterprise up in Milwaukee. The company's diversification into the beer business—its first major foray outside its traditional province of cigarette making—surprised many on Madison Avenue, especially since Miller was considered by most observers to be such a minor force in the brewing world.

Despite this industry skepticism, however, Philip Morris forged ahead. Having acquired the floundering concern, the large tobacco merchant undertook an exhaustive psychological research study that revealed the inner needs of American beer drinkers. With the help of Ad Alley, the corporation went on to develop its well-known campaign for Miller High Life—"Miller Time." These empathetic commercials were aimed at hard-working Belongers, who were looking for a reprieve from the harsh demands of their blue-collar jobs.

Several years later, in an effort to expand its influence in the beer market and to capture a larger portion of the drinking public, Philip Morris created Lite, diet suds for paunchy middle-aged men. The company's incisive research revealed that many Belongers felt like sissies drinking the watered-down brew. To remove this stigma, the firm's advertising agency at the time, McCann-Erickson, produced a series of humorous television commercials that featured brawny ex-athletes drinking Lite. By 1982, Miller Lite represented about 60 percent of all low-calorie beer sold in the United States.

This double-barreled Belonger strategy helped Philip Morris close the gap and almost draw even with Anheuser-Busch in 1982—just twelve years after its acquisition of Miller. The company then decided to update its popular "Miller Time" campaign. Philip Morris's research department was at it again. When data showed the firm's executives that the balance of power among beer-drinking Belongers was shifting from traditional family men to a younger, more restless group—a blue-collar elite consisting largely of disgruntled Vietnam veterans—the marketers immediately yanked anybody over thirty-five off Miller High Life's commercials. Instead of middle-aged men slumping at the bar after a hard day in front of the blast furnace, the ads now showed animated young workers slurping beer while playing cards, shooting pool, or bowling. The upbeat spots were filled with the sounds of pulsating rock or hard-driving country music rather than mellow ballads.

While Philip Morris provided facts, figures, and psychological insights about the beer business, it was two Madison Avenue executives, Bill Backer and Carl Spielvogel, who transformed these important bits and pieces of marketing information into cohesive, convincing, and creative advertising campaigns. This productive agency-client collaboration, which resulted in all of the Miller High Life and Miller Lite commercials of the past decade, began in the early 1970s.

At that time, the two veteran ad men were still working at McCann-Erickson—then the second-largest ad agency in America. Spielvogel, a former *New York Times* financial reporter, was considered by many on Madison Avenue to be the smartest marketer on the street. He was one of the men who oversaw the demanding Coca-Cola account, which required McCann to produce and place ads in forty-eight countries around the globe. Backer was McCann's creative whiz, the talented copywriter who gave us "Things Go Better with Coke," "It's the Real Thing," and "I'd Like to Buy the World a Coke."

The pair's colleagues at McCann were always surprised by how well the middle-aged Backer and Spielvogel—known as Madison Avenue's odd couple—got along and how smoothly they handled Coke's advertising needs, even under the worst kind of pressure.

Backer, a courtly southerner, studied music at Yale. After graduation he came to New York and started writing jingles for several ad agencies. Unable to support himself as a freelance songwriter, he joined McCann-Erickson as a clerk. Over the next twenty-odd years, he gradually worked his way up from

the mailroom to the executive suite. When he wasn't developing commercials at McCann, Backer could be found living the
life of a gentleman farmer on his large spread in the Virginia
countryside. Raising horses is still his passion, and he often
spends his lunch hour hunched over *The Daily Racing Form.*

Spielvogel grew up in Brooklyn during the Depression. He
landed a job as a copyboy at *The New York Times* after attending City College, and that led to a ten-year stint as a writer
at the paper. After a decade of observing businessmen from the
sidelines, the promising newspaperman yearned to join the corporate game himself. His move from journalism to commerce
was a natural one—after all, he had been closely associated
with the marketing community as a reporter for many years and
was intrigued by the ins and outs of the advertising industry.
Spielvogel joined Interpublic, McCann's parent company, and
began a steady climb to the top of the firm's hierarchy.

The ad man's biggest break, the one that catapulted him into
the upper reaches of Interpublic, came in early 1970, when
George Weissman, then a top executive at Philip Morris (he
later became chairman), offered him the opportunity to handle
the $20 million Miller Beer account.

Over the next nine years, Backer and Spielvogel changed the
way millions of men think about beer. In the process, they
proved the worth of Philip Morris's investment in its brewery,
by helping to transform Miller into a prosperous company. But
the story doesn't end there. In 1979, Spielvogel was certain that
he'd be named chairman of Interpublic—especially after his
successes with Coke and Miller—but instead, the top job went
to his archrival, Philip Geier. To no one's surprise, Spielvogel
resigned from Interpublic after more than two decades on the
payroll. One month later, Backer left his post at McCann, because Interpublic's new management began telling him how to
write commercials.

Initially, it seemed that there was no life after advertising for
either man. For a while, they traveled—Spielvogel went to
China; Backer went down to his farm. When they returned,
each executive began a round of lunches with agency chairmen

eager to hire them. None of the offers—and they were all very lucrative—was appealing.

Finally, Backer and Spielvogel met to discuss their situation. They reminisced about the past while sitting at Spielvogel's regular table upstairs at "21." Over an elegant meal, Backer reminded Spielvogel that their track record as a team was unparalleled on Madison Avenue. By the time dessert and coffee came, the two men had decided to start their own agency, Backer & Spielvogel.

Having set up offices in a small suite at the Gotham Hotel, off Fifth Avenue, Backer and Spielvogel spent June and July of 1979 beating the bushes for accounts, but none turned up. As with most fledgling agencies, potential clients were hesitant to get involved with an unproved start-up operation—even if the principals had been Madison Avenue stars. By the time the August doldrums rolled around, the two ad men had begun to wonder whether they had made a mistake. Then one day they got a call from George Weissman, Philip Morris's leader, who had admired Backer's and Spielvogel's work on the Miller account when they were still at McCann. Weissman asked the pair to take over Miller's advertising. Spielvogel told the Philip Morris executive that they would be glad to pitch in.

When word leaked out about McCann's $100 million loss of Miller later that afternoon—the second-largest account change in advertising history—Interpublic stock dropped five points. Bad news for Interpublic was good news for the recently established Backer & Spielvogel. Once Philip Morris "certified" the new agency, other companies followed suit. Today, five years after Miller came aboard, the shop's client list includes such major marketers as the Campbell Soup Company and J&B Scotch. With almost $400 million in billings, Backer & Spielvogel is the fastest-growing enterprise on Madison Avenue.

The 1970s were heady years for George Weissman and Philip Morris. The company entered the beer business with no experience and a broken-down brewery, but it eventually was able to pose a serious challenge to the longtime industry giant, Anheuser-Busch. At the same time, the corporation reversed its

declining fortunes in the cigarette market with the help of sophisticated advertising.

Philip Morris was struggling in the cigarette industry—
trailing the front-runner, R.J. Reynolds, by a wide margin—as
late as 1970. To help offset its languishing tobacco brands, the
concerned company purchased Miller, hoping that a diversification into beer would bring in additional revenue. At the heart
of the marketer's problem, however, lay Marlboro, a cigarette
that had been in search of an identity for half a century.

When it was first introduced, in the early 1920s, Marlboro
was sold as a woman's smoke. Ads touted the brand's soft taste,
calling it "Mild as May." This demure approach didn't catch on,
so Philip Morris resorted to gimmickry by adding an ivory tip to
the cigarette. This didn't do much good either; women complained that their lipstick stained the new mouthpiece. The
company responded by transforming Marlboro into a red-
tipped cigarette during the late 1930s. But by this time, the
damage had been done—Marlboro no longer appealed to the female consumers toward whom it had been geared. Philip Morris took Marlboro off the market in the 1940s.

When the filter revolution began, during the 1950s, the company resurrected the cigarette. The brand's ads now ignored
taste and promoted instead Marlboro's unique crushproof, flip-
top box. Like its predecessors, this strategy proved to be inef-
fectual. Finally, in the mid-1950s, Philip Morris decided to re-
position Marlboro as a man's filter cigarette. This move didn't
make much sense, since women represented close to 75 percent of all filter smokers at the time. (Men were still too macho
to give up their full-bodied smokes: Camels, Lucky Strikes, or
Chesterfields.) Nonetheless, the company and its advertising
agency, Leo Burnett, tried several television campaigns aimed
at the male market. In one of them, Julie London, a sexy cabaret
singer, crooned, "Why don't you settle back and have a Marlboro?" When this didn't achieve the desired effect, a new pitch
was devised: "Marlboro delivers the goods on flavor," rasped a
seductive female announcer. This also failed to win men smokers over. And while Philip Morris bumbled along, other filters—

notably Winston and Salem from R. J. Reynolds—were making
great strides in attracting cigarette buyers.

When Weissman assumed responsibility for Marlboro in the
late 1950s, the always analytical executive, who wanted to
learn more about the tobacco market, felt that a research study
of American smoking habits was in order. The results of this investigation were fascinating. The one group of consumers that
cigarette manufacturers had neglected was the impressionable
young Emulators. In search of an identity, these postadolescent
kids were just beginning to smoke as a way of declaring their independence from their parents. But until now, marketers
hadn't addressed their special needs. Weissman thought that if
Marlboro could somehow appeal to them, then maybe the
brand could be turned around and made profitable.

Jack Landry, a brilliant advertising mind at Philip Morris, was
given the job of working with Leo Burnett to produce commercials that would turn rookie smokers on to Marlboro. Landry's
team spent months trying to come up with the right image to
capture the youth market's fancy. At last, it latched onto the
concept of a weathered-looking cowboy riding off into the
sunset—a perfect symbol of independence and individualistic
rebellion.

The Marlboro Man, as he was called, was an immediate hit.
Insecure young adults flocked to the brand because they
wanted to be as cool and confident as the cowboy—they, too,
wanted to be tough and free. Flushed with success, Landry expanded the scope of the ads—with the unforgettable line
"Come to Marlboro Country." This wasn't an invitation to visit
Wyoming or Colorado; it was a call to Emulators to get it together by smoking Marlboros. Landry's cowboy campaigns
demonstrated the real power of psychological advertising. By
1976, Marlboro, the once-floundering brand, had become the
best-selling cigarette in America, and today it provides Philip
Morris with close to $4 billion a year in revenue.

Although obviously pleased with Marlboro's revival, the restless Weissman refused to stand still. During the mid-1970s, he
again asked Philip Morris's research department to study the
cigarette industry. Its findings revealed that during the 1980s

the number of Emulators in the United States would remain static, but the percentage of Societally Conscious Achievers would almost double. This was hardly good news for Marlboro, which was getting approximately two-thirds of its smokers from those eighteen to twenty-four years old. Clearly, the big brand's salad days wouldn't continue into the next decade.

To take up the slack, Philip Morris began developing Merit, a new low-tar cigarette, for the growing inner-directed population. Weissman positioned this brand as the Volvo of the tobacco business, with advertising that was serious and authoritative without being too clinical. Health-oriented Societally Conscious smokers had to be convinced that lighting up a Merit was the next best thing to not smoking at all, that it was the first cigarette that not only tasted great but also wouldn't fill you up with tar or nicotine. Philip Morris's campaign accomplished this by characterizing the introduction of Merit as an important scientific discovery. "There's Nothing Halfway About It," proclaimed one of the ads. "The One That Rewrote the Book," boasted another. This dramatic approach helped persuade concerned and thoughtful inner-directed smokers that the company had produced something truly remarkable—a safe cigarette.

No other tobacco manufacturer has been able to compete against this unspoken advertising claim. R. J. Reynolds, always formidable, tried—but it got blown away. In 1977, it introduced Real, which was touted as the granola bar of the cigarette business. Unfortunately, Real turned out to be more like the Edsel. Reynolds advertising, showing the cigarette package and an "all-natural" tobacco leaf, just didn't excite or energize experimental Societally Conscious Achievers, and the company lost millions of dollars trying to compete with Philip Morris's space-age smoke.

Although Merit is currently one of the most popular cigarettes of the inner-directed 1980s, it may soon face a challenge from the increasing number of brands targeted at Societally Conscious women. Lorillard, for example, spent close to $100 million in 1983 to persuade active contemporary female smokers to switch to its new cigarette, Satin. Its pitch is simple. Busy women today want—and need—time alone, without interruptions from the kids, boss, or husband. Now they can spoil themselves with the "Satin Moment," a luxurious low-tar interlude in an otherwise hectic day. Early reports indicate that this strategy is appealing to many inner-directed women, who are always on the move, trying to juggle careers and family.

Philip Morris could probably offset this invasion by transforming Virginia Slims, its female Emulator brand, into a Societally Conscious cigarette. Slims advertising ("You've Come a Long Way, Baby"), selling glamour, liberation, and success, seems dated. Most young American women today are more secure about their abilities and don't need injections of confidence from marketers. To protect Merit, the company should update Virginia Slims as a more contemporary smoke.

Once Philip Morris rejuvenated its cigarette and beer businesses, it was ready to enter an even more competitive arena—the $30 billion soft-drink industry. Profits from Marlboro, Merit, and Miller enabled the firm to purchase the Seven-Up beverage company in 1978 for half a billion dollars, an astronomical price that made Wall Street cringe. Why pay so much for Seven-Up, asked the skeptics, when it could never expect to compete on even terms with Coke or Pepsi, which controlled 60 percent of the soda market? Why acquire an also-ran? Weissman had no immediate answer, but he did have a long-term strategy. In time, he would bring the cola giants to their knees and make his large investment pay off.

Philip Morris's cigarette research, which had successfully spawned Merit, revealed that the number of postadolescent Emulators (among America's biggest soda guzzlers) would remain constant over the next ten years. Other data indicated that the percentage of old-fashioned Belongers (heavy Coke and Pepsi drinkers) would decline during the same period. These reports made one thing perfectly clear: the soft-drink industry's large outer-directed audience would not grow in the coming decade.

Although Coke and Pepsi are still riding high in the early 1980s—with billions of dollars in annual sales and with the av-

erage American citizen drinking 40 gallons of soda per year—
they will very likely lose some of their momentum in this country by the 1990s. A shrinking of their domestic consumer base
and the rise of health-oriented Societally Conscious Achievers
will almost certainly weaken the companies' future hold on the
soft-drink business.

Weissman and his staff concluded that Coke and Pepsi were
out of touch with the emerging psychographics in this country, that they were vulnerable in the marketplace. The executive plotted an entirely new course for Seven-Up, one that he
hoped would exploit America's growing inner-directedness. He
would leave the increasingly less profitable ranks of Belongers
and Emulators to Coke and Pepsi and aggressively pursue the
previously untapped—and expanding—Societally Conscious
segment.

Weissman understood that this audience of adults in their
late twenties and thirties had largely forsaken soda pop in favor
of more wholesome beverages such as apple juice, seltzer, and
Red Zinger tea. Nevertheless, Philip Morris's chairman sensed a
major opportunity in this apparent defection from soft drinks.
Maybe, he thought, he could get these counterculturalists interested in Seven-Up. After all, he reasoned, his soda—with its
clean lemon-lime taste—was different from Coke or Pepsi. In
the past, Seven-Up had always been successful when it had
clearly distinguished itself from other soft drinks in the consumer's mind. Back in the late 1960s, for example, it took an
antiestablishment position and billed itself as the Un-Cola. The
Woodstock Generation loved this rebelliousness, and Seven-
Up's sales zoomed upward for a short time. Then the novelty
wore off and many young citizens returned to organic beverages once again.

Despite this once productive marriage—and the distinctive
Seven-Up flavor—Weissman was under no illusions. He knew
how difficult it would be to convince the inner-directed to purchase a sugary, super-fizzed soft drink—no matter how good or
refreshing it tasted—unless he found the right psychological
hook.

He soon got the ammunition he was looking for. One day,

while thumbing through an issue of *Consumer Reports,* the executive stumbled across an article on the growing public concern about caffeine intake. The piece noted that 66 percent of all American adults wanted to cut back on or eliminate the caffeine in their diets.

Weissman's researchers confirmed the *Consumer Reports* findings; they also provided information on the large number of common, everyday products containing caffeine. The executive scanned the list—five ounces of instant coffee, 53 milligrams; twelve ounces of Coca-Cola, 34 milligrams; twelve ounces of Pepsi-Cola, 37 milligrams. There it was: the opening he had been seeking. Coke, Pepsi, and nearly all the other sodas were weak on the caffeine issue. Not only was Seven-Up caffeine-free, but, unlike the colas, it contained no artificial flavors, preservatives, or coloring. This was an environmentally sound soft drink, one that Societally Conscious Achievers could believe in.

Other marketers had tried to sell low-caffeine or no-caffeine soda in the past. Canada Dry introduced Sport in 1968 and Spur in 1979, but both beverages failed in the marketplace. In the mid-1970s, Anheuser-Busch came out with Chelsea, a drink with lemon, lime, ginger, and apple flavoring and just a hint of alcohol. The concoction contained no chemicals, no caffeine, one-third less sugar, and one-third fewer calories than regular soda. Despite its inner-directed potential, the promising cola alternative also quickly disappeared from supermarket shelves. A combination of unfocused and uninspired advertising and an unexpected consumer protest centering on Chelsea's minuscule alcoholic content led to the beverage's downfall. Many parents were concerned that the refreshment would encourage teenage drinking.

Weissman hoped to avoid a similar fate with Seven-Up. He was determined to separate the beverage from Coke and Pepsi. He would position the lemon-lime drink as a contemporary soda, one that had the added health advantage of being caffeine-free.

Seven-Up's hard-hitting commercials were produced by N. W. Ayer, the agency known primarily for its "Reach Out and

Touch Someone'' ads, created on behalf of AT&T. Ayer followed Philip Morris's instructions to the letter. In each 30-
second spot, a variety of sodas was lined up—including Coke
and Pepsi. The camera panned across can after can after can.
Tug McGraw, an extremely popular relief pitcher for the Philadelphia Phillies, then appeared and challenged viewers to identify the beverage without caffeine. One by one, he pointed to
the cans. "Not this one, not this one, and not this one," he said.
Finally, a single can stood alone in all its decaffeinated glory.
"It's Seven-Up," exclaimed McGraw, "with no caffeine. I mean
zero. Never had it, never will."

   The $45 million campaign's impact was felt almost immedi-
ately. During its first six months on the air in 1982, Philip Morris received close to a million encouraging letters and telegrams
from people all over the country. At the same time, supermarkets were flooded with consumers loading up their shopping
carts with six-packs of Seven-Up. Weissman had succeeded
where others had failed. Today, more than two years later, his
inner-directed soft drink's popularity continues to grow. Although Seven-Up has lost its number-three position in the marketplace to the recently introduced diet Coke, Philip Morris's
"healthy" beverage is still expected to increase its sales to approximately 350 million cases in 1984, a 5 percent unit gain
over 1983. To sustain this momentum, Seven-Up recently rein-
stated Geoffrey Holder—the soda's affable and offbeat spokesman of the hip, counterculture 1960s—to solidify its individualistic image.

   Not surprisingly, Seven-Up's initial no-caffeine commercials
did not endear Philip Morris to either Coke or Pepsi. Predict-
ably, the managements of both companies were furious when
they saw their products criticized over and over again on national television. They discussed the possibility of taking legal
action against Seven-Up, but what could they do? The new advertising may have been controversial, but it told the truth—
Coke and Pepsi contained caffeine; Seven-Up didn't.

   The frustrated cola kings couldn't stop the embarrassing TV
spots and they couldn't sue Seven-Up, so they tried to under-

mine Weissman's strategy in other ways. Pepsi, for instance, contacted bottlers that carried its drink as well as Seven-Up. They were encouraged to complain to Philip Morris about the caffeine-free soda's new ads or face the possible loss of their Pepsi franchise rights. This threat scared many of the bottlers, who depended on the cola for much of their business. Despite the warning, however, most of the franchisees saw the merit of Philip Morris's new marketing strategy and backed the company.

Coke then tried to take its case to consumers, issuing a statement claiming that caffeine in soft drinks posed no health hazard. The company also accused Philip Morris of using scare tactics to mislead the public. But this broadside didn't deter inner-directed shoppers from purchasing Seven-Up; sales for the newly positioned no-caffeine soda continued to rise.

Seven-Up's growth soon began to alarm the two large cola corporations. They knew that Philip Morris had fought its way to the top ranks of the beer industry by aggressively promoting Miller High Life and Lite, and they were concerned that Weissman would employ similar tactics to take over the soft-drink business. In an effort to head the bold executive and his colleagues off at the pass, Pepsi quickly developed its own decaffeinated soda, Pepsi Free, which was introduced just several months after Seven-Up's anti-cola campaign first aired. Coke eventually followed suit; almost a year later, it came out with caffeine-free versions of all its carbonated beverages. In early 1984, Pepsi began selling Slice, a new lemon-lime drink that contains fruit juice and vitamins, in an apparent effort to attract health-conscious consumers.

Thus far, joining the no-caffeine crusade hasn't made it much easier for Coke or Pepsi to win over Societally Conscious Achievers. For hip counterculturalists, colas are a cliché, old-fashioned beverages that don't fit into their contemporary lifestyle.

Part of the reason that Coke and Pepsi are considered old hat has to do with their advertising. Both brands' commercials have traditionally portrayed a world that, for the most part, has already passed us by—a world of small towns, large families, and unrestrained joy, tenderness and togetherness, simplicity and stability. These nostalgic spots have usually been set to such syrupy songs as "Have a Coke and a Smile," "Have a Pepsi Day," "Coke Is It," and "Pepsi Now"—anthems that a large number of inner-directed citizens have apparently tuned out.

But instead of changing the direction or target audience of their campaigns, Coke and Pepsi have generally responded to this consumer apathy by simply spending more than the competition on their television messages. Last year, for example, the cola giants' combined advertising and promotion expenditures in this country reached an astronomical $900 million. Their commercials, which tend to look and sound alike, cost approximately $300,000 each and are closer to Hollywood extravaganzas than Madison Avenue sales pitches. The companies believe that such big-budget spectacles will grab the attention of all American drinkers—including the Societally Conscious. So far, however, this lavish advertising hasn't achieved this ambitious—and unrealistic—goal. A confidential study, recently conducted by a Madison Avenue research company, revealed that Coke and Pepsi commercials had to be seen twice as often as Seven-Up spots to be remembered by counterculture shoppers.

Although the cola kings' commercials often seem out of date in today's increasingly inner-directed society, their all-American advertising was once considered quite relevant. From 1960 to 1980, these campaigns were instrumental in helping Coke and Pepsi corral herds of Emulators and Belongers—the folks who dominated America's consumer culture at the time.

During the 1960s, the emphasis was on recruiting restless postadolescents in their cola-drinking prime and molding them into a large loyal gang—the Pepsi Generation, for example. The object was to get kids to join the crowd, so Madison Avenue's soft-drink commercials repeatedly showed masses of youngsters having a wonderful time together while drinking soda pop. One typical 30-second spot of the era showed a bunch of guys driving a dune buggy into a lake at full speed on a hot summer's day while a group of tawny blond California girls cheered them on—in between gulps of Coke.

Another classic featured hundreds of college students dancing on a raft in the middle of the ocean somewhere. A camera attached to a helicopter zoomed in to reveal a Pepsi in each person's hand, and, without missing a beat, the dancers tilted their bottles to the sun and downed twelve ounces of carbonated pleasure in unison. An announcer then told viewers that Pepsi was "for those who think young," and a chorus began singing this bouncy refrain:

> *The lively crowd today agrees,*
> *Those who think young say, "Pepsi please";*
> *They pick the right one, the modern light one,*
> *Now it's Pepsi for those who think young.*

This advertising was so effective that by the mid-1960s just about everyone under twenty-five in America was hooked on cola. A poll taken in 1965, for instance, revealed that almost 70 percent of those between thirteen and twenty-four considered themselves part of the Pepsi Generation.

As the war in Vietnam began to escalate, and the youth of this country started getting a taste of reality, Coke and Pepsi responded to the tumultuous times with sweet, innocent campaigns designed to bolster the shell-shocked Emulators. In one famous spot, Coca-Cola assembled 500 children from nations all around the globe up on an Italian hillside. There they sang Bill Backer's ode to peace, love, and carbonation—"I'd Like to Buy the World a Coke."

Not to be outdone, Pepsi countered with its own set of lofty commercials. The good news they brought to Emulators was, "You've Got a Lot to Live, and Pepsi's Got a Lot to Give." The embattled young and their favorite cola would face up to things together—unafraid. As the chorus from one of these 1969 ads suggests:

> *There's a whole new way of living,*
> *Pepsi helps supply the drive;*
> *It's got a lot to give*
> *For those who like to live,*
> *'Cause Pepsi helps 'em come alive.*

It's the Pepsi Generation,
Comin' at ya, goin' strong . . .

Another major shift in soft-drink marketing took place in the
early 1970s, when Richard Nixon was President. Cola companies turned their attention away from the youthful Emulators of
Kennedy's New Frontier and toward the Belongers of the Silent
Majority. This new strategy marked the first time since the early
1950s that the soda giants had appealed directly to adults as
well as their offspring. Donald Kendall, president of Pepsi and
one of Nixon's corporate patrons, was so caught up in the new
conservative mood sweeping America that he asked Pepsi's ad
agency, BBDO, to develop ads that would feature members of
the "Smiling Majority." This uplifting advertising, generally
targeted at Belonger families, offered emotionally charged nostalgic vignettes of everyday life and provided grown-up citizens, burdened by life's hardships, with 30 seconds of psychic
relief.

Each of Pepsi's campaigns during the 1970s was filled with
what Madison Avenue called "warm fuzzies": adorable children romping in the backyard with puppies, kindly grandmoth-
ers celebrating their birthdays on the front porch with the entire clan, and immigrant cousins stepping off the boat to a
loving embrace.

One of the biggest tearjerkers the brand produced was its
"Marry Me Sue" spot of several years ago. In this 30-second
soap opera, folks from a prairie town are out under the broiling
midday sun watching a skywriting show. Among the spectators
is a cowboy and a young woman. As the camera pans the crowd
(drinking Pepsi), we notice that these two are exchanging shy
glances at one another. There's definitely something going on
between them. The viewer is then shown some of the skywriting and more shots of the perspiring audience drinking Pepsi.
Finally, the camera scans the heavens where the skywriter's ultimate message—"Marry Me, Sue"—takes form. Sue, with tears
welling up in her eyes, nods her head. The cowboy reaches
over and hugs her. The theme music, which has been playing
throughout this half-minute, suddenly builds to a crescendo:

Come and taste it,
Pepsi's got it;
Pepsi's got your taste for life.
Come and taste all that life can be,
That Pepsi spirit in you and me.

A picture of the newly engaged couple holding bottles of Pepsi—as well as each other—is frozen on the screen with a final reminder: "Catch that Pepsi spirit! Drink it in."

Coca-Cola's executives had received advance knowledge of Pepsi's impending "Spirit" campaign from well-placed intelligence sources almost six months before "Marry Me, Sue" initially aired. In an effort to beat their cola rivals to the punch, Coke's marketers informed their agency, McCann-Erickson, that it would have to develop and run an equally mushy and moving set of commercials first—if it wanted to hold on to the account. When this ultimatum arrived at McCann's New York headquarters, there was near-panic in the halls. The agency was still reeling from the recent departure of Backer and Spielvogel, not to mention the $100 million Miller Beer business they took with them.

To make matters even worse, Backer & Spielvogel had hired away some of McCann's most experienced executives. The shop's prospects were bleak, and morale was low. And now, Coca-Cola, a $750 million account worldwide, was threatening to drop the ax. If McCann lost Coke, it would almost certainly go under.

Recognizing the seriousness of the situation, McCann immediately began work on a new campaign for the brand. There wasn't much time, however. Coke wanted to quickly preempt Pepsi's dramatic new advertising before it was presented to the public. McCann was given ninety days to come up with an answer.

The agency called in its best art directors and copywriters. The group worked around the clock for several weeks, pausing only for brief catnaps on office couches. The pressure to produce was intense; one young wordsmith cracked under the strain and had to be taken home to recuperate. The team's spirits sagged when it learned that executives from Ted Bates had flown to Atlanta to confer with Coke's management about possibly handling the soft-drink account. Nonetheless, the hard-pressed staff kept at it. With only a few weeks to go before the final presentation at Coke's Atlanta headquarters, McCann's creative stars gathered to exchange the fruits of their labor. Many interesting ideas were bandied about at this meeting, but one theme line eventually took hold—"Have a Coke and a Smile."

The storyboard accompanying this umbrella slogan illustrated a commercial set in a cavernous football stadium. After a brutal game, Mean Joe Greene, the six-foot-eight lineman for the Pittsburgh Steelers, is trudging back to the dressing room. He's sweating, bruised and beaten. In one hand, he's carrying his battle-scarred helmet; in the other he has a torn jersey, which has been ripped off his back during the contest.

A boy suddenly emerges from the shadows. He looks up at Mean Joe and sees a warrior in distress. The youngster timidly offers the football star a Coke. At first, the athlete refuses the boy's kind gesture, but after a moment of reflection he accepts the bottle. Mean Joe grabs the Coke, turns it upside down, and drinks it all in one long gulp. Suddenly his scowl turns into a broad smile. Coke—and the kid—have brought him back to the land of the living.

The youngster turns away and heads off into the night. Mean Joe calls to him. "Hey, kid." "Yeah?" "Here." The football hero tosses the little guy his shredded jersey. The boy's face lights up, and a chorus chimes in: "Have a Coke and a Smile."

McCann decided to go ahead and film the commercial. When it was completed, the agency presented it to Coke's executives in Atlanta. There wasn't a dry eye left in the screening room, and it was immediately decided that McCann would keep the huge account. Armed with its own heart-wrenching campaign, Coke now set out to destroy Pepsi in the marketplace.

The cola wars have continued on into the 1980s, with Coke and Pepsi each employing the same type of free-floating emotional advertising as their main marketing weapons. In 1983, Pepsi came out with its "Now" campaign and spent almost

$300 million on advertising and promotion to drum this message into the heads of Americans:

> *Now is the time*
> *For all the taste you can find;*
> *Now is the time*
> *C'mon and let that Pepsi spirit shine.*

Coca-Cola has its own upbeat claim. The soft-drink company laid out close to $400 million in 1983 to inform American soda lovers in the United States that "Coke Is It." After twenty years, very little seems to have changed. The brand is still using all-American imagery in its ads—community softball games, farmers at work, and cheerleaders at play—as well as corny music and lyrics:

> *It's the smile you can't hide*
> *'Cause it comes from inside;*
> *Like the time you spend*
> *With your family and friends;*
> *It's the way you feel*
> *When you know it's real;*
> *Coke is it!*

Coke and Pepsi's emotional advertising has become so entrenched that both companies appear incapable of switching gears and appealing to the growing inner-directed market in this country. In a recent effort to reestablish a youthful audience for its cola, Pepsi launched its "Choice of a New Generation" campaign featuring super pop star Michael Jackson in several commercials and new-wave imagery in a handful of others. But while the energetic and entertaining spots may appeal to adolescent Emulators, it's unlikely that they will influence the larger and more crucial counterculture segment. Coca-Cola's upbeat new campaign for diet Coke also showcases celebrities—including media mogul Ted Turner and football star Marcus Allen—but it, too, seems to be directed at a stagnant target audience. Early reports indicate that the low-calorie soft drink is doing well among male Belongers, many of whom have switched from fattening regular Coke.

The future winners in the soda business will almost certainly be those—like Seven-Up—that can communicate with the emerging Societally Conscious majority. Nutrition, not nostalgia or break-dancing, is a key factor in motivating counterculture consumers to purchase soft drinks today.

5 PATRIOTS ON WHEELS

Detroit Starts to Fight Back

Time is beginning to run out for companies that are unwilling or unable to recognize the growing Societal Consciousness among this country's consumers. Upstart enterprises in tune with the times are slowly taking sales away from outer-directed corporate America, and if old-fashioned businesses don't respond to this marketing challenge soon, they could find themselves in some financial difficulty by the early 1990s.

The domestic auto industry has already experienced hard times. For much of the past fifteen years, it has buried its head in the sand as the number of imported cars entering the United States has steadily multiplied. This prolonged paralysis has prevented Detroit from competing on even terms against foreign manufacturers, and, as a result, almost an entire generation of young American drivers has gone with Japan, Germany, and Sweden. Unless there's a sudden burst of inner-directed thinking at General Motors, Ford, and Chrysler during the late 1980s, the situation could deteriorate even further.

It's hard to believe that America's once-powerful automobile business could break down, but the signs of decay are unmistakable. In 1972, for example, domestic auto makers sold just over 9 million new cars to the American public; in 1982, their annual sales amounted to less than 6 million vehicles. During these ten lean years, Detroit's share of the U.S. automobile market slid from 90 percent to a little more than 70 percent. About one out of every four cars on American highways today is imported.

This large defection has had a disastrous effect on the $100 billion auto industry's bottom line. In 1980 and 1981, for example, Detroit lost over $7 billion in operating profits. Financial setbacks of this kind have resulted in a great deal of human suffering, too. During the past decade, approximately one-quarter of all auto workers in the United States have been laid off at least once. Since 1972, more than 10 percent of all domestic-car dealerships have been forced to close or start selling foreign makes.

Detroit rebounded from its prolonged slump in 1983, registering an 18 percent increase in cars sold over 1982. The combined sales of domestic auto makers last year totaled almost 7 million vehicles. Despite this resurgence and the gains made in 1984, however, Motown's long-term prospects remain uncertain. A recent consumer study revealed that almost 70 percent of those who had purchased an imported car in the last three years were pleased with their choice and had little or no intention of switching to an American-made vehicle. The satisfaction quotient dropped precipitously, however, among owners of American cars. Only 35 percent of them said they were content with their selection, and almost half of the General Motors, Ford, and Chrysler drivers interviewed indicated that they might consider buying an import the next time around.

Executives in Detroit have blamed almost everyone but themselves for their failure to hold on to American consumers. They complain about unions, claiming that the average American laborer on an assembly line works half as hard but earns twice as much as his Japanese counterpart. This negative productivity, they say, drives the price of their cars way up and makes it virtually impossible for them to undersell those bargain-mobiles from abroad. They also castigate Congress in Washington for not erecting airtight trade barriers that would make it a crime for auto importers to market their products in this country. And they bridle at the government's expensive safety program, which requires every vehicle to have seat belts and pollution controls. According to automobile industry leaders, these regulations contribute unnecessarily to the high price of cars today.

The Federal Reserve Board's tight-money policy of the early 1980s, aimed at reducing inflation, was another target of the car manufacturers' discontent. This strategy, says the Motown majority, raised interest rates, made financing cars more difficult, and inevitably scared the buying public away from showrooms. Even the American educational establishment is chided for not producing as many bright engineers as, say, Japan or Germany. Without this talent, according to Detroit, United States auto manufacturers can't match the foreigners' sleek car designs, which generally appeal to younger consumers.

Unruly union members, uncooperative government officials, and an unsophisticated engineering corps—to some extent, all of these factors have contributed to the domestic auto industry's recent hard times. But Detroit's problems are minor when compared with the obstacles that Japanese car manufacturers had to overcome in order to sell their vehicles in the United States. For three decades following Pearl Harbor, Tokyo was branded in this country as a purveyor of shoddy merchandise—a reputation that was difficult to live down, even when Japan had first-rate products to offer. During the 1970s, against enormous odds, the foreigners finally succeeded in changing the way Americans viewed their goods by harnessing the power of television advertising.

The Japanese understood what most of Detroit has yet to grasp: A large percentage of consumer purchases are based on perceptions, on images. Millions of folks are cruising around in Datsuns, Toyotas, and Subarus today because they were influenced by television commercials that portrayed these cars as practical but spiffy driving machines.

Apart from a small price gap—Japanese cars tend to be slightly less expensive than their American counterparts—the only major differences between vehicles made in Tokyo and those made in Detroit are the ones Madison Avenue has established. When you get down to it, Chevy's Chevette is virtually the same car as Honda's Accord. The two vehicles have similar gas mileage statistics, an equivalent amount of interior space, and generally the same performance ability. But Honda ads have been more successful than Chevy's in conveying an aura of stylish simplicity that appeals to so many younger car buyers today. Last year, Honda Accord sales outpaced Chevette sales by 20 percent.

Ironically, things have finally come full circle. Fifteen years after their refusal to buy "tacky" Japeanese cars, many American consumers seem to have developed an emotional block against purchasing from Detroit. Now it's domestic automobiles that are viewed as poorly made, inefficient, and stodgy. This current negativism, like our former anti-Tokyo bias, has little, if any, basis in hard facts. One of the main reasons we have fallen out of love with American-made cars is that foreign auto manufacturers—unlike General Motors, Ford, or Chrysler—have been flooding our living rooms with psychologically appealing commercials.

In the meantime, Detroit's television campaigns appear to have lost their effectiveness, their edge. A research study recently revealed that although American auto makers spend the same amount as their Japanese competitors on advertising and promotion (approximately $1 billion annually), United States manufacturers' commercials had to be seen twice as often to gain the same level of attention among viewers. The typical 30-second spot from Motown shows Mom and Dad out with the kids for a leisurely Sunday drive around the neighborhood. The shiny car is a symbol of togetherness, and it signifies further that this clan owns a small piece of the American dream. Mileage statistics and seating dimensions punctuate this nostalgic family portrait, but unless you're a middle-aged traditionalist, the cozy message isn't likely to inspire you to visit the showroom.

Most viewers seem to be more excited by Tokyo's campaigns, which stress fun and adventure. This exuberant advertising features streamlined driving machines scooting up hills, bolting around treacherous mountain curves, and flying down highways as if they were airborne. Along with high-speed performance and maneuverability, these commercials also point out the quality, durability, and efficiency of Japanese automotive technology—an appealing equation for the burgeoning number of inner-directed consumers in this country. Unlike Detroit, the importers are selling a bold and personalized driving experience.

Only one domestic auto maker, Ford's Lincoln-Mercury division, has come close to emulating the foreigners' commercials. The company's surreal campaigns of the late 1970s, developed by Young & Rubicam, were created to show what a space-age car Mercury is. This jazzy approach helped Mercury gain a distinctive identity among drivers and separated it from Detroit's old-fashioned image.

Despite Lincoln-Mercury's innovative and highly stylized advertising, however, most domestic car makers' commercials continue to take viewers on a journey down memory lane. Motown's failure to reach the inner-directed driving public with insightful and energetic ad campaigns has been a costly one.

With their business turning sour and inventories building up in the early 1980s, American auto companies were forced to shift gears somewhat by offering consumers cash rebates for buying cars. Unfortunately, this approach backfired, and the results were devastating for Detroit. Many people became so conditioned to the generous giveaways that they wouldn't even think about purchasing a vehicle unless there was a sale on. Approximately 40 percent of all domestic automobiles sold in America between 1980 and 1982 were discounted.

In an effort to lure consumers into the showrooms without those damaging dollar incentives, several U.S. auto manufacturers resorted to waving the flag. Over the past few years, Detroit has been calling upon citizens to do their patriotic duty by driving American. You don't hear the national anthem or see George C. Scott as General Patton in these commercials—and there aren't any obvious anti-German or anti-Japanese slogans either—but the message is clear anyhow: Support the home team!

Chevrolet has been at the forefront of this chauvinistic crusade. In the mid-1970s, it came up with a campaign based on the theme "Baseball, hot dogs, apple pie, and Chevrolet." But this Yankee Doodle Dandy appeal fell mostly on deaf ears; it wasn't persuasive enough to prevent the young folks of this country, traitors in Detroit's eyes, from defecting to the enemy—Toyota, Datsun, Volvo, and BMW. So Chevy decided to get tough. The establishment car maker's latest ads throw down the gauntlet and announce that it will defend a besieged America against the onslaught of imported cars. As a squadron of Cavaliers, Celebrities, Camaros, and Corvettes races across the television screen in formation, an authoritative announcer asserts that "Chevrolet is challenging the world; U.S.A. 1 is taking charge."

The underlying message is clear: The Japs will be pushed off the beach at Malibu and driven all the way back to Tokyo, once Chevy digs in and gets to work. The only problem with this gunboat advertising is that it inspires the middle manager at Chevrolet more than the man on the street. To most consumers, imported cars provide a choice, not a threat; it's the executives running Detroit, frightened about losing their jobs, who benefit from these tough-talking commercials.

If Chevrolet and its Detroit brethren want to compete effectively in the auto market of the 1980s and 1990s, they will have to develop ads that do more than just bolster their nervous employees. The Japanese, Germans, and Swedes have proved that the only way to sell cars to the increasingly powerful Societally Conscious Achievers is by talking in the new generation's language. Inner-directed people respond to campaigns that stroke and flatter. To win customers over, marketers must tell them that they are innovative, that they are intelligent and individualistic, that they have integrity. BMW, for instance, has ingratiated the new superclass by using subtle, psychologically targeted advertising. One ad for the car describes BMW as "the epitome of truth in packaging"; another says it's "the car that thinks its way to higher performance"; a full-page magazine insertion notes that this is a "personal car that won't depersonalize its owner''; and a newspaper spread says that BMW ''doesn't scream wealth—it just quietly rewards insight.''

While Detroit must address the Societally Conscious drivers in this country to avoid further financial losses, it must also start paying closer attention to one other essential group of car buyers: working women, a growing segment of the market. This consumer audience is currently going through a transition period, and if domestic auto makers don't appeal to it in just the right way, it may be tempted to join the millions of inner-directed people who drive imported cars.

Working women are American car manufacturers' great hope for the future. For decades—beginning with the Model T back in the 1920s—auto makers targeted their sales pitches at men. Women had no income of their own, so as far as Detroit was concerned, they didn't exist.

In the 1970s, however, women began their mass exodus from the kitchen, and suddenly, over half the United States female population had paying jobs. This shift created a lucrative opportunity for Motown; after all, the new workers had to have a method of transporting themselves to and from the office or factory. Women, who had never purchased their own cars before—and thus had no negative preconceptions about domestic vehicles—needed wheels. Yet despite this opening, General Motors, Ford, and Chrysler failed to make any significant overtures to the growing female car-buying public. No commercials were developed and no ads were produced to specifically persuade working women to buy from Detroit. Foreign auto manufacturers haven't pitched their cars directly to women either, yet the importers' commercials project a more contemporary image to the female populace.

Women today demand respect from advertisers. Motown needs to create campaigns that recognize the female struggle to balance professional careers and personal lives. If it continues to ignore working women, Detroit runs the risk of alienating them for good.

Perhaps no other individual's career symbolizes the trials and tribulations of the American automobile industry better than

Lee Iacocca's. A forty-year veteran of Detroit, the charismatic executive first made his mark during the 1950s, when Motown's big-finned status symbols were the rage. Iacocca continued his corporate climb through the 1960s as head of Ford Motor Company, capitalizing on the Pepsi Generation's exuberant life-style with the creation of the sporty Mustang. Suddenly, in the 1970s, however, America's once invincible car business fell into bad times—and with it went one of its leading lights. Faced with an onslaught of foreign competition and the American public's resistance to big, gas-guzzling cars, Iacocca found himself struggling to hang on. But the scrappy and resilient auto marketer bounced back and brought new hope to the ailing Motor City with his rescue of the Chrysler Corporation in the early 1980s.

Lido Anthony Iacocca first learned about automobiles and consumer purchasing behavior from his father, Nicola, an Italian immigrant who made a living renting cars in Allentown, Pennsylvania. Later, at Lehigh University, where he received an engineering degree, the young man mastered the complexities of auto mechanics. A gruff old sales manager in Chester, Pennsylvania, one of Iacocca's first bosses at Ford, then taught his eager employee about the politics of getting ahead in a large corporation.

After toiling in the field for nine years as a Ford salesman, Iacocca, who had learned the car business from the ground up, was promoted to assistant eastern district manager. One year later, in 1956, he scored his first major marketing coup. Ford was losing customers to General Motors' Chevrolet division at the time, and Iacocca's territory was particularly hard hit by these defections. In an effort to turn this potentially disastrous situation around, the young executive devised his "56 for 56" program, which enabled the average citizen to buy a new Ford for just $56 a month. Sales immediately picked up, and Iacocca's district, which had traditionally been one of Ford's least profitable areas, soon became a big income producer.

This dramatic improvement didn't go unnoticed in Detroit. Robert McNamara, then running Ford, plucked Iacocca from virtual obscurity and brought him to Motown to serve as his protégé. During the three years that he worked for McNamara, the whiz kid quickly developed a reputation as a corporate cobra—an arrogant, aggressive climber who would step on anybody to get to the top. As he swaggered down the halls in those days, wearing an expensive mohair suit and puffing on a fat Cuban cigar, Iacocca boldly predicted to friends that he'd be running Ford by the time he was thirty-five. Actually, he was only one year off schedule. In 1960, when McNamara left Detroit to become Secretary of Defense in the Kennedy administration, his thirty-six-year-old underling was named head of Ford's automotive operations.

Over the next decade—the last one before the foreign car assault—Lee Iacocca revolutionized the way Ford conducted business. He believed that the company could increase sales if it took the time to study the various consumer segments in society and then built and marketed cars to fit each individual group's life-style. Motown's research up to this point had been one-dimensional, focusing almost exclusively on how much people were willing to pay for a car. Iacocca argued that the typical American driver cared more about the image his car projected—whether it was practical, sporty, or status-oriented, for example—than about the machine's cost.

After several months at the top of the Ford hierarchy, Iacocca, who had watched as the cola kings capitalized on the Emulator market, decided that his company could profit from the postadolescents' patronage, too. Nobody else in Detroit was catering to this group of young consumers during the early 1960s, so the field was wide open for Ford. He ordered his engineers to begin designing an automobile that would appeal to the Pepsi Generation's fantasies, a car that embodied the idea of freedom and independence, perfect for Emulators who were trying to break away from their parents and get their adult lives started.

Ford's technicians labored on this project for almost a year before they reported back to Iacocca with a prototype. The executive decided to test-drive the vehicle himself. Motown legend has it that he left Detroit in the spirited machine and headed off into the night. Stopping only for gas, Iacocca reached Connecticut thirteen hours later. When he finally got out of the car, he found a telephone booth, called his design team, and proclaimed their creation a winner.

Ford's leader next met with his marketing people to decide on a name for the new product. There were at least 150 suggestions, ranging from Astro (the space program was just taking off) to Zodiac (the Age of Aquarius was about to unfold). Finally, after three weeks of deliberation, Iacocca chose Mustang, because it conveyed the spunky image he wanted the car to project.

Then J. Walter Thompson, Ford's longtime advertising agency, was called in to develop a series of commercials that would further communicate Mustang's feisty personality to millions of restless and rebellious young drivers. JWT devised a dramatic campaign to introduce the vehicle. One spot, for example, opened with a dreamlike vision of a white mustang galloping loose and free across a beach through the early-morning mist. This shot gradually dissolved into a picture of a college-age student cruising along behind the wheel of Ford's new car with the top down and the wind ruffling his hair. Sitting beside him, along for the ride, was a pretty young woman. The couple were obviously having a wonderful time. This automotive exhilaration was summed up in one line, inserted at the end of the 30-second sales pitch: "Mustang—it can take you as far as you want to go."

The message couldn't have been clearer. JWT's advertising for Mustang caused an immediate stampede at Ford showrooms across the country, and by 1965, one year after it hit the market, the car was parked in almost 1 million U.S. garages. It became the best-selling vehicle in Detroit's post–World War II history.

Iacocca had other major marketing victories while he was at Ford's helm. A few years after Mustang took off, he began to examine ways to tap the lucrative Emulator-Achiever segment. He realized that affluent consumers wanted more than just a big car like the Cadillac—they were interested in elegance and style as well as size—so Ford's chief put his engineers to work again, instructing them to come up with a handsome luxury car that didn't look like a boat.

After six months, the designers presented their ideas to Iacocca, but none of the blueprints satisfied him. Each of the proposals called for a hulking steel chassis, which was exactly what the executive was seeking to avoid. He sent the technicians back to the drawing board to develop a sleek, graceful vehicle, but for some reason, they kept concocting armored tanks. Needless to say, Iacocca was frustrated.

One day in 1968 he had a brainstorm. Why not take the slender body of Ford's Thunderbird, which wasn't selling very well, and graft onto it a Rolls-Royce-type grill? Ford would then have a classy, contemporary-looking car to offer the upwardly mobile. Iacocca told his engineering department to assemble this automotive hybrid overnight. He would check it out when he returned to the office the next day. On seeing the car for the first time, the executive knew it could be marketed as the ultimate status machine, and he immediately ordered it into production. The Mark III, as it was subsequently called, helped Ford cut into Cadillac's customer base and turned out to be one of Iacocca's greatest moneymakers.

In the late 1960s, before foreign automobiles landed on American shores, Ford was riding high. Once the invasion began in earnest, however, selling cars in this country became a whole new ball game. Iacocca, like so many of his Motown associates, was surprised and unprepared for this attack. That anyone other than Detroit could provide American consumers with their transportation came as a rude shock to this proud veteran of the automotive wars. It was obvious that he didn't fully understand the inner-directed movement's new value structure or its disaffection with the Motor City's mass-production mentality. He caught on quickly, however, and began to fight back against the imports. In 1970, Ford introduced two jaunty new cars—the Maverick and the Pinto—designed primarily for Societally Conscious Achievers. Iacocca believed that the vehicles were just what alienated young drivers were looking for. Unfortunately, however, his high expectations were never met. From the outset, the Pinto was plagued by safety problems, which made enlightened inner-directed consumers wary. Advertising for the new models, emphasizing many of Detroit's traditional values, also left counterculture auto buyers uninspired.

Even though Iacocca came up short in his bid to capture the inner-directed market, Ford flourished under his stewardship in the early 1970s. After three decades of runaway success, however, the executive finally encountered a roadblock—Henry Ford, his boss. According to many Detroit insiders, Ford felt threatened by Iacocca's abilities and was jealous of his accomplishments; more important, he was tired of watching his marketing magician hog the limelight. In an effort to bring Iacocca down a notch or two, the envious automotive patriarch turned against his underling. It was reported in *The New York Times,* for example, that Ford had Iacocca's travel and entertainment accounts audited; the auto tycoon also slashed his executive's research budget by a hefty $2 billion, making it almost impossible for Iacocca to pursue his career objectives.

Despite these formidable obstacles, however, Iacocca refused to submit to Ford's tyranny. It was difficult, but he managed to conduct business as usual, which only enraged his superior further. Things came to a head during the summer of 1978, when Iacocca was summoned to Ford's office and fired. When the fallen executive asked why he was being let go—especially in view of his excellent track record—Ford responded curtly by saying, "I just don't like you." It was over that quickly. After having worked and charmed his way to the top for thirty-two years, Lee Iacocca was out on the street without a job.

He wasn't unemployed very long. Four months after his dismissal from Ford, the fifty-four-year-old executive was back in the race, as chairman of the ailing Chrysler Corporation. Iacocca paid a heavy price for accepting this position, however. His final agreement with Ford stated that if he went to work for a competitive automobile manufacturer, he would forfeit $1.1 million in deferred bonus payments. In addition to this personal financial loss was the fact that after years of mismanagement, Chrysler, his new employer, was on the verge of bankruptcy.

Undaunted by the risk of assuming Chrysler's leadership, Iacocca took charge of the beleaguered company. Part of the auto
executive's confidence stemmed from his understanding of
what had gone wrong at Chrysler in the past. As he saw it, the
firm had been out of touch with consumers for decades. When
large vehicles were in vogue, Chrysler downsized its entire
line; when deluxe models were favored, Chrysler stripped its
cars; when fuel economy was needed, Chrysler offered gas
guzzlers—and so it went, until the vast majority of the driving
public had given up on the company. The only Chrysler supporters left by the late 1970s were aging Belongers in their fifties and sixties who lived in America's heartland. Iacocca believed that these loyal customers were essential to the battered
auto maker's future. But before he could launch any grandiose
marketing strategies, he had to take care of more pressing matters.

Chrysler was caught in a Catch-22. The firm's previous management had misjudged the kind of wheels people in this country were after. As a result, the auto maker was saddled with
80,000 unwanted cars, which were gathering dust in its parking
lot. In order to manufacture new vehicles that were more appealing to consumers, however, the company needed massive
amounts of cash to modernize its outdated factories. The only
way it could raise this much capital was by unloading its previously produced—but unsold—vehicle inventory.

Unfortunately, there were few buyers. If Chrysler was to survive and compete effectively against General Motors and Ford
in the American automobile market of the 1980s and 1990s, it
would have to borrow money to rebuild. But the banks were reluctant to lend large sums to an auto maker with such a long history of marketing failures. Even with Iacocca at the controls,
there was no guarantee that the firm could, at last, come up
with cars that people would want to drive. The oil-rich Arabs
were invited to invest in the company, but they declined.
Buying up real estate was a much safer way to protect their
petrodollars.

In a last-ditch effort to raise money, Iacocca turned to the
federal government for help. Chrysler was losing close to

$1 billion a year and would go down the tubes unless Uncle Sam bailed the company out. At first, Congress was unenthusiastic about rescuing the dying auto maker; many senators believed that if a corporation couldn't make it on its own, it deserved to go out of business. But then Iacocca, the ultimate salesman, entered the picture and began a lobbying effort that was unprecedented on Capitol Hill. He told legislators that if his company was forced to declare bankruptcy, thousands of laborers would be put out of work. He described in detail the human misery that would result from a shutdown.

And finally, he revealed his plans to produce the conservative little "K-Car," which had won rave reviews from Belongers who had already test-driven it. Iacocca predicted that his latest automotive invention would be an instant success among Chrysler's traditionalist consumers. The K-Car was the executive's ace in the hole, his promise to congressmen that prosperity was just around the corner. The government bought Iacocca's arguments, and in 1979 it helped Chrysler obtain $1.5 billion in loans so that the auto maker could begin manufacturing its new car.

Once Chrysler received a new infusion of capital, its leader was able to return to his specialty—selling cars to the public. Iacocca's first act was firing the company's two advertising agencies—BBDO and Young & Rubicam. He then turned to Kenyon & Eckhardt, a longtime Ford agency, and gave it Chrysler's entire $110 million account. K&E's job was twofold: It had to help Chrysler retain its aging Belonger base, and at the same time it had to attract a large number of Chevrolet's or Ford's Middle American customers.

The agency believed that the only way to achieve both goals was by talking to people on a very personal level. Current Chrysler consumers needed to be reassured, and potential prospects needed to be romanced. Before developing television advertising, the shop devised a direct-mail campaign to say hello to folks on a more informal basis. Almost a million drivers—of both Chrysler and Chevrolet/Ford—were selected by computer. Each received a friendly letter from Iacocca, in which he told them all about the "new Chrysler Corporation" and its solid, reliable K-Car. Attached to every note was one of the executive's business cards. In his message, Iacocca informed people that they would receive special treatment if they presented his card to their local Chrysler dealer. Recipients of the letter eagerly headed down to the Chrysler lot to reap the rewards of this new relationship.

They weren't disappointed when they got there. Those who were willing to test-drive a K-Car were sent a check for $50 if they eventually bought a Chrysler or a competing make; the people who purchased one of Iacocca's vehicles were promised their money back if they weren't completely satisfied with their acquisition; and the folks who kept their new Chrysler wheels were given five-year free-maintenance policies. This daring program, which cost Iacocca's company over $10 million a month, proved to be a drain on the auto maker's already depleted treasury. But it was a price the ailing firm had to pay if it wanted to reestablish contact with a public it had ignored for too long. The generous giveaways did, in fact, succeed in bringing customers into Chrysler's showrooms.

Slightly less expensive and more effective in boosting Chrysler's sales were the television commercials K&E produced featuring Iacocca as spokesman. Even though he wore a flashy pinky ring and shiny alligator shoes, Iacocca came off in those ads as a man traditionalists could trust; he seemed to be one of them—honest, dependable, the salt of the earth. When he walked through the Chrysler factory in each 30-second pitch, down the assembly line and past the bodyworks, he projected total command of automobile production. Viewers believed that they would never get a lemon from Lee, because he seemed to be on top of things—helping his guys put each and every vehicle together.

Iacocca's aura of industrial invincibility, his image as a proletarian knight in shining armor, has given Chrysler a new lease on life. Its share of the American automotive market, which dropped from 16 percent to 9 percent between 1967 and 1979, has inched its way back to a respectable 13 percent during the early 1980s. And just five years after staring down into the dark abyss of bankruptcy, the company has recorded a profit. Above all, however, is the consumer confidence factor. A recent survey of Belongers in this country revealed that almost half of them preferred Chrysler over all other domestic cars.

Iacocca's success as a corporate media personality has been one of the key factors in Chrysler's turnaround. Now chief executive officers of every hard-pressed company in America want to get on the tube and play savior. Unfortunately, few of the embattled business leaders who have made TV commercials have become stars. (Remember David Mahoney of Avis Rent-a-Car or Frank Sellinger of Schlitz Brewing?) Often the chairmen who are most forceful in the boardroom fail to make a convincing presentation on the screen; they come across as cardboard characters in pinstripe suits. Most of the time, the viewing audience has no idea who these guys are or what they're trying to sell. Just because you run a company doesn't mean you can stand up in front of the camera and talk about quality, excellence, and dependability. The public won't buy it.

The trick to bringing these spots off is persuading people that the CEO is truly tied to his corporation's fate. The audience has to believe that the spokesman is on the firing line—if he doesn't deliver on his television promises of better service or improved products, sales will drop and he could end up without a job.

The ever-seen-a-grown-man-cry strategy works beautifully for Frank Perdue, the chicken entrepreneur, for example. Perdue looks and sounds as if he spends most of his day with his chickens. When he peers into your living room and rambles on about how hard it is to raise first-class fowl, you feel sorry for him. Being in the poultry business isn't easy. You'll buy one of Perdue's oven roasters for dinner tonight—partly out of sympathy, but mostly because you know he's a tough man who makes a tender chicken.

The majority of CEO presenters don't make that human connection, however. Take Frank Borman, who runs Eastern Airlines, for instance. On paper, he seems like the perfect spokesman for an aeronautical enterprise. Who wouldn't fly with a former astronaut? If he made it up to the moon and back, surely he can get us to Miami in one piece. But just because Borman was a NASA whiz doesn't mean he's got the right stuff for television celebrity. Rather than projecting a warm, calm, and trust-worthy image for Eastern, the airline head appears stiff and un-comfortable on the screen—a bit cold and mechanical. When Borman says, "We've got to earn our wings every day," he sounds like a technocrat; he sounds as if he's still talking to mission control in Houston from outer space. Eastern's probably a terrific outfit, but the company has lost close to half a billion dollars since its leader went show-biz six years ago.

Over the past five years, Lee Iacocca has demonstrated the power of television advertising by using 30-second commercials to keep his company alive, but now that this struggle for survival appears over, the question is whether Chrysler can flourish in the late 1980s and into the 1990s. If it continues to follow its current Belonger strategy, the auto maker may lose its newfound momentum as it enters the Societally Conscious era.

The average Chrysler driver—age fifty-five, family-oriented, a blue-collar worker—is a dying breed. To continue to grow in the marketplace of the future, the company will have to broaden its consumer audience considerably. In addition to Mom and Pop buyers, it must also appeal to the inner-directed.

Iacocca is hard at work trying to create a line of vehicles that will excite these hard-to-please customers and challenge the Japanese and Germans at the same time. If all goes according to plan, his counterculture "H-Cars" (*H* as in Honda look-alike)—the Lancer and the Commander—will be introduced sometime late in 1984. But regardless of how dynamic these new autos are, Chrysler will have to change its entire advertising approach in order to sell them. Iacocca is a working-class hero, but he doesn't have much clout among the Societally Conscious, who view him as a corporate bulldozer. To succeed, the company's H-Car commercials will have to feature a younger, more mellow spokesman.

As Chrysler struggles to remain competitive, Ford's Lincoln-Mercury division is cruising into the inner-directed 1980s and 1990s at full speed. More than any other domestic auto maker, Mercury has attempted to establish a relationship with Societally Conscious America, and it's this overture toward the nation's most influential consumer group that makes it Detroit's great hope for the coming decade.

One of the driving forces behind this counterculture rapprochement is a man named Lester Wunderman, Madison Avenue's quietest genius. The head of a direct-marketing firm, Wunderman Ricotta Kline, which is owned by Young & Rubicam, the executive has developed a technique for modifying people's buying habits—no matter how ingrained the patterns may be. Over the past few years, Wunderman has spent a large amount of time studying the Woodstock Generation's resistance to American-made cars. It hasn't been an easy task, but the marketer, a student of behavioral psychologist B. F. Skinner, has finally come up with a method he believes will get inner-directed drivers interested in Motown's products.

His approach, which has been successfully tested among small groups of consumers in several cities, doesn't produce overnight results. It's a slow process that gradually dissolves the barriers between advertisers and Societally Conscious Achievers.

Wunderman's research proposal for Young & Rubicam's Mercury account, which he hopes to implement nationwide in the near future, is designed to help the auto maker win back disenchanted inner-directed customers.

As he explains it, his work for the manufacturer will begin with a computerized list of baby-boomers across the country who have defected to foreign cars. With these names and addresses on file, the executive will send each driver a letter with a stamped, self-addressed return envelope. In his note, he will ask each recipient to fill out a questionnaire on American-made vehicles. People will be queried about which cars they like, which they dislike, and why. Nothing will be mentioned about the great advantages and joys of cruising around in a Mercury. Not yet, anyway.

Wunderman plans to follow this opening gambit by writing back to those consumers who replied to his first message. This time, he will ask them to rate their imported driving experiences—in terms of performance, service, gas mileage, etc. He still won't try to sell anybody anything. His main interest at this point will be making contact with people, listening to what they have to say and creating a rapport with them.

This subtle and seductive massage of the Societally Conscious will continue when Wunderman sends a free gift certificate to respondents. The present is the executive's personalized way of saying, "Thanks for your help; we appreciate the information you provided us; you're a good friend—let's stay in touch."

Several months later, the marketer will resume his correspondence. Now that he has established a dialogue, he can begin to push a bit. The Societally Conscious Achievers who have become his pen pals will now be invited to a gathering at a health club or department store in their city. There, over wine and cheese, they can mingle with Mercury dealers.

A few months after the wine and cheese parties, Wunderman will finally be ready to pop the question. He will have carefully cultivated his inner-directed consumers for a full year, slowly conditioning them to think favorably about Mercury; now he can put his plan to the test. Letters will go out to the citizens who have participated in the twelve-month project, inviting them to visit their local Mercury showroom. Based on his earlier, small-scale tests, the executive estimates that he can attract several thousand drivers of imported cars to the Mercury dealerships. These people, who deserted Detroit a decade ago for Datsun, Toyota, and Mazda, the marketer believes, will now take a serious look at a domestically built vehicle. Wunderman's intricate and involved selling theory promises to open up a direct line of communication between Mercury and the Societally Conscious public.

The direct-marketing whiz has helped the auto manufacturer devise other innovative sales techniques as well. He has suggested, for example, that Mercury dealers pick up consumers at their homes for test drives, rather than making people come to the showroom. Selling cars, Wunderman says, is a service, and you've got to cater to the public if you want its patronage.

The executive has also proposed that Mercury create a new, more lasting relationship with its drivers. Instead of dealing with them on a one-car-at-a-time basis and possibly losing out to the Japanese or Germans, he believes the company should begin thinking of each person as a lifetime customer. To retain consumer loyalty over the long term, Wunderman has devised an incentive plan that would offer a free vehicle to anyone who does business with the auto maker for twenty-five consecutive years.

In 1983, the marketer recommended that Mercury use direct-mail techniques to help sell the Topaz, its new car for the inner-directed. The manufacturer had spent five years and $2 billion developing this state-of-the-art vehicle, and its futuristic aero-dynamic design, built-in computer, and technically advanced suspension system made it one of the most sophisticated sets of wheels on the road. A traditional 30-second commercial couldn't possibly do this machine justice, Wunderman argued, even though Young & Rubicam had created an insightful slogan for it—"A Car as Advanced as Those Who Own It."

The marketing guru urged his auto maker client to run advertising that would provide consumers with a toll-free telephone number to call for further information about Topaz. Since Mercury adopted this unique idea, the phones have been steadily ringing in Detroit. Wunderman also prepared a booklet, which people could write away for, describing the vehicle's space-age features. After a year, close to 1 million of these brochures have been sent to prospective buyers. Wunderman's thinking was clear. Unlike so many on Madison Avenue, he understood that you can't rush Societally Conscious Achievers into a purchase. These prickly individualists need plenty of attention and information before they plunk down a penny.

6 FALLING ARCHES
America Gets Burger Fatigue

After a decade of spectacular growth, the fast-food business—like the soft-drink and domestic automobile industries—has come to a crossroad.

During the 1970s, McDonald's and other fast-food chains used psychological advertising to convince America's Belongers that their restaurants were havens for family harmony rather than greasy-spoon truck stops. The traditionalists reacted positively to these warm, emotional commercials, and their loyal patronage enabled the fast-food enterprises to spread across the nation's highways.

Today, however, the burger boom appears to have gone bust, and the future prospects of the roadside eateries are shaky. Fast-food sales in this country have lost their sizzle, remaining flat over the past two years. The number of franchises being built has declined. And several companies have even been forced to close some of their outlets.

McDonald's and most of its fellow fast-food purveyors seem to be suffering from the same malady that has plagued Coke and General Motors—psychographic indifference. The hamburger champs, like the cola king and the automotive giant, sat back during the early 1980s and watched as their market eroded bit by bit. To compensate for this loss of business, they often raised their prices, creating a problem for consumers who wanted to purchase their products. And to make matters worse, the firms virtually ignored the emerging superclass of Societally Conscious Achievers.

The soda and domestic auto industries only recently made their first overtures toward the inner-directed; thus far, however, neither has succeeded in winning over a majority of counterculture customers. When (and if) the major fast-food chains follow suit, they will encounter even more resistance from the Woodstock Generation than the soft-drink and automobile people did.

Health-oriented Societally Conscious consumers view burgers, shakes, and fries—high in fats and calories and low in vitamins—as nutritionally unsound. A current Madison Avenue survey reveals that the inner-directed eat half as much red meat as Belongers, so it's no wonder that they shun the Golden Arches and the Home of the Whopper.

Counterculturalists also like to cook for themselves or friends. Preparing meals from scratch and then sharing the homemade food experience has become one of the main ways that inner-directed folks socialize these days. The Societally Conscious enjoy sitting around the kitchen table with a group of people much more than going to restaurants. When they do eat out, it's at cozy cafés or bistros, not at roadside hamburger joints. McDonald's and Burger King, with their plastic swivel seats, garish orange-yellow-red interiors, and hurry-up-and-eat attitudes, lack the relaxing dining ambience that members of the Woodstock Generation prefer.

In addition to inadequate aesthetics and nutritional values, sensitive Societally Conscious Achievers disdain the fast-food ethos for another reason, too. Wherever they look in this country, they are confronted by a tangle of neon lights, a strip of jerry-built brick shacks, or hulking cement malls that symbolize the encroachment of the burger chains. To many inner-directed people, McDonald's, Burger King, and Wendy's are more synonymous with environmental blight than good eating. Counter-culturalists, it seems, can't forgive the fast-food industry for spoiling so much of the nation's landscape.

The burger chains' antiseptic and automated methods have reinforced the Woodstock Generation's negative feelings about the fast-food experience. Societally Conscious consumers want to be treated as individuals, and they demand personalized service—something that McDonald's and Burger King are not designed to provide. Hamburgers, fries, and shakes are mass-produced on sophisticated computerized assembly lines hour after hour, and the people behind the counter are reduced to robot status. This sterile and standardized approach to dining gives indigestion to even those inner-directed citizens with the heartiest of appetites.

The fast-food industry has generally done very little to ac-commodate the burgeoning Societally Conscious movement. It has set up token salad bars here and there and even tried to mar-ket a pita-pouch vegetable sandwich, but other than that, most chains have stuck with their old-fashioned strategies. Rather than improving the nutritional content of its products or sprucing up its austere franchises—two important ways it could appeal to the large number of inner-directed consumers in this country—McDonald's, for example, continues to stress family togetherness in its sales pitches. The company's latest cam-paign, "McDonald's and You," is no different from the ads it has been running for the past fourteen years. Mom, Dad, and Ju-nior still discover that the happiest moments of their day take place under the Golden Arches.

McDonald's commercials appeal primarily to the country's shrinking Belonger segment. In a recent attempt to hang on to the dwindling number of traditionalist consumers, the fast-food leader resorted to the sponsorship of a multimillion-dollar sweepstakes contest. Such desperate moves would have been unthinkable for McDonald's a decade ago, when the fast-food industry was in its prime. During the big-bottom-line years of the mid-1970s, the typical American family was eating three meals a week at the burger chains and spending about 20 percent of its total food budget on Quarter-Pounders, Whoppers, and other snacks along the highways.

With all this munching, fast-food sales in the United States skyrocketed—from $5 billion to $30 billion between 1970 and 1980. Business was so good that the number of domestic road-side outlets quintupled to 150,000 during this period; each day, throughout those ten years of prosperity, an average of four new franchises were opened somewhere on the North American continent. At one point in 1976, the federal government estimated that fast-food companies were responsible for four of every ten new jobs created in this country.

No chain contributed more to the mobile eating revolution of the 1970s than McDonald's, and no chain profited as much either. At the beginning of the decade, the firm's 2,000 outlets around the United States provided it with annual sales of approximately $600 million. Then its famous series of cathartic television campaigns, including "You, You're the One" and "You Deserve a Break Today," was launched. McDonald's initial advertising and promotion budget in 1970 was a respectable $10 million. Over the course of the next ten years, the company dramatically increased its marketing expenditures, to approximately $300 million, making it the fifth-biggest commercial user of television among American corporations. This spending surge also helped the Chicago-based firm become the largest single private-sector dispenser of meals in the world by 1980, with 6,500 franchises blanketing this country alone and domestic gross earnings of over $6 billion.

The extraordinary success of McDonald's can be measured even more graphically. Between 1970 and 1980, the flourishing fast-food enterprise sold a staggering 30 billion hamburgers to Americans, or 8.2 million beef patties each day throughout the entire decade. If you stacked up the total number of burgers the chain produced in this period, the pile would stretch beyond the stratosphere, halfway to the moon. Five million steers gave their lives during the booming 1970s in support of the McDonald's cause, and in its heyday, the company stripped 300 square miles of forest annually so that the people who stopped at the Golden Arches could have napkins and paper plates.

The pervasive impact of McDonald's on American society over the last decade can be gauged in other ways as well. A confidential research study completed for a leading Madison Avenue agency reveals that by 1978, almost 70 percent of all citizens in the United States had eaten a meal at one of the chain's franchises. Another survey taken in 1977 indicates that the McDonald's advertising theme song, "You Deserve a Break Today," was second only to the national anthem in terms of public awareness. In another poll, the company's mascot clown, Ronald McDonald, was chosen—along with Santa Claus—as the most likeable adult in America by children under ten years of age. Over 60 percent of the youngsters interviewed had met Ronald at least once.

The powerful McDonald's television commercials created a new American tradition, influencing what, where, and why the average citizen ate. Until "You Deserve a Break Today" or "You, You're the One" hit the airwaves and descended into the living rooms of this country, people thought of the hamburger as a thin pattie of ground meat to be barbecued at a backyard picnic and eaten on a roll with a blob of ketchup. Once the marketers at the Golden Arches began sending out their electronic sales messages, however, this perception changed dramatically.

By the mid-1970s, traditionalist consumers were driving miles down the interstate in search of something called a Big Mac, a caloric concoction consisting of a sesame-seed bun, two all-beef patties, and dollops of onion, pickle chips, cheese, lettuce shreds, and a special sauce, the formula for which was guarded like an atomic secret. Madison Avenue and McDonald's had redesigned the hamburger, but more important, they had transformed it from a mere sandwich into a symbol of family unity.

The founding father of the fast-food business was Ray Kroc, the man who, in 1954, created McDonald's. Up until the time of his death, in early 1984, at the ripe old age of eighty-two, Kroc was still supervising his company's hamburger production and monitoring its french fry sales. The burger baron lived a life that resembled the Horatio Alger story. Combining a fanatic devotion to hard work, an obsessive eye for detail, a generous dose of Yankee ingenuity, and perpetual optimism, he took several beat-up old drive-ins scattered around Southern California and, against enormous odds, turned them into an awesome multinational food enterprise in just three decades.

Kroc's success didn't come easily. He was born at the turn of the century in Chicago, the son of Bohemian immigrants. His father, who worked for Western Union, wanted his son to become a butcher in the stockyards, but young Ray wasn't interested in learning the meat trade—not yet, at least. Instead, he dropped out of school after the ninth grade and drifted through several odd jobs until 1916, when he enlisted for overseas duty in World War I. Kroc wasn't involved in direct combat during his two years in France, but he experienced plenty of action anyway, as the driver of a Red Cross ambulance. His running mate in the medical corps was a young man named Walt Disney, who would prove to be a lifelong friend.

When the war was over, the two Americans headed home. Disney went out to Hollywood and joined the fledgling motion picture business; Kroc returned to Chicago, where he hoped to earn a living doing what he loved best—playing the piano. He made the rounds, auditioning at bars and restaurants all over the Windy City, but he ended up with just a handful of bookings. After struggling for several months to break into the cabaret scene, the aspiring musician threw in the towel. He was broke, unable to pay his rent, and in need of a real job.

An old acquaintance of Kroc's was working for Lily-Tulip, a paper-product company, and arranged to get him an interview. The former piano player was hired as a paper cup salesman and soon began to draw a decent salary. A few years later, he was named the firm's Midwest manager, a position he retained through the 1930s. But despite the financial security that his post at Lily-Tulip afforded him, Kroc was restless and unfulfilled as an employee. He wanted to strike off on his own and make his mark in the world of commerce. He wanted to get rich.

In 1937 he left behind the paper cup business for the world of milkshake mixers, putting up $10,000 of his own money to gain the exclusive American sales rights to the Prince Castle Multimixer. The Prince, as it was called in the trade, was considered a revolutionary machine at the time because of its ability to mix six malts or milkshakes at once. During the 1940s, Kroc traveled all over the country promoting his high-powered blender. He visited almost every soda fountain in America, and by the end of the decade he had made a fortune.

One day in 1954, the milkshake mogul received a check for eight multimixers from a previously unheard-of restaurant chain in Southern California. This was the largest single order he'd ever gotten. Kroc wanted to establish a rapport with his new client, so he flew out to Los Angeles and personally delivered the mixers himself. When he arrived at the company's flagship franchise, he was shocked. The parking lot surrounding the run-down wooden shack and its neon golden-arch sign was filled to capacity with hungry people sitting in their cars eating lunch. The food was cheap and simple—15-cent hamburgers, 10-cent french fries, and 20-cent milkshakes—and it was obviously pleasing to the customers. As the motorists in each automobile finished their meal and pulled out of the lot, new drivers cruised in and took their places.

In all his years on the road, Kroc had never seen such a busy restaurant operation. This was the first time he'd experienced the fast-paced action of a drive-in; outside of sunny California's freeway culture, folks usually ate at a counter or table, rarely behind the wheel. Later that day, the executive from the Midwest met the dynamic owners of this thriving business, Richard and Maurice McDonald.

The McDonald brothers had moved west in 1928—from New Hampshire to California—with dreams of making it big in the film industry. But after spending several years as menial laborers, building and moving props, the pair left Hollywood bitter and disillusioned. They soon opened a movie theater in Pasadena, and somehow kept it going despite the Depression's strong undertow. During the early 1940s, the McDonalds sold their theater to a real-estate concern. They took the proceeds from this deal and set up several barbecue stands just outside Los Angeles. Word quickly spread about their mouth-watering ribs, pork, chicken, and ham, and the quaint little roadside restaurants were soon jammed with customers day and night.

After World War II ended, the wholesale development of California began. The state filled up with both cars and people, and to attract the motorized masses, the brothers expanded their small eateries into larger drive-ins. To accommodate the hungry crowds that pulled into their freshly built parking lots, they decided on a new, simpler menu of fast foods—burgers, fries, and shakes.

Under their old system of operation, the McDonalds cooked each meal to order. When someone came in and requested barbecued ribs, for example, he waited patiently while the meat was prepared and grilled. Now, however, hamburgers and french fries were precooked and kept warm under infrared lights. Drivers sat in their automobiles and gave their orders to carhops, who quickly returned with the food. The speedy new approach to dining enabled the brothers to move people in and out of the lots in a flash.

Ray Kroc had made millions of dollars selling his milkshake mixer over the years, but now he sensed an even greater financial opportunity. The fifty-two-year-old executive persuaded the McDonald brothers to give him the exclusive rights to franchise their Golden Arch drive-ins around the country. According to the agreement, Kroc would collect 1.9 percent of the gross sales from the franchisees, and he would turn over about a quarter of that to Richard and Maurice. The ambitious businessman constructed his first McDonald's outlet near a new interstate in Des Plaines, Illinois, a Chicago suburb. From the moment it opened, the place was mobbed. Like Californians, midwesterners on the go loved the freedom of pulling into McDonald's for a quick bite to eat.

Spurred on by his initial success, Kroc began erecting his Golden Arches on highways throughout Middle America. He picked out potentially lucrative locations for his chain by flying

over a neighborhood and counting its schools and church stee-
ples. By 1959, his 225 McDonald's franchises were generating
annual sales of close to $50 million.

Despite the strength of his new business, Kroc, the quintessential capitalist, was dissatisfied; he resented giving away even
a small portion of his earnings to the McDonald brothers each
year. In 1960, he flew to Los Angeles and tried to buy the pair
out. The brothers refused to sell their share of the enterprise,
and Kroc returned to Chicago with the partnership still bind-
ing. Several weeks later, however, Maurice McDonald had a
change of heart and made the executive an incredible proposal—Richard and he would give up their interest in McDonald's
for $2.7 million. Kroc quickly accepted the terms and began ex-
ploring ways to raise the money. He eventually decided to borrow the entire sum from a group of college endowment funds
at the then exorbitant interest rate of 6 percent. By 1961, the
Bohemian immigrant's son was the sole owner of a lucrative
string of hamburger drive-ins stretching from coast to coast.

During the early 1960s, Kroc spent most of his time trying to
improve the operations of McDonald's. To increase the number
of people who could be fed at one time, he added indoor seat-
ing at many outlets. This move was particularly helpful in stimulating the sales of franchises located in cities where car ownership was relatively low. The fast-food executive also began an
employee training program. Each of his managers was required
to take a series of demanding courses at McDonald's Hamburger
University, near the company's headquarters outside Chicago.
This school taught students how to run a fast-food franchise,
and nobody could get promoted within Kroc's corporation unless he or she had earned a Bachelor's Degree in Hamburgerol-
ogy.

Upon graduation from HU, each individual was given a book
written by the company's leader, titled *QSC* (for Quality, Service, Cleanliness). This was the Burger Bible, which included
the belief that men behind the counter should keep their hair
cut at military length and sport polished black shoes, and that
women should wear no makeup on the job. The guidebook also
stipulated that no franchise should have a cigarette machine or

newspaper rack on its premises, because these conveniences only created a litter problem.

One of Kroc's Ten Commandments was that the manager of each outlet had to keep the floor of his restaurant spotless by mopping it every hour during the working day. Kroc often toured McDonald's facilities to make certain that his rules were being observed. Once on a visit to a franchise in Montana he discovered a piece of chewing gum stuck to the bottom of a table. He got down on his knees and began scraping the nasty glob off.

Cleanliness wasn't Kroc's only obsession. As McDonald's expanded throughout the country, its chairman channeled more and more energy into the automation of his fast-food chain. An efficient, mechanized operating system was essential, the executive believed, for two reasons. First, it would ensure that consumers received burgers and fries of the same consistent quality—no matter which franchise they ate in. Second, it would eliminate waste and boost profits.

By 1965, special equipment, designed to standardize food preparation, had been installed in almost every McDonald's outlet in America. Machines cut huge portions of ground beef into precise patties that were $3\frac{5}{8}$ inches wide and weighed 1.6 ounces each. Ovens baked hamburger rolls, $3\frac{1}{2}$ inches in diameter, to just the right level of brownness. And grills with winking lights on them told countermen when to flip each fried burger over. Sensitive cybernetic deep-fryers were also used. These devices adjusted to the moisture in every potato stick and guaranteed that each batch of french fries would come out cooked evenly. Once they emerged from the fat, the hot potatoes were handled with customized scoops, which made it impossible for an employee to put too many or too few of the fries into a paper container at one time.

With only minimal advertising support at this time—mainly billboard displays and local radio announcements—McDonald's and its high-tech kitchens achieved annual sales of over $200 million. This prosperity encouraged Kroc to take his company public in 1966. The move made the executive one of the richest men in America. By 1969, his stock in the burger business—for which he had paid approximately $3 million in 1960—was worth close to $100 million.

Despite this initial bullishness, however, McDonald's go-go period on the Big Board was short-lived. The early 1970s brought the fast-food enterprise face to face with several seri-ous problems that threatened its continued growth. Kroc's chain had succeeded during the previous decade largely be-cause it had attracted curious consumers who had never eaten under the Golden Arches before. Now, just several years later, the novelty of dining at McDonald's had worn off, and many customers were starting to eat at home again. There also seemed to be a growing burger backlash, a feeling among cer-tain Middle American members of the populace that fast-food franchises were unfriendly and uncomfortable places to bring the family for a meal.

The steady loss of once-loyal patrons stunned Kroc. He had worked for fifteen years to build his business, and now it ap-peared to be coming apart at the seams. The executive couldn't understand why the public now perceived the Golden Arches so negatively; more important, he didn't know what to do to help his company regain its shiny image. He turned to advertis-ing. In 1970 he decided to increase his media budget and to en-trust his account to a new, more creative agency.

Kroc made this move somewhat reluctantly, however. He had always viewed Madison Avenue marketers as slick hustlers who weren't to be trusted. He felt uneasy about having to rely on their sleight of hand to keep his business going. Not surpris-ingly, the skeptical fast-food chieftain rejected the large num-ber of agency executives who came clamoring for his lucrative account. It wasn't until after he had met with the key members of Ad Alley's twenty top shops that Kroc finally found one young copywriter he felt comfortable with.

Keith Reinhard of Needham Harper & Steers, then a small Chicago-based agency, was thirty-five years old when he first met Ray Kroc. As Needham's designated new-business getter, Reinhard was responsible for developing the shop's presenta-tion to the burger baron. Unlike many of his Madison Avenue colleagues, who had been quickly dismissed by Kroc for not having done their homework, the enterprising executive from Needham came well prepared for his meeting.

First, he had taken his wife and children to the Golden Arches for several meals and had immediately sensed how these eating experiences had brightened their day. Then he had conducted a hamburger taste test. He asked hundreds of consumers to try three burgers from unidentified fast-food chains and then pick their favorite one. The results were inconclusive; no hamburger—including McDonald's—emerged as the definitive winner. Reinhard proceeded to formulate an advertising strategy for Kroc's company. He concluded that the chain couldn't promote its food directly, because consumers didn't believe its hamburgers were really different from, say, Burger King's or Wendy's; but it could stress the joy of eating at McDonald's and promise happier times if families frequented the Golden Arches.

Several weeks before he was scheduled to present Needham's campaigns to McDonald's management, Reinhard sat down at his typewriter and tried to translate his strategic thinking into copy. Somehow, he had to come up with advertising that would help transform the Golden Arches from a cold, austere purveyor of food into a warm, emotional provider of domestic bliss. This was the only way Kroc's chain of restaurants could lure back its defecting Middle American customers—and regain its sales momentum.

The executive's thinking resulted in a series of commercials using the theme "You Deserve a Break Today." Reinhard believed that these five words would have a powerful impact on the burdened working people of America if McDonald's used them in its new television spots. In essence, the company would be empathizing with Belongers, telling them that it understood their plight and offering them a respite from their daily travail.

To make this soothing message even more effective, the copywriter decided to tug at viewers' heartstrings. One of his first commercials for the fast-food chain featured an exhausted blue-collar laborer trudging home at the end of a hard day. The tired man is met at the front door by his children, who plead for a meal out at McDonald's. Of course Dad can't refuse his kids, so despite his bone-crunching fatigue, he heads off to the Golden Arches with the entire family. Once he digs into a Big Mac, his weariness suddenly disappears, and a look of relaxed pleasure spreads across his face as he watches his little ones gobbling up their french fries. Clearly, coming out to McDonald's has been the high point of this man's day. Reinhard set this and several other emotional spots to sympathetic songs with the refrain "You Deserve a Break Today," making certain that Belongers understood how much Kroc's company cared about them and how wonderful a place McDonald's was for the entire family to eat.

Reinhard and the Needham team took their commercials to McDonald's corporate headquarters and screened them for Kroc and his lieutenants. When the presentation was over, it was unanimously decided that even though the agency was small in size, it was large in creative talent and could handle the fast-food chain's advertising.

Winning the $10 million McDonald's account in 1970 firmly established Needham Harper & Steers as a force to be reckoned with on Madison Avenue. The victory also moved Keith Reinhard to center stage at the agency. Once his sensitive "You Deserve a Break Today" campaign restored the Golden Arches to prominence, the dynamic executive began producing other commercials for the rejuvenated burger enterprise. Over the next eleven years, he supervised all McDonald's advertising and helped the company increase its sales tenfold, from approximately $600 million to over $6 billion. By 1980, the chain controlled about 20 percent of the fast-food market and was spending almost $300 million each year on advertising and promotion.

Reinhard was successful in handling the McDonald's business for all those years primarily because he understood his client's audience so well. He was a Belonger himself. Raised in the small Swiss Mennonite community of Berne, Indiana, in the 1930s, the ad man experienced enormous hardships as a child. His father, an upholsterer in a furniture factory, died from the flu at the age of thirty-one. Young Keith Reinhard was only four years old and his baby brother was just ten months old when this tragedy struck. Their mother, Agnes, was left with nothing but a $1,000 life insurance policy and a monthly check of $92 from the federal government.

To make ends meet, she was forced to leave her small sons and begin work as a cashier at the local grocery store. Keith held jobs after school and during the summer from the time he was eight. He spent many boyhood hours employed as a weed puller on a farm. The youngster was often lonely, but he received a good deal of affection from his grandparents, who lived nearby. The church also provided solace, and he attended Bible class, chorus practice, and Sunday school each week until he was eighteen.

Reinhard couldn't afford college after graduating from high school, so he began to work part-time as a photographer's assistant in order to learn a craft. He eventually became a commercial artist, but he barely earned a living at it. In late 1963, the struggling illustrator—who now had a wife and two children of his own—learned of an opening for an art director at Needham Harper & Steers. He applied for the job and got it.

When the designer reported to work in January 1964, however, he was in for a surprise. The agency's personnel department had somehow made a mistake; the shop needed copywriters, not art directors. Reinhard was given a typewriter, and even though he had never written an ad before, he was told to start developing copy for a new State Farm Insurance campaign. Despite this mix-up, the artist was determined to succeed in his new job. He knew very little about the insurance industry, so he drew upon his own experiences to create his first set of commercials. He remembered how callously an insurance company had treated his mother after his father's death and decided that this was exactly the image that State Farm was seeking to avoid.

After several weeks of work, Reinhard came up with a group of gentle ads that showed how much the firm catered to its policyholders in their time of need. Later, to go with these new sales messages, he worked with colleagues on a song that told viewers, "Like a Good Neighbor, State Farm Is There." This campaign helped change State Farm's reputation as an insensitive company. It also won Keith Reinhard a slew of advertising awards and launched his career as a copywriter.

Over the next decade, Reinhard continued to write commercials targeted at Middle America. Unlike Mary Wells or Leo Burnett, who relied primarily on gimmicks, or Bill Bernbach, who used tongue-in-cheek humor, Needham's rising star employed emotion to sell even the most mundane products—even cake mixes.

When the Betty Crocker division of General Mills found itself losing business to Procter & Gamble's Duncan Hines brand, it called in Reinhard and asked him to give the old lady an advertising facelift. After much thought, the executive came to the conclusion that the existing campaigns had gone stale because they were too factual—they bored the average homemaker, who was tired of hearing about creamy frostings and moist cakes. To regain the attention of America's traditionalist women, Reinhard once again took a page from his childhood. He remembered the many sweet moments he had spent as a youngster in his mother's kitchen, watching as she made rich chocolate cake, and he tried to inject some of these nostalgic sentiments into the new commercials.

Rather than mentioning the specific attributes of Betty Crocker's products, one fresh spot featured a little boy and girl busy helping Mom prepare a cake. This group activity was a joyous one; everyone was having fun collaborating on the project. When the dessert was served later that evening at dinner, the entire family was present. Smiles abounded as each member of the clan bit into the cake, and Dad was especially appreciative that his wife and kids had taken the time to bake for him. The 30-second commercials ended with a picture of father hugging the children and the sound of a song, "Bake Someone Happy." Reinhard had emotionalized something as basic as cake mix.

As a result of his understanding of such Belonger clients as McDonald's, State Farm, and General Mills, the copywriter was promoted up Needham's corporate ladder during the mid-1970s. By 1975, he was making close to $150,000 a year and was clearly in line to succeed Paul Harper, the agency's chairman, when Harper retired. Then, all of a sudden, disaster struck Keith Reinhard's career. Out of the blue, McDonald's—Needham's largest client—decided it was unhappy with "You Deserve a Break Today." Though its sales were booming and research showed that people liked and remembered its commercials, the company's marketing executives—bored with the same old campaign—wanted a new advertising approach from Needham, and nothing Reinhard could say would dissuade them. The agency was given ninety days to come up with another set of television spots, or it would lose the Golden Arches account.

Developing a sequel to "You Deserve a Break Today" wasn't easy. Reinhard knew that McDonald's would lose its Middle American constituency unless it continued to project a warm Belonger image, but the chain's management was adamant in its belief that new advertising was necessary. Finally, after going through nearly a ream of paper, the copywriter came up with a compromise solution, one that might satisfy both client and agency. McDonald's could use a different theme to communicate the same traditional family-oriented strategy that had been successful for the past five years. The memorable slogan that Reinhard created was "You, You're the One."

With only a month to go before Needham's crucial presentation to McDonald's, Reinhard called in one of Madison Avenue's best songwriters, Ginny Redington, a tiny woman with long blond hair and blue eyes. In the 1960s, Redington had been a Peter, Paul, and Mary type of folk singer, playing for $10 a gig in coffeehouses. During the early 1970s, however, when music started to become more prevalent in commercials, the composer sold her act to Ad Alley. It was a smart decision. By 1975, she had written and sung hundreds of 30-second spots and was making close to $100,000 a year.

Redington worked best under pressure, and that's why ad people liked her and called upon her often. In recent years, she and her husband, Tom Dawes, had created music that helped Doyle Dane Bernbach on the American Airlines account ("Doing What We Do Best") and Ted Bates on the Colgate Toothpaste business ("The Smile on Your Face, the Clean in

Your Mouth''). Maybe, thought Reinhard, the talented song-writer could now assist Needham in its effort to hold on to McDonald's.

Soon after receiving the big assignment from the Chicago agency, Redington completed her soulful song for its fast-food campaign, incorporating Reinhard's "You, You're the One" lyrics. In front of a small audience of Needham executives attired in gray flannel suits, the denim-clad musician sang the song. Reinhard and his associates were so pleased by Redington's earthy rendition of the score that they asked her to record the sound track for their commercials.

After Redington completed her studio session, the music was synchronized with footage of happy blue-collar families eating at McDonald's, which had been shot earlier. Then, to get a better idea of their effectiveness, the finished spots were shown to groups of Middle Americans. In interviews conducted a day after the screenings, viewers had trouble remembering exactly what they had seen, but they were able to sing Redington's tender song without any difficulty. The results of this research pleased Reinhard tremendously. He realized that once the new McDonald's television campaign aired, millions of consumers would be walking around the streets with Redington's voice reverberating in their heads; soon afterward, they'd be whistling or humming the burger chain's soothing sales message—portable advertising.

The Reinhard/Redington commercials were finally shown to McDonald's marketers as part of a dazzling presentation, which Needham staged at the Civic Opera House in Chicago. When the curtain came down on the agency's one-hour show, the chain's executives were suitably impressed. They quickly decided that their account would stay at Needham.

The dramatic musical rescue of the McDonald's business, orchestrated by Keith Reinhard, soon became the talk of Madison Avenue. Songs had become an increasingly important part of Ad Alley's repertoire over the years, beginning in the mid-1960s, when the cola kings started using them in their television spots. But with Reinhard's well-publicized accomplishment, agency executives discovered just how potent a marketing device music could be—especially in persuading sentimental Belongers to purchase their products—and by the late 1970s, a vast majority of the commercials aimed at traditionalists in this country contained an emotional theme song.

Even the most conventional advertisers began relying on "heartsounds" in their sales pitches. The Army, for example, started losing recruits to the Navy and Air Force, so it developed the rousing "Be All You Can Be" campaign. Maxwell House dropped its spokeswoman, Cora, who used to lecture viewers about bitter coffee, and moved out of the confining kitchen with Ray Charles's stirring rendition of "Good to the Last Drop Feelings." And General Electric, once a hard-edged nuts-and-bolts marketer, softened its image by running the inspirational "We Bring Good Things to Life" spots, which promoted appliances as joyous accouterments rather than boring necessities.

From 1975 to 1980, Keith Reinhard's trend-setting musical advertising for McDonald's was consistently among the best work produced on Madison Avenue. Agency people regularly cited his commercials for their creative excellence; trade associations showered him with Ad Man of the Year awards; and, with sales rapidly approaching $5 billion at the time, McDonald's was once again praising the modest executive's efforts. Needham, now the twentieth-largest shop in the country, rewarded its ace copywriter for all this success by naming him president of its Chicago office in 1979. He was forty-four.

But soon after Reinhard was promoted to the top of Needham's hierarchy, the psychographics in the United States began changing, and McDonald's bastion of Belonger strength started to crumble. During 1980 and 1981, for the first time in a decade, the chain's burger sales were flat, and consumer traffic in many of its franchises decreased. Despite this loss of business, however, the company still showed a profit—largely because of the price hikes it passed on to loyal customers, the real estate it was able to sell off, and the success of its foreign outlets.

Even though McDonald's remained in the black in the early 1980s, its executives were alarmed by the slowing of the American fast-food market, which accounted for almost two-thirds of the chain's total earnings. In an effort to come up with a new advertising approach that would bolster the sagging Golden Arches, the burger enterprise's marketing department met with Reinhard's creative team. Unfortunately, neither the client nor the agency understood the fundamental changes that were taking hold in our society; they didn't see that McDonald's Middle American base was shrinking and that the inner-directed market was expanding. So naturally, when Needham recommended a fresh Belonger-oriented campaign, nobody objected.

The agency's cheery new conformist spots—basically a variation of the old "You Deserve a Break Today" campaign—ran for almost a year, but they didn't do much good. McDonald's continued to lose momentum in the marketplace.

During the latter part of September 1981, the McDonald's board met to discuss possible solutions to the chain's problems. One member of the group suggested that the franchises run cents-off coupons in newspapers to stimulate consumer activity. Another participant urged the research and development department to speed up its testing schedule for the McFeast Sandwich, which would offer people a real bargain—30 percent more meat than the Big Mac for about the same price. A third said that Needham should be fired and replaced by a new agency. This last idea was bandied about, and because it seemed like the easiest way to improve the company's stagnating domestic business, it received a good deal of support. A vote on the matter was put off for ten days. When the board reconvened, it was unanimously decided that the chain needed more innovative advertising and marketing help than Needham was providing. A new shop had to be found.

The decision to terminate Needham was kept confidential for several days, until a replacement for the agency could be lined up. Reinhard finally received the bad news with a phone call on a Sunday afternoon. Needham would no longer be handling the fast-food account; Leo Burnett, the largest shop in Chicago, which had briefly worked for Kentucky Fried Chicken in the mid-1960s, would be taking over.

After eleven years, one of the advertising world's most successful relationships had ended. Keith Reinhard's Belonger campaigns had helped transform the Golden Arches into a national symbol of family unity during the 1970s, and McDonald's had blossomed into a multibillion-dollar company. Unfortunately, however, both the ad man and the fast-food chain became stuck in time.

The new McDonald's advertising agency hasn't improved the chain's business over the past few years. The erosion of the fast-food purveyor's Belonger base has continued, especially since its archrival, Burger King, began intensifying its marketing efforts targeted at Middle America. And a new group of inner-directed restaurants—such as Bennigan's, Chi-Chi's, and Red Lobster, which serve a variety of foods from Mexican dishes to fresh fish—has recently sprung up to capture the loyalty of many Societally Conscious Achievers, making it even more difficult for the Golden Arches to attract members of the discerning superclass.

The most immediate problem that McDonald's currently faces is holding on to its faithful patrons from the heartland. These last remaining fast-food fans are currently being wooed away by a seductive advertising campaign—"Aren't You Hungry?"—that J. Walter Thompson produced for Burger King. Thompson's commercials show beautifully filmed close-ups of its client's food and claim that Burger King's menu is superior to McDonald's. Unlike the family-oriented ads for the Golden Arches, these taste-oriented spots are intended to make viewers salivate and switch to the Home of the Whopper.

Burger King's decision to step up its fight against McDonald's for the shrinking Belonger market was made out of desperation. Although both chains were founded at the same time, thirty years ago, Kroc's company grew much faster than its second-ranked competitor. Today, McDonald's has twice as many franchises as Burger King, and it spends almost three times as much on advertising each year. The only way the smaller fast-food enterprise can survive with fewer hamburger-hungry consumers out there is by attacking the front-running Golden Arches.

This comparative advertising strategy has been a longtime

Madison Avenue staple. It helped Avis pull closer to Hertz in the 1960s, for example, and it enabled Bic to gain ground on Gillette in the disposable razor market during the 1970s. Now, in the 1980s, Burger King is brazenly trumpeting the fact that its flame-broiled beef patty is 20 percent larger than McDonald's fried hamburger.

One spot from the sarcastic hard-sell campaign, known along Madison Avenue as "Burger Meltdown," features an adorable four-year-old girl standing in front of a Burger King franchise. "Do I look 20 percent smaller to you?" asks the child, as she peers irritably into the camera. "I must to McDonald's. When I order a regular hamburger at McDonald's, they make it with 20 percent less meat than Burger King." The peeved youngster then shows viewers a primitive crayon drawing she did in her preschool class. It reveals the difference in size between a Burger King hamburger and a McDonald's hamburger. A real-life picture of a juicy, delicious beef-filled sandwich from Burger King appears next on the screen, looking good enough to eat. The crabby little princess finally returns. "Luckily," she says, "I know a perfect way to let McDonald's know how I feel about things. I go to Burger King."

J. Walter Thompson's cutting commercials have succeeded in helping Burger King take traditionalist customers away from McDonald's. Over the past year and a half, the McDonald's share of the fast-food market has dropped from 20 percent to 17 percent, while the Home of the Whopper has increased its standing from 10 to 13 percent. McDonald's must find a way to respond to Burger King's cheeky campaigns in order to hold on to the declining number of Belongers still cruising the American highways in search of a quick bite to eat.

In addition to combating Burger King's current advertising onslaught, McDonald's must also contend with the aggressive television spots that Wendy's, the third-largest burger enterprise in the United States, is now running. Not satisfied with being a fast-food also-ran, the Ohio-based chain has revised its once conservative marketing strategy and decided to go for broke. Wendy's biting new campaign portrays both McDonald's and Burger King as cold, impersonal marketers of assembly-line hamburgers, while positioning itself as the only road-side eatery that treats its customers as individuals and makes them fresh, customized meals.

To drive home its point, the company uses a caustic sense of humor in its commercials. The 30-second sales pitches take viewers into the competition's franchises, which, according to Wendy's, resemble sterile scientific laboratories—empty gray spaces devoid of charm or character. The people behind the counter in these austere, antiseptic chambers function as robots—cooking, wrapping, and serving food in unison, without cracking so much as a smile. And the burgers that these automatons mass-produce are more like frozen bricks than broiled or fried beef.

In a recent spot that got an extraordinary reaction from the public, a trio of elderly women examine a typical fast-food hamburger. Lifting up the large, fluffy bun, the ladies find a paltry portion of meat. The group's cantankerous leader asks, "Where's the beef?" Before this half-minute is up, however, Wendy's reminds viewers that it caters to its discerning clientele with a warmth and sincerity that neither McDonald's nor Burger King can match. The last image we are left with is a striking picture of one of Wendy's healthy-looking hamburgers, garnished with loads of lettuce and plenty of tomatoes.

By disassociating itself from both the Golden Arches and the Home of the Whopper—the establishment—and stressing its own personalized service and nutritious burgers, Wendy's is trying to reach out to inner-directed consumers. The feisty chain has created a humorously satirical advertising message that appeals to the Societally Conscious, and there is reason to suspect that this campaign is strong enough to overcome the counterculture's built-in resistance to hurried highway eating. Wendy's still holds a strong number-three position in the marketplace, and in the first quarter of 1984 its sales rose 15 percent.

Increasingly, inner-directed citizens who dine out are frequenting a new type of restaurant, created especially with them in mind. These Societally Conscious eateries are slightly more expensive than fast-food franchises, but they offer a cozy, relaxing ambience and a more health-oriented menu. Most of them also serve wine and some even provide no-smoking sections. Bennigan's, a chain of bistros in the Sunbelt, has prospered, for example, because of its wide variety of quiches and salad plates. Chi-Chi's, serving simple Mexican food, is doing well in the Southeast. Oriental noodle bars and gourmet pizza places are popping up all over California. And Red Lobster and Long John Silver's—two fish enterprises long established in the Northeast—are expanding throughout the country.

This proliferation of informal eating establishments, appealing to a wide range of palates, signals the end of the fast-food era as we've known it. Societally Conscious Achievers would rather munch on nachos or lo mein than on Big Macs or Whoppers, tired Middle American products of the 1970s. Even with Madison Avenue's magical manipulation at work, it's questionable whether members of the emerging superclass can be persuaded to get into their cars and drive down the interstate for a hamburger and fries. If they want to flourish during the late 1980s and 1990s, McDonald's and Burger King are going to have to change their entire way of thinking about food and the people they serve it to. Unless the chains develop and market a McTofu Sandwich or a Guacamole Whopper, the industry may well continue its downslide.

7 GENDER GAP

Mrs. Olsen Gets an American Express Card

Packaged goods, those ordinary products we regularly purchase at the supermarket or drugstore, are the backbone of the American consumer society. Just about everyone in this country uses toilet paper, toothpaste, soap, cleansers, and detergents; millions of people stock up on instant coffee, paper towels, and disposable diapers; and most citizens depend on dandruff shampoo, mouthwash, or deodorant to get them through the day. These near-necessities are essential weapons in our never-ending battle against dirt, grime, body odor, and halitosis.

In addition to feeding and cleansing the nation, packaged-goods manufacturers keep Ad Alley afloat. Food, toiletry, and household items, staples for American shoppers, are also the lifeblood of Madison Avenue. Media expenditures for kitchen and bathroom products amounted to $35 billion last year, almost half the total billings of the advertising business. These accounts provide the often volatile industry with a solid financial underpinning. Unlike many other clients, blue-chip packaged-goods companies—such as Procter & Gamble, General Foods,

General Mills, Kellogg's, and Colgate-Palmolive—are rarely forced to cut their marketing budgets. With their relatively steady year-in, year-out sales, they make it much easier for agencies to profit from their patronage. This is why shops that produce the most campaigns for laundry bleaches or cooking oils are also usually the ones that make the most money.

The packaged-goods bonanza that has fueled so much of Madison Avenue's recent growth may soon taper off, however. Like soft-drink, fast-food, and domestic automobile advertisers, these manufacturing giants have failed to recognize America's changing psychographics. They've lost touch with the attitudes, values, and experiences of their consuming public. In essence, that means they've neglected women—who purchase almost 80 percent of all the products sold in American supermarkets and drugstores.

Over the past decade, the packaged-goods conglomerates have stood idly by as the world of the American woman changed. Up to now, the huge enterprises have virtually ignored the growing number of influential Societally Conscious women in this country—almost 35 percent of the nation's feminine population. Their commercials rarely portray the inner-directed woman's experience, which is a careful balancing of career and family. Instead, most of these manufacturers have created two diametrically opposed female stereotypes in their ads. The first (and most enduring) of these is the stay-at-home housewife, who is often depicted as a dirt-obsessed fanatic who spends all day on her knees cleaning bathroom tiles. She is a staple of commercials during daytime television, appearing between soap operas and game shows. Her prime-time counterpart—less prevalent perhaps but just as exaggerated—is an entirely different species. Dressed for success, this striving Emulator-Achiever woman is always on the go. Appearing on-screen as a busy television news anchorwoman or high-powered corporate executive, she is a single-minded careerist who needs a hair spray, deodorant, or shampoo that will help keep her cool businesslike image intact.

Unfortunately, these conflicting views of today's female consumer audience fail to take into account the reality that a large number of women in this country are inner-directed—seeking fulfillment from both their jobs and their home lives. Purveyors of packaged goods need to revise their current female sales strategies if they want to appeal to women in the emerging Societally Conscious marketplace. Right now, there is growing resentment among these customers toward Madison Avenue for its disregard of their varied life-styles, and they are starting to avoid the products of advertisers who ignore them. If this marketing myopia continues, it will almost certainly result in the loss of business for many companies during the late 1980s and 1990s.

Fourteen years ago, in 1970, slightly more than one-third of all American women were earning a living. This provided Madison Avenue with a substantial television audience of home-bound females. These "sitting ducks," as they were called by ad executives, became easy targets for inane commercials that showed wives fretting over their husbands' ring around the collar or squeezing Mr. Whipple's toilet paper to test its softness. Today, over 50 percent of the adult female population in this country works outside the home in a wide variety of fields.

During the mid-1970s, as more and more women began spending their days at either the office or factory, ad executives shifted gears; they started running some of their television campaigns at night, during prime time—to catch the "sitting ducks" when they came home to roost. This new media ploy wasn't entirely successful, however, because a growing number of women in the United States were adopting an inner-directed perspective on life. The new woman had a much better self-image than the traditional housewife—largely because of her ability to combine a career she liked with a family she loved—and she was becoming a bit cynical.

What's more, Societally Conscious women were generally too busy juggling their personal and professional lives to pay attention to the advertising industry's prattle. Even if they did happen to tune in to one of Madison Avenue's commercials, they were usually affronted by its narrow-minded and outdated view of the female experience.

According to several confidential agency research studies, many of these new inner-directed citizens were former homemakers who had left the cozy confines of the kitchen for the workplace, where they discovered that there was more to life than baking the perfect Apple Brown Betty. These defections helped deplete Belonger ranks considerably. As the studies show, traditionalists made up over 50 percent of the American female population in 1970, but a decade later this figure had shriveled to a mere 30 percent of the total number of women in this country.

The steady rise of the Societally Conscious woman and the sharp decline of the Belonger homemaker will continue through the next decade. By 1990, say Madison Avenue researchers, the inner-directed segment will total approximately 50 percent of the female market, while the number of Belongers will drop even further—to 20 percent. Most significant, however, is the fact that in ten years' time only a very small percentage of women in this country will be spending their days slaving away over a hot stove or cleaning bathroom floors. It appears that a long-standing American icon, the housewife, is about to become an extinct marketing creature—and that she will be replaced by a new female exemplar: the active, energetic woman who leads a full life, both at home and at work.

Despite the obvious signs of psychographic change, Madison Avenue and its packaged-goods clients have done surprisingly little to improve their reputations among inner-directed females. Television commercials reflecting Societally Conscious values and attitudes of women are few and far between. Ad Alley's women never seem to exhibit both professional strength and personal softness when they're on the tube making a sales pitch. For some reason, marketers are reluctant to portray the woman who can negotiate a deal with a tough-minded businessman as easily as she can solve a homework problem for her daughter or prepare a delicious meal. Advertisers have yet to show a female executive busily working at an office desk that's cluttered with files, memos, and telexes as well as framed pictures of the family. If we are to believe Madison Avenue's current mythology, women in this country aren't creating both recipes and five-year plans.

The fact that so few advertisers understand the inner-directed woman's multifaceted life-style can be seen in several recent attempts to bring this new feminine experience to television. For example, one commercial for Enjoli perfume, which first aired in 1978, featured an attractive woman dressed in a three-piece gray flannel suit. As a version of "I'm a Woman—W-O-M-A-N" played in the background, the female executive was first transformed into a housewife and then into a seductress. Meanwhile, she informed the audience that today's woman can "bring home the bacon, fry it up in a pan, and never let you forget you're a man." This suggestive 30-second spot may have soothed masculine egos, threatened by the female exodus to the workplace, but it also presented a crude caricature of the women it sought to portray.

It's hard to believe that the majority of agencies on Madison Avenue haven't gone beyond Enjoli's primitive advertising approach and appealed to inner-directed women in a more sophisticated way. After all, there are millions of Societally Conscious females out there just waiting to respond to a savvy advertiser's campaign.

Jane Fonda, with her health and fitness programs, is an example of one marketer who has proved how lucrative the inner-directed female segment can be. The movie star promises women that her training regimen will give them the stamina and muscle to deal with the triathalon of work, motherhood, and marriage. This shrewdly crafted pitch has helped Fonda rake in millions of dollars in profits and royalties. At last count, her exercise studios were being frequented by 10,000 women a week; her workout book, which has sold almost 2 million copies, was about to celebrate its hundred-week anniversary on *The New York Times*'s best-seller list; and receipts from her body-building tapes, records, and videocassettes were rapidly approaching the $8 million mark.

Rather than following Fonda's example and targeting their sales messages at the large, untapped inner-directed female market, most advertisers have continued to reinforce the quickly vanishing values and attitudes of the traditional all-American housewife.

Agency executives view homemakers as zealots in endless pursuit of antiseptic cleanliness. Television ads for Lysol, Spic and Span, and Lemon Pledge, for example, show these ladies frantically spraying and polishing everything in sight—from refrigerator doors to dining-room tables to kitchen floors. Women in these commercials attack dirty toilet bowls with Sani-Flush, the kids' grass-stained blue jeans with Spray 'n Wash and hubby's graying shirt collars with Wisk. They aren't satisfied until they're able to see their faces reflected in counters and furniture.

After they've spent the morning conquering bathroom mildew, Madison Avenue's happy homemakers attempt to make the perfect pot of coffee or cure the common cold. This is when helpful, friendly neighbors generally drop by for a casual, matter-of-fact chat about bitter grinds or postnasal drip.

To get the conversation going, one woman may start bragging to her friend about how shiny her dishes are. The power of new lemon-scented liquid Joy does all the work for her. When the scene shifts to the laundry room, the gals discuss their secrets for attaining a whiter, brighter wash. They exchange notes and compare detergents to see who has the best warm- or cold-water technique. After they do a load together, pulling soft, fluffy towels, fresh-smelling sheets, and clean underwear together, it's obvious that the woman who uses improved Tide is the better housewife. Often Mom will be joined at the washing machine by her daughter. This is laundry legacy time, when the older generation passes on the tricks of the domestic trade.

At dinnertime, the man of the house arrives home from work—and he's a mess. Not only is he exhausted after a hard day at the factory, but he's also got a stuffy head, runny nose, and fever. It looks as if he's coming down with something. Ad Alley's all-American housewife must now nurse her husband back to health. She administers such packaged-goods panaceas as Dristan, Vicks Formula 44, or Contac. Later that evening, she gives him a cup of Nyquil, "the nighttime cold remedy," or two Sominex, so that he can "sleep, sleep, sleep."

Naturally, the man feels great the next morning. He's been magically cured of all his ailments and is ready to return to his job. After a quick shower and shave, he's faced with a major dilemma, however: which mouthwash to use—Scope or Listerine? He knows that Listerine "kills germs and helps fight plaque"; but, according to Scope's ads, it also gives him "medicine breath." Luckily, his wife once again comes to the rescue. She slices an onion in half and pours Scope on one side and Listerine on the other. Then she asks her spouse to sniff both parts. The Listerine-laced section smells awful, but the Scope-saturated portion gives off a delightful spearmint scent. "If Scope can make a smelly onion minty-fresh," he says, "imagine what it can do for your breath."

In commercials for the past thirty years, homemakers have been trying to gain the approval of men. In the late 1950s and 1960s, such stern disciplinarians as Mr. Clean or the Ajax White Knight would drop into Middle American kitchens and censure women for allowing their counters and floors to become dirty. When the Man from Glad appeared on the scene, ladies had their knuckles rapped for wasting leftovers.

During the 1970s, these male authoritarian spots continued to proliferate, taking even more irritating forms. In one campaign, for example, a man went to a business meeting or social event only to have people quietly snicker at his dirt-tinged "ring around the collar." Without directly saying anything, Lever Brothers, the manufacturer of Wisk detergent, was sending each housewife in the country a strong message: If you don't properly attend to your husband's laundry needs, he's going to be the laughingstock of the community.

Advertisers of shortening and cooking oil use the same approach to sell their products. One recent spot has a man inviting his boss home for dinner, hoping to make a good impression on him. Everything goes swimmingly until a pie is brought to the table. The very important guest barely touches his dessert, and later in the kitchen, the hostess realizes that she forgot to bake with Crisco. This gaffe may eventually hurt her husband's career, and he'll remember it—especially if he fails to get that promotion.

Another campaign designed to strike fear into the hearts of homemakers was created for Stove Top Stuffing Mix. Several families are out for an afternoon barbecue when an announcer asks a wife whether her husband prefers potatoes or stuffing with his meat. The lady is sure that her man favors potatoes. But, lo and behold, he chooses another woman's stuffing. Obviously, the housewife has failed to satisfy her spouse's appetite, and as a result, she's lost his palate to someone else. He never would have wandered if she had served him Stove Top instead of potatoes.

A handful of coffee makers have successfully imitated Stove Top's tactics to get insecure homemakers to buy their products. Folger's, which features Mrs. Olsen in its commercials, is the prime practitioner of this coffee coercion. In one of the brand's spots, a young wife knocks at Mrs. O's door and asks if the sagacious woman has time for a chat. Once inside the kitchen, the depressed bride explains that she can't seem to make her husband a decent cup of coffee. Naturally, Mrs. Olsen has the perfect solution: The relationship can be saved if the wife starts using Folger's. Several weeks later, the homemaker returns to Mrs. Olsen's kitchen and happily reports that her domestic life is now wonderful. The moral of the story for housewives is clear.

Many of the most manipulative packaged-goods commercials targeted at homebodies today promote health and beauty aids. Each of these spots preys on women's vanity and fear of aging, subtly informing traditionalist female viewers that unless they use the advertised product, they risk being rejected by their husbands.

Young & Rubicam's long-running campaign for Oil of Olay, which promises women that they can look younger if they simply smear sticky pink cream on their faces each day, is perhaps the most notorious example of this slick salesmanship. Olay, a perfumed substance that's 80 percent water, is known among cynical Y&R executives as the "magical mystery fluid"—because they don't really believe it helps retard aging. But their

doubts haven't stopped them from persuading vulnerable
women that the moisturizer is a veritable fountain of youth.

Y&R's Oil of Olay advertising never explains the product or
lists its attributes. Instead, each current commercial creates a
dreamlike world, a fantasy, in which a fifty-year-old man redis-
covers his wife's beauty and sex appeal. In one of these spots, a
man behind the wheel of a car looks over at his sleeping wife in
the seat next to him. The sight of her pretty face prompts a nostalgic reverie of the couple's earlier years together. For this sentimental spouse, his mate looks as youthful today as she did
thirty years ago. A voice-over informs the viewing audience
that the secret behind this woman's smooth, unlined skin is her
faithful use of Oil of Olay. The soulful words and sounds of
Roberta Flack's "The First Time Ever I Saw Your Face" provide
a touching background to this midlife love story. These moving
half-minutes give homemakers hope; there's still a dance or
two left for them.

Oil of Olay's campaigns, exploiting aging women's natural
resistance to growing older, have resulted in a sales jump for
the brand from $40 million to approximately $100 million
since 1970. The product now leads the moisturizer market, oc-
cupying the huge gap between Vaseline and Elizabeth Arden.

While commercials targeted at homemakers play on their desire to be good wives and mothers, the few ads aimed at career-
centric Emulator-Achievers present products as essential accouterments for job security and advancement. Recent spots for
Final Net Hair Spray, for example, show us an active professional woman scurrying through her daily round of appoint-
ments. Nearing exhaustion at the end of this busy day, the executive still looks good, thanks to Final Net's staying power. Her
unruffled appearance symbolizes this employee's ability to handle even the most difficult assignments under stress. In other
words, with a strong-holding hair spray like Final Net, upwardly mobile working women can fulfill career aspirations.

In their portrayals of women as either homemakers or career-
ists, Madison Avenue's executives demonstrate a schizophrenic
attitude toward females in American society today. Few commercials address the melding of work and family interests. Ad

Alley's inability to come to terms with the emerging female counterculture is largely linked to a pervasive sexism in the advertising industry itself.

Madison Avenue is a powerful bastion of male dominance. According to a trade association survey taken in 1981—which, for obviously embarrassing reasons, has never been released—almost 65 percent of America's 150,000 marketing and sales executives are Caucasian men, mostly between forty and fifty-five years of age. The study also points out that many advertising women are languishing in junior positions in media or production departments, the "pink ghettos" of Ad Alley. Female agency employees place commercials on television—but they rarely share in the decision-making process with clients.

This inequality is surprising, especially in view of the fact that almost three-quarters of all consumer dollars spent in this country come from the pocketbooks of women. Since so many purchases are made by the female population, one would logically assume that male marketing leaders—in search of a better rapport with their female buying public—would move more women into top management positions. But this has not been the case thus far.

In addition to being outnumbered and underchallenged in their jobs, advertising women are also grossly underpaid. The average male working on Madison Avenue currently earns 60 percent more than the average female. This remuneration gap remains constant, even when employees of differing sex bring identical experience levels to the same post. Put another way, 80 percent of all Ad Alley women earn less than the industry-wide median salary for their position.

The results of several trade publication polls indicate that many female marketers resent the unequal treatment they've received from male agency executives over the years. They also disapprove of Madison Avenue's portrayal of women in commercials. The strongest protests about the female television image come from younger—and consequently more junior—female employees. These women, in their twenties and early thirties, would like to change the way women are depicted in

Ad Alley's campaigns, but they have little influence or input because they're usually at the bottom of the agency totem pole.

Ironically, older—and more senior—advertising women don't believe that their industry has given feminism a black eye; they say that Madison Avenue's sales pitches accurately reflect the female's role in our society. The reason for this conservative point of view is simple: In order to climb Ad Alley's corporate ladder, women executives have traditionally had to adopt the ideas and world view of their male counterparts. This is a dismaying thought, but it's always been a fact of life in the often repressive advertising business. There has never been a feminist agency head, and the few women who have risen to the top of Madison Avenue's hierarchy have somehow distanced themselves from female reality.

There will probably never be a feminist revolution on Madison Avenue; advertising doesn't seem to be the kind of profession that nourishes inner-directed women. That doesn't mean, of course, that females can't be portrayed realistically in commercials. The male power structure that currently controls Ad Alley isn't ideologically committed to or opposed to the woman's movement. It is committed to the principles of profitability. If giving women characters in television spots a sense of dignity means that the female population will purchase more products, then marketing executives can be counted on to improve the feminine image in their sales pitches sometime soon.

There are subtle indications of change along Ad Alley. A few bottom-line-oriented agencies have recently begun to depict the contemporary American female experience more accurately in their campaigns. Although these "enlightened" shops are clearly in the minority on Madison Avenue, their willingness to jettison out-of-touch commercials for honest, inner-directed ones represents a giant step forward for commonsense marketing.

Take Ted Bates's recent Colgate toothpaste spots, for example. Rather than continuing its old commercials, in which Mom touts Colgate's cavity-fighting power, the agency's 30-second pitches star Dad as nurturer.

One opens with a five-year-old pajama-clad girl brushing her teeth before going to sleep. Since her mother is working late at the office, she asks Daddy to tell her a bedtime story. Midway through the tale, the child dozes off. The father, who obviously shares household responsibilities with his liberated wife, gives his daughter a kiss on the forehead, pulls up her covers, and turns out the light. An announcer then comes on the air to assure us that "Colgate protection doesn't fall asleep when she does—it stays wide awake fighting cavities."

This kind of earnest, soft-spoken commercial has helped Colgate gain the loyalty of many Societally Conscious women because it rings so true; it's a perceptive slice of inner-directed American life, which also promotes toothpaste. Counterculturalists appreciate it when advertisers portray them as thinking, caring individuals, and, more often than not, they'll reward these insightful marketers with their business. As a result of its sensitive advertising approach, Colgate has recently closed the gap between itself and Crest, the category's longtime leader.

General Foods, like Colgate, has followed this intelligent sales strategy—and achieved excellent results. Its new campaign for International Coffee, which features women immersed in serious conversations about their lives, is light-years beyond Mrs. Olsen. Rather than moaning about how difficult it is to make a decent pot of coffee, the women in this original advertising talk about the challenges of their jobs and the pleasures of their families. They share laughter and intimacy, and they clearly have a positive view of things.

One of these commercials takes place in a cozy living room, where two friends in their late thirties are enjoying a brief coffee interlude. The women are chatting easily about their careers, when suddenly one turns to the other and proudly announces the fact that she's just been granted a tenured teaching position at the local university. The second woman is so pleased for her friend that she gives her a hug. The high-spirited women continue talking and sipping until an announcer breaks in and reminds us to "celebrate the moments of your life" with General Foods International Coffee.

A recent study conducted by a large packaged-goods agency

on Madison Avenue revealed that this General Foods campaign was one of the most popular series of television commercials among inner-directed American females. Societally Conscious women view themselves as successful but sincere people, and they respond to warm, unaffected advertising that humanizes their lives.

Not surprisingly, Nestlé has picked up on the emotionally realistic coffee campaign from General Foods, and it has created a series of similar television spots for its Taster's Choice brand. Over the past decade, Taster's Choice offered a more fact-oriented advertising message—telling viewers that it looked, smelled, and tasted like ground roast coffee. Now the product's commercials have a different feeling. Each 30-second sales pitch focuses on a man and woman coping with one of life's many small problems. Somehow the couple work their trouble out, and to celebrate the resolution of the dilemma, they adjourn for a cup of soothing hot coffee. A musical score lets us know, "Times like these are made for Taster's Choice."

The coffee drinking, in this case, is slightly less festive than in the General Foods spots, but it is an equally revealing expression of how Societally Conscious Achievers actually live. Although Taster's Choice still lags behind General Foods' Maxwell House and Procter & Gamble's Folger's, the product's new ads have helped it to establish a more distinctive brand identity among consumers, according to industry analysts.

By portraying inner-directed women honestly in their television commercials, both General Foods and Nestlé have recently regained a small number of female counterculturalists for their coffee franchises. Many of these nonconformists dropped the caffeine-laced drink during the late 1960s and early 1970s, when the health, nutrition, and fitness movement first began, but some have been lured back to the fold by advertising. Despite its new born-again drinkers, however, coffee will never surpass juice, wine, or tea in popularity among members of the superclass, but the fact that a handful of adults have resumed sipping the beverage should indicate to marketers the advantages of dealing fairly and squarely with Societally Conscious females in this country.

The Campbell Soup Company recently learned this important lesson, too. After promoting itself for more than six decades as the Belonger's best friend, Campbell's sales began to drop in the 1970s, when women first started adopting inner-directed values and attitudes. By 1980, things had gone from bad to worse, and the firm's red-and-white soup line was in trouble. So Campbell went out and hired a new agency, Backer & Spielvogel, and decided to change its marketing strategy.

Instead of continuing its home-and-hearth advertising, which had traditionally featured an all-American apron-clad Mom ladling out "m'm, m'm good" Chicken Noodle, the company began stressing soup's nutritional value in its commercials—an attempt to win over the Societally Conscious. Each spot was aimed at physically active inner-directed women, telling them that everything they ever believed about the goodness of soup was true.

One 30-second pitch explained that a bowl of Campbell's Vegetable Beef had more vitamin A than nine eggs and as much protein as a peanut butter sandwich and that a cup of Tomato Rice had as much Vitamin C as half a grapefruit. Backer & Spielvogel's inner-directed "Soup Is Good Food" campaign has helped boost sales for Campbell's red-and-white line for the first time in a decade. The ads have succeeded because they talk to women in respectful contemporary language and treat them as bright, nutritionally aware consumers.

Several nonpackaged-goods companies, whose clientele was once almost exclusively male, have similarly begun to romance Societally Conscious women in their commercials. Beer marketers, for example, traditionally believed that their consumer constituency was masculine—no brewer in his right mind sold suds to the "fair sex" on the tube. But now, Anheuser-Busch is doing just that.

A current Budweiser Light commercial features an introspective female skier, determined to succeed against great odds as she takes on a challenging slalom course. We understand from an interior monologue that the athlete is afraid of confronting the steep downhill run, fearful of falling and hurting herself. Nonetheless, she summons up her courage and starts flying down the mountainside, giving it all she's got. She eventually crosses the finish line in record time and wins a medal—a bold overreacher who has fulfilled her potential and achieved excellence. By linking the victorious inner-directed skier with Budweiser Light, Anheuser-Busch is attempting to attract Societally Conscious females to its newest beer product. The gutsy athlete in the company's "Bring Out Your Best" spot is a positive symbol for contemporary women in this country. She represents the triumph of a new liberated feminine life-style over the confining world of house and home.

Anheuser-Busch is also targeting another of its beers, Michelob Light, at females. To accomplish this, the brewer has created a series of ads that show women competing on even terms with men. One commercial, for instance, takes place by the seashore, where a co-ed group is in the middle of a volleyball game. But this is no remake of "Beach Blanket Bingo." The women play as hard as the men and buy as many rounds of Michelob Light when the hotly contested match is over. This campaign sells beer to Societally Conscious females by featuring them in active, physically demanding roles and portraying them as equal partners with their male friends.

Like Anheuser-Busch, American Express—another advertiser with a predominantly male consumer base—has recently discovered how lucrative the growing inner-directed female market can be. Since the mid-1970s, the big financial conglomerate has been running its famous "Do You Know Me?" campaign, which has increased the number of its credit card holders in this country fourfold. But most of the anonymous celebrities starring in these commercials have been men—Luciano Pavarotti, Benny Goodman, Tom Landry, Pelé, George Gallup, Roy Jacuzzi, and Sam Ervin, to name just a few—and male cardholders outnumber their female counterparts four to one.

To correct this imbalance, Amex television spots began including such female luminaries as Sarah Caldwell, Joan Cooney, Roberta Peters, and Cynthia Gregory—in the hopes of encouraging Societally Conscious women to apply for its green plastic credit card. Unfortunately, however, these 30-second sales pitches didn't accomplish much. In 1982, American Express's female cardholders still represented only 20 percent of the women in this country who were eligible to benefit from the company's charge privileges.

Finally, last year, the marketer conducted a research study among inner-directed women to determine why they were using Visa and MasterCard rather than American Express. The survey revealed that Societally Conscious females disliked the "Do You Know Me?" campaign because it equated having an American Express card with prestige and material success. Counterculture women aren't just after fame and fortune. They define attainment differently from most male executives; to them, it's living a rich, interesting, and personally fulfilling life—a life that doesn't necessarily include becoming the chief operating officer of a Fortune 500 corporation.

American Express got the message and created new advertising especially for inner-directed women. The female-oriented campaign's umbrella headline is "American Express. It's Part of a Lot of Interesting Lives." In one magazine spread, a young mother is shown cross-country skiing with her baby resting snugly in a papoose on her chest; a second ad features a woman leaving a sporting goods store with a lacrosse stick in one hand and a briefcase in the other; another commercial takes place at a restaurant where a busy female executive is having lunch with her three kids. After just one year, this new marketing strategy—focusing on confident, independent, and physically fit women—seems to be paying off for American Express. Female credit card applications are up almost 25 percent.

In addition to creating fresh advertising campaigns that will appeal to the growing number of Societally Conscious women in this country, several packaged-goods companies are also hard at work trying to develop new products for this increasingly important and influential group of consumers.

Inventing and marketing new products is a dicey process at best. Only twenty of the 10,000 new items launched in supermarkets and drugstores between 1970 and 1982 achieved and sustained annual sales of $100 million or more—Madison Avenue's benchmark for a successful packaged-goods introduction.

And many terrific ideas never even made it out of the lab. Some of the past decade's most notable new-product concept failures include Ketchips (potato chips that tasted like ketchup and french fries), Cough Whip (an aerosol-dispensed whipped cream that helped fight colds), and the Go-Nut (a vitamin-enriched breakfast doughnut).

But despite the staggering odds—and the average $50 million developmental cost—there have recently been several important new-product breakthroughs, especially in the crucial female counterculture market. Campbell's, which for years has sold the Swanson line of frozen foods, has recently updated the unhealthy old-fashioned TV dinner, a longtime Belonger staple, and transformed it into a nourishing meal for Societally Conscious families. The new product is called Le Menu.

Inner-directed consumers used to turn their noses up at the thought of tin trays filled with frozen food. Mystery meat sloshing around in puddles of thick gravy! Soggy french fries! Mushy peas and carrots! Some people said that there was more nutritional value in the box than in the meal itself. Even Gordon McGovern, Campbell's youthful chairman, once called his own company's Swanson TV dinners "junk food," according to *The Wall Street Journal.*

After recognizing Swanson's poor quality and the large number of working women who were interested in serving their families wholesome meals in a hurry, McGovern created Le Menu. Each of these gourmet dinners comes on a classy-looking plate and provides consumers with a healthy dose of vitamins, minerals, and protein. There's fish—lobster, red snapper, and salmon; vegetables—asparagus, mushrooms, and snow peas; and even real meat—veal, chicken, and turkey. The response to this new dining experience has been overwhelming. Le Menu has reached $125 million in sales after just fifteen months in national distribution.

Kellogg's, the Middle American cereal maker from Battle Creek, Michigan, has also shifted gears and created a nutritious new product for Societally Conscious female shoppers. The company flourished during much of the twentieth century by selling sugar-filled cereals—such as Frosted Flakes and Froot

Loops—to Belongers. But several years ago, in the late 1970s, its bright prospects began to dim. Kellogg's loyal traditionalist market was evaporating while the expanding inner-directed segment of society remained faithful to organic granola purchased at the health food store.

Sensing a bleak future, the firm's top management decided to pour millions of dollars into the development of a truly nourishing cereal. For months, Kellogg's technicians experimented with every known strain of wheat, corn, barley, and rye. Finally they came up with Nutri-Grain, a pure breakfast food with no sugar or artificial preservatives—a perfect knockoff of the natural-fiber mixes that health nuts around the country were eating each morning. The marketer packaged its new product in a simple, clean white box, to distinguish it from the circus of cereals sitting on the supermarket shelf.

In addition to shrewd packaging, Kellogg's wholesome cereal succeeded for another reason—smart advertising. Rather than running ads in such conventional homemaker magazines as *Good Housekeeping* or *McCall's,* the company's media selection focused on sports and fitness publications, including *Self* and *Runner's World.* Less than a year after Nutri-Grain went into national distribution, it had achieved a strong 1 percent share of the American cereal market, where even a leading brand like the venerable Kellogg's Corn Flakes controls only 5 percent of the business.

General Foods, like Campbell's and Kellogg's, has seen the psychographic handwriting on the wall. As a result, the big packaged-goods conglomerate has committed itself to a multibillion-dollar new-product-development program, designed to attract the emerging female majority. The most successful item to come out of the company's test kitchen thus far has been its Pudding Pops, which, in just two years on the market, have accumulated sales of close to $250 million.

The enormous popularity of this frozen milk dessert on a stick stems from its unique positioning. Many of the product's commercials, aimed at Societally Conscious parents, promote it as a healthy alternative to ice cream, pointing out its nutritional advantages. One spot, for example, shows both adults and children enjoying the new dessert while informing fitness-oriented viewers that a dish of chocolate ice cream has seventy more calories and ten more grams of fat than a chocolate Pudding Pop. With this clever strategy, General Foods has helped provide Societally Conscious families with a special sweet treat they can believe in.

Despite the positive steps taken by Colgate, Campbell's, General Foods, Nestlé, and Kellogg's, all is not well in the world of packaged goods today. Most advertisers of food, household, and toiletry items have yet to come to terms with the growing number of intelligent and independent inner-directed females in America.

Procter & Gamble, the nation's largest packaged-goods advertiser, is a good case in point. P&G's sales increased thirty-fold between 1945 and 1975, but as the Societally Conscious movement gained momentum over the past decade, the $13 billion company's growth slowed. In recent years, Procter's biggest brands have been battered by the competition at the retail level. For example, Tide has seen its market share decline from 26 percent to 20 percent since 1977. Crest's share has dropped from 40 percent to 36 percent during the same period. And Pampers, which once accounted for 70 percent of all the disposable diapers purchased in the United States, now represents 40 percent of this category's sales. The Cincinnati-based conglomerate has lost its way for two main reasons: Its television campaigns are out of touch, and its new-product-development program is based on rigid technology rather than psychographics.

P&G's advertising has been criticized by many inner-directed women for its reactionary portrayal of the contemporary female experience. After all, this is the company that's given us Mr. Whipple for Charmin toilet paper and Mrs. Olsen for Folger's. It's also one of the companies that relies on the unimaginative Burke measurement system to gauge the potential effectiveness of its commercials. Burke research estimates how memorable a television campaign will be by asking consumers to recall brand names from specific ads twenty-four hours after they've seen them on the screen. The reasoning behind this exercise is that if people can identify a product, they'll be more inclined to buy it. Burke is P&G's Bible—unless an ad passes this test with flying colors, it doesn't appear on the air. Copywriters at the company's agencies are aware of this strict criterion, and as a result, they've been forced to devise commercials that repeat an item's name five or six times in 30 seconds.

Burke's "scientific" process sucks the creative life out of a campaign and leads to annoying advertising that inner-directed viewers tend to tune out. P&G's TV spots for Pampers disposable diapers, Bounty paper towels, and Downy fabric softener, for example, are so busy drumming brand identity into our heads that they neglect to show how the products can help us.

Procter & Gamble has neglected Societally Conscious women in the development of new products, too. Take the case of Pringle's. During the mid-1970s, the manufacturer's lab wizards came up with a way to make the perfect potato chip—one that would stay fresh longer, break less easily, and store more conveniently than the normal variety. Each of these superchips would be cut by a machine into exactly the same size and shape and then stacked in a cannister resembling a tennis ball can. On paper, the idea was terrific—consumers could enjoy big, crunchy chips that wouldn't get stale or soggy for months. But in reality, Pringle's, as the product was called, turned into a disaster—largely because Procter & Gamble forgot to analyze the way its buying public lived.

It turned out that the enormous amounts of additives and preservatives in this processed chip alienated millions of health-oriented women. P&G lost half a billion dollars on this nutritionally unsound item—three times more than Ford squandered on the Edsel of the late 1950s. But Pringle's was more than a large, one-time financial loss for P&G. The debacle helped confirm for counterculture females—who were serving their families more natural and organic foods—that the company wasn't on their wavelength. The canned potato chip is still on supermarket shelves today, yet, despite a newer, more natural formula and a new television advertising campaign, the product has not been able to gain a following. Too many people remember its artificial origins.

Unfortunately, Procter & Gamble didn't seem to learn much from its experience with Pringle's. Recently the company repeated the same mistake when it tried to introduce Certain, a lotion-laced toilet tissue, in selected test markets around the country. This product was hailed by P&G's laboratory staff as a real technological breakthrough—the softest toilet paper ever manufactured. The only problem was that the greasy tissue clogged household plumbing and wreaked havoc in municipal sewer systems. When word of this environmental hazard leaked out, women began to shun Certain, ensuring its failure. Undaunted, P&G sent waste disposal experts into neighborhoods in an effort to convince people that its new toilet paper was ecologically sound. The manufacturer even got the National Sanitation Foundation to give the bathroom tissue its seal of approval. But the damage was done, and inner-directed females felt betrayed by Procter & Gamble's insensitive approach to marketing.

If packaged-goods purveyors want to continue to grow over the next decade, they will have to improve their credibility with contemporary counterculture women in America. A company can no longer market chemical-filled potato chips or environmentally disastrous toilet paper and expect the majority of this country's women to buy them. Financial self-interest demands a more enlightened approach to feminine consumer needs today.

8 GOLD MINE
Computers Get Personal

While the marketers of colas, fast foods, domestic cars, and many packaged goods remain bogged down in their Belonger past, most personal computer companies are moving smartly ahead into the future.

Silicon Valley's microchip—the tiny postage-stamp-sized circuit board inside the new desktop mini-brains—is a smashing technological innovation that is changing the lives of millions of Americans. For the first time, the average consumer can harness computer power right in his own living room, and some of life's most time-consuming tasks—writing, accounting, and filing, for instance—suddenly seem effortless, and even enjoyable.

Personal computers are one of the fastest-selling products in the country today. Over 6 million of the sophisticated machines have been purchased since 1977, and demand is expected to remain strong for at least the next ten years. It's estimated that by 1990 half of all American households will own one of these small electronic wizards. This positive momentum can be measured in another way, too. The personal computer industry, launched less than a decade ago on a shoestring budget, has become a thriving $7.5 billion business in its first seven years of existence. During the next seven years, according to analysts, this phenomenal growth will continue, as the category mushrooms to $60 billion.

Attaining this level of success hasn't been easy for marketers in Silicon Valley. Despite its convenience and practicality, the personal computer was initially greeted by a skittish and skeptical public. Most people were frightened that the brilliant machine would eventually take over society, automating even the most basic functions and making talented human beings obsolete. Many consumers were also high-tech illiterates—they didn't understand how to use a computer or what it could do for them. As a result, the vast majority of Americans harbored negative feelings toward the new hardware.

To help eradicate this national fear and loathing of computer technology, Silicon Valley companies turned to the image transformers on Madison Avenue and began to increase their media expenditures. In 1980, for example, the computer industry spent a total of $20 million on all forms of advertising and promotion; by 1983, it was investing close to $100 million on television commercials alone.

The computer makers didn't just throw money at their problem, however. After watching big marketers such as Procter & Gamble, McDonald's, and General Motors squander huge sums on ineffective campaigns, they realized that the quality of their advertising mattered as much as the quantity. Silicon Valley knew that it couldn't hope to sell its complex machines by simply describing their functional details. Thirty seconds of bits, bytes, rams, and disk drives would only further alienate consumers—technospeak or specsmanship just wouldn't work. Facts weren't enough. Each PC (personal computer) brand had to be targeted at a specific group of people on the basis of its image or personality—not on its technical merits.

This sales strategy worked exceedingly well, and it's one of the primary reasons for the growth of many Silicon Valley enterprises today. Apple, for example, has made friends with Societally Conscious Achievers by positioning its computers as part of their inner-directed life-style. The company's commercials stress the fact that its machines do more than just word processing or financial analysis.

Owning an Apple, according to the company's mellow spots, fosters creative thinking and helps a person become more self-reliant while contributing to his overall sense of well-being. The introspective ads portray young and independent-minded entrepreneurs who have integrated the firm's computers into their rich and varied lives. A woman architect, a musically inclined executive, and a bicycle-riding businessman are among the characters appearing in these commercials. For each of them, Apple's computers bring personal satisfaction and ease to their individual pursuits.

On the other hand, IBM addresses striving executives by linking corporate prestige and promotion with ownership of one of its PCs. The firm's television campaign features Charlie Chaplin's enduring character, the Tramp, whose frantic attempts to survive in the contemporary business world mirror the real-life experiences of people in every American company today. In each 30-second commercial, however, the Tramp always seems to get a handle on things and is able to move ahead—thanks to his small IBM computer, a tool for coping with difficult modern times. The message of these pinstripe parables is clear: Without IBM's prowess, the middle manager doesn't stand a chance.

Commodore has adopted a marketing approach much like IBM's—only it uses the threat of parental, rather than corporate, failure to sell its machines. The company's hard-hitting commercials, which promote computers as if they were encyclopedias, tell anxious Emulator-Achiever adults that unless their kids start using the intellectually nourishing hardware early in life, the youngsters will never amount to anything.

In one of these ads, a little girl celebrating her fifth birthday receives a Commodore computer. She is absolutely delighted. An announcer informs viewing adults that giving a child access to the new technology today will ensure his success tomorrow. This advertising is extremely effective because it pushes the guilt button in upwardly mobile parents. These people, who want their kids to become doctors and lawyers, will do almost anything to help them attain this respectability—even if it means purchasing a complex computer system for a second-grader.

Atari recently appealed to these same status-conscious Emulator-Achievers in another way—by tapping their materialistic instincts. The firm's advertising positioned its machine as a faddish electronic toy, a dazzling high-tech novelty that, like the Betamax or Walkman, conspicuous consumers absolutely had to have. In the company's campaigns of several years ago, for example, families and friends were shown huddled around a television console having a wonderful time with the newest video game. The ads' refrain—"Have You Played Atari Today?"—reminded viewers that they would be left behind if they didn't own the latest in computer gadgetry. Most Atari purchasers enjoy flaunting their money. Unlike Apple's clientele, which views the personal computer as a device for self-enrichment, most of Atari's customers see the tabletop machine as a symbol of financial accomplishment.

Atari and most of its Silicon Valley brethren have taken the low road in their television commercials so far. They've built their companies up by preying on the public's insecurities, and it's now clear that the fear of failure scares people more than the fear of high technology. The microchip has won by default; it's the lesser of two evils, and that's one of the reasons so many consumers are purchasing computers today.

These negative advertising strategies ("Buy this machine or you'll never move up the corporate hierarchy"; "Buy this machine or your kids won't get into college"; "Buy this machine or people will think you haven't made it") work well when they're aimed at uncertain Emulator-Achievers. But they don't influence Societally Conscious Achievers, who represent the largest nonbusiness computer market in the United States. If Atari, Commodore, and even powerful IBM want to capture this significant audience, they'll have to shift marketing gears soon and, like Apple, begin selling to counterculturalists in a positive and innovative way.

* * *

Apple is one of the fastest-growing corporations in the history of American commerce, expanding even more rapidly than Bell Telephone did in the 1880s or Ford Motor did in the 1920s. Founded in a Northern California garage in 1977 by two nonconformists with just $1,300 between them, the computer firm is now a $1 billion enterprise.

Unlike the vast majority of businesses in the United States today, Apple has an integrated inner-directed persona—it is one of the quintessential corporations for our times. For example, each of the firm's employees has benefited tremendously from its meteoric rise to fame and fortune. In addition to a traditional profit-sharing program, the egalitarian computer maker regularly distributes large chunks of its stock to workers, and, as a result, Apple's payroll now includes several hundred millionaires—most of them under forty years of age.

There's an aura of casual informality at the company's Northern California headquarters, too. Almost everyone, from top-level executives down to the janitorial staff, wears open-necked shirts and jeans; three-piece suits or ties might inhibit the free-flowing corporate dialogue that Apple seeks to encourage. Apple's values are reflected in other small but significant ways as well. The firm's name, which some say is derived from the Beatles record label of the early 1970s, for instance, helps to project a friendly, nonthreatening, down-to-earth image. The company's logo, a rainbow-striped apple that looks like a pop-art emblem of the late 1960s, also communicates warmth and integrity.

However, it's more than gestures and symbols that make Apple what it is today. Quite simply, the high-tech enterprise has captured the loyalty of millions of inner-directed consumers because it has made personal computing easy, fun, and productive.

First, it created a small, trim, and inexpensive machine that was sophisticated yet simple to program and operate. And once it had established affordability and accessibility, the firm launched its now-famous marketing plan, which positioned its little brains as mind-expanding assets rather than materialistic possessions. In the resulting ads, "Apple People" don't use their computers strictly for such outer-directed ends as financial gain or career advancement. Rather, these counterculturalists plug in for intellectual challenge and nourishment—microcomputers are just one facet of their energetic lives. A recent commercial for the company featured a solitary executive playing his clarinet in a deserted part of the office in order to loosen up his mind before returning to work and his computer. By taking the bite out of the bit in its advertising, Apple has gained a reputation as one of the most sensitive American companies of the 1980s.

The man at the core of Apple's success story is a twenty-nine-year-old student of mysticism turned romantic capitalist named Steven Jobs. He's the daring entrepreneur, the electronic advanceman, who first came up with the idea of computerizing this country a decade ago—before anyone thought it was possible. He planted Apple's corporate seed in 1977, against enormous odds, and by combining a smooth sales pitch and blind faith in his product, he helped his company grow. By 1983, Apple's unimposing microcomputer was the toast of Societally Conscious America, and its high-tech visionary had become extremely wealthy—worth over $200 million.

One of the reasons for Apple's enormous popularity among inner-directed consumers in the United States is that its leader understands this group so well—he's a product of the same counterculture. Adopted by a middle-class California family in 1955, Steve Jobs spent his early years going it alone, detaching himself from elementary school life and making few friends in the small bedroom community outside of San Francisco where he lived. His one interest was electronics, and it became a consuming passion. Jobs, a born tinkerer, devoted much of his childhood to the designing and building of primitive gadgets. Whenever he needed parts for his bizarre inventions, he'd pick up the phone and make collect calls to such suppliers as Burroughs or Texas Instruments. Once, as an eleven-year-old, he visited the engineering laboratories of nearby Hewlett-Packard and persuaded senior executives there to lend him sophisticated equipment for a project. Jobs's crowning achievement as an adolescent came when he assembled a frequency counter in his bedroom. This device measures electronic impulses and introduced the whiz kid to the concept of timing, which is critical for understanding how computer systems work.

After graduating from high school in 1971, he interrupted his scientific pursuits to begin a four-year odyssey that took him halfway around the world. Jobs spent that first summer of freedom living with his girl friend in a quaint wooden cabin nestled high atop the Santa Cruz Mountains. In the fall, he descended from his aerie and matriculated at Oregon's Reed College. On campus, the engineering star showed little interest in attending classes. Instead, he hung out at the Hare Krishna house in Portland and explored the finer points of mysticism, meditation, and I Ching. He also became a vegetarian. After several semesters, Jobs left Reed.

The young man returned to the Bay Area in 1974, when he landed a low-paying job at a fledgling video game enterprise called Atari. Run at this time by Nolan Bushnell, an eccentric entrepreneur, the company was just beginning to capture national attention. Bushnell and his small staff had been in business for only two years, but their challenging electronic version of table tennis, Pong, was rapidly replacing pinball as the favorite diversion of drinkers in bars across the country. Jobs helped design some circuitry for Atari, but he never really became an integral part of the company. Over the years, members of the firm have been quoted as saying that they were put off by the young engineer's arrogant attitude and his brash manner.

In order to maximize the cocky—but talented—nineteen-year-old's productivity, Atari's flexible management arranged for Jobs to come to work late at night—after everyone had gone home. For the next few months, the difficult adolescent genius labored in solitude. Eventually, however, he grew tired of the grind and the regimented life-style—and he quit.

Seeking personal solace and spiritual enlightenment, the disaffected youth set off on a pilgrimage to India, where he wandered around for several months hefting his heavy backpack. Unfortunately, Jobs found few answers in Calcutta, Madras, Delhi, or Bombay, and he again returned home to San Francisco.

In 1975, he resumed a "normal" life and began frequenting the Homebrew Club, where the best computer brains in the Bay Area spent their free time. It was here that Jobs met a young man named Stephen Wozniak. Woz, as he was called by almost everyone, thought of himself as an "electronics nerd," but the microchip mafia of Silicon Valley gave him much higher marks than that. The precocious engineer was regarded as one of the computer industry's bright stars of the future, a wizard who could design a complex circuit board as well as anyone in the business.

The son of an aeronautical technician, Wozniak, like Jobs, had been drawn to electronics at an early age. He built hundreds of small computers, including a sophisticated binary adding and subtracting machine, while still in high school. And after scoring a perfect 800 on his math SAT, he was recruited by colleges and universities around the country. Woz chose to stay home, however, and began studying at Berkeley. After three years of college, he became bored and took an $18,000-a-year job with Hewlett-Packard as a designer of calculator chips.

When he wasn't working at H-P, the gifted computer whiz was busy using his technical skills to engineer offbeat inventions. Having read about "Blue Boxes"—devices that shortcut phone company circuits, allowing someone to call anywhere for free—Woz built one. He showed the gadget to Jobs, who immediately recognized his new friend's talent.

It soon dawned on Jobs that Wozniak's bizarre inventions might be worth something; maybe there was money to be made from them. He proposed that the two go into business together, manufacturing and selling Blue Boxes to the university students around Berkeley. Woz loved the idea and began to crank out the electronic gizmos. The small-scale commercial venture proved to be quite profitable. A partnership had begun.

Promotiong Wozniak's Blue Box helped Jobs discover how lucrative the practical application of technology could be. In an effort to come up with a new moneymaking idea, the fledgling entrepreneur began analyzing the consumer marketplace for areas of opportunity. After considerable thought, he decided that computers were where the action was.

On the surface, Jobs's thinking made very little sense; there were hundreds of Silicon Valley companies already in the data processing field—and the last thing the world needed was another hardware enterprise. But the shrewd young man had a unique vision. He realized that although many American companies had been using large mainframe computers for over two decades, few people outside the corporate world had access to this kind of intricate technology.

Woz, like Jobs, believed that a simple new computer that could be used at home would be enormously popular—especially among their counterculture peers across the country. But there was just one problem: the building of such a small machine. The duo began spending nights in Woz's office at Hewlett-Packard, trying to design a desktop wizard for the general public. Finally after several months of trial and error, they came up with a plan that enabled them, in essence, to scale down a big mainframe into a box weighing just twelve pounds. Unlike those sizable corporate machines, which often took up large amounts of space and required cumbersome power and cooling devices in order to operate, this baby brain was based on a small sliver of silicon circuitry and could be housed in a trim, light casing.

In addition to fitting onto a desk, the diminutive new computer was easy to use, too. Instead of coping with a tangle of heavy-duty mainframe cables, the operator needed just one wire, and it could be plugged into a wall outlet. Nobody was needed to program the microcomputer either. After hooking the mini-machine to a television console, the user could insert a software disk of his choice and get right to work.

The major difference between this creation and the larger data processors, however, was price. Because the compact new machine was smaller, less powerful, and less complicated, and because its microchip, which stores and processes data, was mass-produced, it could be sold at a fraction of the cost of a mainframe. The big computers of the mid-1970s were leased for an average of $11,000 a month; a person would now be able to purchase the new hardware outright for approximately $2,000.

In 1977, Jobs and Wozniak began to assemble sample models of their computer in the Jobs family garage. They sensed that they were sitting on a potential gold mine. When the machines were operating properly, the pair showed them to several engineering friends, who were quite impressed. The small boxes that the two young men demonstrated were complex, yet they ran so simply and smoothly. Those who saw the mini-machines compared them to the original Volkswagen, predicting that they would revolutionize Silicon Valley the way the VW had shaken up the automobile business almost twenty years earlier. Heartened, Jobs and Wozniak decided to get their computer into production as soon as possible, and they came up with a name for their newborn enterprise—Apple.

Wozniak submitted his resignation at Hewlett-Packard, and Jobs began lining up electronics suppliers in the Silicon Valley area. Parts for Apple's computers would be purchased from other companies, and the two young men would then assemble the machines in their garage warehouse. After several months, the partners had built up a small inventory of computers, which were quickly sold to friends.

Word soon spread throughout the Bay Area about Apple's machine, and the pair were quickly swamped with orders. To keep up with demand for their product, Wozniak and Jobs were forced to hire additional employees, who worked around the clock putting the small company's computers together. Business was so brisk during these early days that Apple's cofounders were unable to do much more than eat, sleep, and supervise their booming enterprise. There wasn't even enough time to go to the bank, and Jobs kept stuffing the firm's weekly receipts into a desk drawer. At the end of a year, the two engineers had sold their dazzling new machine to customers up and down the West Coast. This success continued over the next twenty-four months, and by 1980—just three years after setting up shop—Apple had sales of $140 million.

Wozniak and Jobs had made a lot of money in a hurry; more important, however, they had taken the Silicon Valley establishment by surprise. In 1977, no electronics firm thought it was possible to manufacture and distribute a personal computer on a large scale in this country, but Apple's triumph proved the doubters wrong. Many competitive computer corporations now began moving into the marketplace to challenge the profitable upstart.

Despite its track record, Apple was still a fairly primitive outfit at this time. For example, the company continued to sell its machines with only minimal advertising support—most consumers learned about them through the grapevine, and retailers generally discovered them at trade conventions. Jobs realized that in order to compete with such better-funded firms as Atari, Commodore, and, eventually, IBM, Apple would have to produce and sell its computers much more efficiently. More sophisticated plants would have to be constructed, and big-budget advertising campaigns would have to be created.

These improvements would, of course, require millions of dollars. The only way the three-year-old enterprise could raise such large amounts of money would be by entering the venture capital market and becoming a publicly owned corporation.

Neither Jobs nor Wozniak wanted to give up any control of the company, but they grasped the reality of the situation. If Apple was to retain its momentum, it needed a major infusion of cash, which could come only from the powerful investment community. Despite their reluctance to let outsiders into Apple's decision-making process, the dynamic engineers did receive some consolation for relinquishing a small portion of their power. When Wall Street's stock offering for Apple was issued, it sold out in twenty-four hours—making both Jobs and Wozniak instant multimillionaires.

With this vote of public confidence, Apple entered a new era of respectability and legitimacy. Most of the company's employees still wore jeans and boots to the office each day, but they now worked in a new building, and an ultramodern assembly line was producing scores of finished computers every day. The firm also began spending heavily on television commercials that spread its sales message to all corners of the country.

After an exhaustive review of Madison Avenue's top shops, Wozniak and Jobs chose Chiat-Day, then a tiny California-based company specializing in the promotion of consumer electronics, to create Apple's advertising. As its first order of business, the local agency conducted a major research study among Americans, to determine their attitudes about computers. The project revealed that a large number of inner-directed entrepreneurs would purchase a computer if it appeared to be friendly and not intimidating. The shop created a set of 30-second television spots, featuring Dick Cavett, the talk-show host, who was selected as the computer maker's spokesman because of his mellow, nonthreatening egghead image. Cavett had the ability to put people at ease, and his wry sense of humor added a touch of levity to Apple's sales pitches. His offbeat presence in each of the company's commercials also helped ensure their memorability. One of these half-minutes, targeted at inner-directed women, for example, conveys the tone of the campaign:

CAVETT: I'm here with an average American homemaker with her Apple PC. Jill, do you use your Apple for household budgeting?

JILL: Actually, I'm working in gold futures.

CAVETT: Oh. Well, you could probably put a lot of recipes in there, huh?

JILL: And, you can do trend analyses, generate bar graphs . . .

CAVETT: Are you really a homemaker?

JILL: Well, of course.

CAVETT: So the Apple is the appliance of the '80s for all those pesky household chores?

JILL: I also own a steel mill.

ANNOUNCER: Apple. The personal computer.

Chiat-Day's television spots for Jobs and Wozniak were extremely well received. A confidential research study conducted by a competitive computer maker indicated that close to 70 percent of the inner-directed consumers in this country recalled seeing the Cavett commercials six months after the campaign had first aired. According to the survey, these viewers got the message that Apple was a warm, sincere manufacturer, whose hardware would fit comfortably into their lives. The Cavett spots were so effective that orders began pouring into the company's headquarters.

To keep up with the growing demand for their product, Apple's cofounders had to hire still more employees and began working twenty-hour days themselves. This grueling pace eventually proved to be too much for Wozniak. He had burned himself out, and he decided to take a sabbatical from the high-pressure computer business.

About a year and a half later, Woz began to grow restless. He had enjoyed his vacation—traveling, studying, and thinking had left him immensely fulfilled—but he missed the excitement of his expanding business and wanted to get back into the fray. He and Jobs discussed his return to the computer wars. Apple's cofounders also chatted about the direction their company was heading. They agreed that the firm had to be gradually transformed from a loose, free-swinging entrepreneurial outfit into a more mature, disciplined operation—especially if it was going to compete successfully against IBM during the 1980s and 1990s. The corporate giant had entered the personal computer market with much fanfare in 1981 and was already generating a great deal of competitive pressure. But as much as Jobs and Wozniak wanted to change Apple's structure, they were determined not to let go of the enterprise's unique character. Somehow, the computer manufacturer had to make the jump from cottage industry to big business without losing its innocence.

Despite their strong leadership skills, the two young engineers realized that Apple couldn't handle this enormous leap to corporate faith without outside managerial assistance. They needed a sensitive and seasoned top-level executive, someone who would bring a wealth of professional experience to the company without destroying its special values.

Jobs hired Gerald Roche, the chairman of Heidrick and Struggles, a large executive recruiting firm based in New York, to help him locate the kind of individual Apple required. Roche presented a list of several prospective candidates to the computer company's leader, but he made it clear that John Sculley, a dynamic young president at Pepsi-Cola, was his choice for the position.

Sculley, the headhunter explained, was one of the best and brightest marketers around. He had already earned his stripes in the upper echelons of the corporate world, despite the fact that he was only forty-four years of age. During the 1970s, for example, the soft-drink manager had successfully spearheaded Pepsi's bold attack on Coke and had helped the second-place cola increase its sales. Most important, according to Roche, Sculley was a terrific people person, a down-to-earth fellow who inspired tremendous employee loyalty. The recruiter also believed that the beverage executive was an adventurer, someone who would get along well with Woz, Jobs, and the rest of Apple's counterculture crew.

Initially, Pepsi's president showed little interest in the Silicon Valley post. He told Roche that he had no desire to switch from colas to computers. The persistent recruiter nevertheless managed to set up a meeting between Sculley and Jobs. The soft-drink executive found himself intrigued by the computer maker. He was fascinated to learn how the young engineer had built his high-tech company into a booming enterprise, and even more interested in the coming computer revolution. Selling the electronic brains to America would be one of the major marketing opportunities of the next decade, and this excited Pepsi's leader.

During subsequent meetings with Jobs, Sculley decided he would like to become part of the Apple operation. After lengthy negotiations, it was agreed that the computer company would pay the cola marketer $2 million in first-year salary and bonuses, guarantee him $1 million in severance funds, and offer him options on 350,000 shares of its stock. In the spring of 1983, Sculley, one of the biggest names on Madison Avenue, went west to join Apple in its battle against such heavyweight hardware producers as IBM. Silicon Valley's advertising was about to become as advanced as its machines.

During the newcomer's first months at Apple, Sculley and

Jobs made several important decisions. The two executives agreed that large advertising expenditures would be necessary to compete effectively against IBM in the marketplace. They earmarked about $40 million for television commercials alone, a sum that was more than double the company's total ad budget for the previous year. With the increased finances at hand, Sculley recommended that Apple's TV campaign be updated. He liked the old Dick Cavett spots, but Apple's research indicated decreased viewer involvement with those witty half-minutes. The executive decided that stronger ads were needed in order to capitalize on the firm's status among Societally Conscious consumers. This nonconforming group's unique life-style had to be portrayed more vividly. A celebrity spokesman like Cavett speaking from a studio armchair could take Apple's message only so far; more realistic slice-of-life commercials were required.

Collaborating with Chiat-Day, Sculley developed a fresh advertising approach that showed casually dressed young professionals using the firm's mighty microcomputers. Each of these inner-directed citizens was depicted as an innovative, free-spirited individual, and the sunshine-filled sales pitches suggested that creative brilliance and Apple went hand in hand. To reinforce the inventive campaign's individualistic imagery, Sculley came up with a potent phrase that ended each of the new commercials: "Soon there'll be just two kinds of people. Those who use computers. And those who use Apples."

The introspective "Apple People" spots were considered by many on Madison Avenue to be reminiscent of the exuberant Pepsi Generation commercials that Sculley's former employer had given America twenty years earlier. The marketing strategies for the two ad campaigns were identical—glorify or celebrate the target audience's values and attitudes to make a sale. Only now, instead of beach barbecues, Frisbee flings, or patriotic parades down Main Street, the tube reflected a more sensitive and subdued vision of life in this country.

One of Apple's recent 30-second spots shows a scruffy counterculturalist riding his bike to the office early one morning, a big ungainly dog trotting along at his heels. Once inside his light-drenched office, the young executive settles down in front of one of Apple's sophisticated computers and begins to analyze several complicated-looking graphs and charts. Another half-minute from the computer maker focuses on a lanky blond female architect who is shooting baskets with some of the guys during her lunch hour. The trim, athletic woman symbolizes the bright, energetic, and liberated female user that Apple seeks to attract.

John Sculley's striking campaign for Apple, which first aired in late 1983, is Ad Alley's most definitive Societally Conscious statement to date. His commercials convey a clear understanding and appreciation of the growing number of inner-directed consumers in this country, while offering many insights into this group's mind-set. One comes away after each of these 30-second snippets with a much better sense of the Woodstock Generation's world view.

Although this ingenious advertising strategy has helped Apple to carve out a solid second-place niche in the fiercely competitive personal computer market—behind powerful IBM— there is some concern among high-tech analysts these days about the upstart company's long-term prospects. The antiestablishment computer firm increased its sales by more than 200 percent each year between 1977 and 1982, and many industry observers wonder if this kind of momentum can be regained.

Apple's recent introduction of Macintosh, its extraordinarily versatile and easy-to-use microcomputer, which offers dazzling visual graphics as well as other sophisticated programs, promises to keep consumers interested for the time being. But perhaps more important than its technological innovation is whether the company can retain its special persona, which has contributed so much to its past successes.

The proprietor and protector of this image is Steve Jobs. As long as he remains actively involved in Apple's complex operations, the enterprise stands an excellent chance of maintaining its unique image. Assuming that the mercurial Jobs stays with the company he created, one of the bloodiest marketing battles of the 1980s and 1990s will be between the feisty electronics rebel and the American corporation with the biggest potential byte of all, a goliath named IBM.

"Big Blue," as IBM is known on Madison Avenue, entered the personal computer business in late 1981—four years after Woz and Jobs introduced their microcomputer. Despite its late start, however, the company rapidly made up ground and eventually overtook Apple in the PC market.

IBM has been able to mount such a strong comeback partly because of its size. With approximately $40 billion in annual sales, the corporate behemoth—forty times as large as Apple—can afford to channel huge sums into research, product development, manpower, and capital improvements. This special financial clout allows the company to accomplish major undertakings in a hurry. Silicon Valley analysts are still in awe, for instance, over Big Blue's ability to catch Apple from a standing start in just a few years; closing such a wide gap, they say, might have taken a smaller, less profitable firm over a decade.

It's more than raw dollar power, however, that's behind IBM's dramatic success in the PC category. Over the past thirty years, the conglomerate has developed a reputation—among striving Emulator-Achievers especially—as a safe, secure establishment purveyor of office products. Owning or leasing one of the company's typewriters or mainframes reassured nervous executives; these upwardly mobile businessmen felt more confident about their career prospects with Big Blue's classy machines humming along in the background.

When the firm's personal computer was first introduced, it benefited tremendously from a halo effect—people in commerce thought that the mini-brain would perform miracles, too. As a result, demand for IBM's small-scale hardware often outstripped supply in 1981 and 1982, and an entirely new segment of status-conscious consumers entered the desktop computer market. Big Blue had legitimized the information revolution launched by Apple.

IBM elbowed its way into the lucrative PC industry only after closely monitoring Apple's progress for several years. The huge enterprise's first step was appointing a task force of engineers to develop an easy-to-use machine that could compete against

Apple's successful desktop model. The group worked intensely—twelve hours a day, six days a week—until it perfected its
own computer. Next, IBM built a huge state-of-the-art factory
to manufacture its new data processing product. The automated plant was so advanced that it could assemble an entire
PC in just several minutes. Last, the company broke a long-
standing corporate policy of distributing its products primarily
through IBM representatives when it gave computer stores the
opportunity to sell its personalized hardware, too. This eventually proved to be a very astute marketing move: In 1982 and
1983, Big Blue sold approximately one million PCs.

Of course, advertising also has played a major role in IBM's
successful invasion of the personal computer industry. The
firm's commercials featuring Charlie Chaplin's Tramp, a symbol of get-ahead productivity, have great appeal among ambitious Emulator-Achievers—the people who believe that Big
Blue microcomputers will give them a boost in the business
world.

Like IBM, Commodore has also risen to the top of the competitive personal computer market by appealing to status-
conscious Emulator-Achievers. The company's hard-hitting
commercials, which tell parents that their kids will fail without
the help of a microcomputer, are among the most powerful and
effective spots on the air today. The firm's 30-second commercial "Flunk-Out" is a good example of this kind of salesmanship. The spot opens with a middle-class couple seeing their
son off to college at the railroad station. The young man is
dressed in a coat and tie, and as he boards the train, he smiles
and promises to make his folks proud. The happy parents wave
good-bye to their offspring, certain that he'll go places. Their
expectations are shattered, however, when the boy returns
home several months later. Wearing a frayed sweat shirt and
dirty jeans, the despondent overweight kid schleps his bags off
the train—he's flunked out of school. As the camera focuses on
the dejected mother and father, an announcer tells us that the
youngster didn't make the grade because he lacked the com-

puter skills that come from years of experience on a Commodore microcomputer.

Another recent half-minute, "Perfection," drums in the same message. We are shown two high school students on a split screen. One of the boys is seriously working on a term paper at his Commodore computer; the other is zealously zapping Martians out of the sky at his electronic console. The action freezes, and an announcer comes on the air: "Become great at video games and maybe you can score sixteen million in Space Invaders. Become great at the Commodore Vic 20 and maybe you can score sixteen hundred on the College Boards."

Atari, the video game and computer hardware company, has similarly made its mark by attracting millions of upwardly mobile consumers. Positioning electronic games such as Space Invaders, Missile Command, and Pac-Man as high-tech essentials, the firm amassed annual revenues of almost $1 billion by the early 1980s, selling millions of game cartridges a year. Atari then capitalized on this early success by bringing out a line of spiffy microcomputers. These products, which were aggressively advertised as the latest in Silicon Valley gadgetry, sold well among Emulator-Achievers.

The company, which has a fascinating corporate history, was started just twelve years ago by a young man named Nolan Bushnell. The son of a cement contractor, Bushnell came to Silicon Valley in the late 1960s, after gaining a degree in engineering at the University of Utah. In 1972 he came up with the idea for a new computerized game—an automated high-speed version of Ping-Pong that could be played on a television screen.

Bushnell decided to call his invention Pong, and with $500 of his own money he began manufacturing the coin-operated machines. Within several months, the challenging electronic table tennis game was replacing old-fashioned pinball in taverns and arcades. Bushnell hired a staff and officially formed a company, which he named Atari—a term from the Japanese game of Go that is a polite warning to an opponent that he's about to be engulfed.

In its early days, Atari was a wild, unstructured kind of operation, reminding many Silicon Valley observers of a bawdy fraternity like that in *Animal House*. Despite its free-spirited approach to business, however, the enterprise still managed to make money—by 1973, Atari had profits of $1 million. But even with this success, the video game company's financial situation was often shaky, because of several costly and unsuccessful attempts to expand.

Atari's topsy-turvy balance sheet may have scared several would-be corporate suitors away. Disney Productions and MCA, the Hollywood entertainment conglomerate, were both interested in purchasing the video game outfit—but each company eventually passed up the opportunity. Finally, New York–based Warner Communications stepped into the picture. Warner was involved with films, records, and network and cable television, and it believed that Atari's electronic recreation would complement these businesses perfectly. In 1976, it paid $28 million for the enterprise—a price that would seem ridiculously low four years later, when the firm's annual revenues were approaching $1 billion at the height of the electronic game craze in this country.

Warner gradually began to reorganize Atari. Bushnell was eventually forced out (he had received approximately $15 million for selling his firm), and Raymond Kassar, who had been a top-level fashion marketer at Burlington Industries, was hired to run the video game company. Kassar pumped $120 million of Warner's money into Atari, primarily in an effort to develop a video game cartridge system based on the microchip. This technological breakthrough would open up an entirely new world for consumers, giving them a much wider selection of electronic games to choose from.

Once again, Silicon Valley's engineers triumphed—and Atari began marketing its video game consoles and cartridges with abandon. Under Kassar's aggressive leadership, the company spent close to $100 million each year on television advertising targeted at upscale families, the affluent group that could afford its hardware and software.

Each of the firm's campaigns during the late 1970s tried to create the impression that there were two types of people in the

United States: those who were fortunate enough to own an Atari system—the haves—and those who weren't—the have-nots. In one spot, for example, a woman complained that after her family bought its Atari set, the game became so popular that the neighbors moved in. The message was clear: Stay ahead of the Joneses and you'll bask in neighborhood approval. Kassar drew upon his experience from Seventh Avenue to build a certain snob appeal and trendiness into Atari's brand name. In essence, he believed that the company's commercials, which positioned its games as if they were part of the latest *haute couture* collection from Paris, would help establish a loyal electronic elite.

This marketing strategy proved to be quite successful. By the early 1980s, Atari had become close to a billion-dollar business. But video games were not enough for Kassar. Eager to cash in on the personal computer revolution, he decided that his firm should introduce a line of microcomputers, too.

Atari's computers were advertised as an essential materialistic possession. Clan superiority was the theme of one of these commercials, as two families busily compared the respective merits of their home computers. While the Atari owners rattled off a long list of their machine's functions—from geography lessons to bookkeeping—the other, ''less privileged'' group appeared disconsolate. It seemed they couldn't plug in to nearly as many programs as the Atari family. Not surprisingly, Atari's desktop machines sold well among the company's staunch Emulator-Achiever supporters—the same upscale people who had purchased its video game fun several years earlier.

Despite this initial success, however, Atari suddenly began to lose its fiscal momentum in late 1982. The video game market had finally become saturated, and the company's share of the microcomputer market was not yet strong enough to bolster its sagging financial fortunes. In an attempt to reverse this downward trend, Warner ordered Kassar to expand Atari's consumer base for its personal computers. Unfortunately, the executive's efforts—including his unexpected dismissal of Young & Rubicam, one of the firm's advertising agencies—didn't help mat-

ters much. During the first half of 1983, Atari lost more than
$100 million, and Warner's stock dropped sharply.

With matters reaching a crisis point, Steven Ross, the head of
Warner, let his high-tech manager go. In just six short years,
Kassar had transformed Atari from a tiny Silicon Valley outfit
into a major corporate presence in the home electronics field.
But when it became necessary for the company to compete
more aggressively against the savvy marketing of such formidable computer competitors as Apple and IBM, the former fashion
executive was unable to produce the required results.

Warner's search for a new chief executive at Atari lasted several months. The huge entertainment enterprise spent much of
this time wooing a marketing talent from Philip Morris named
James Morgan, who was widely regarded on Madison Avenue as
the heir to George Weissman's corporate throne. The forty-
two-year-old Morgan—a bold and innovative strategic thinker
—had helped preside over such profitable cigarette brands as
Marlboro and Merit during the late 1960s and 1970s.

Initially, the marketer rejected Ross's suggestion that he take
over at Atari, claiming that his future was at Philip Morris; but
after several lengthy discussions with Warner's chief, the executive became more interested in the leadership opportunity.
The key factor in Morgan's ultimate decision to leave Weissman's fold, however, was almost certainly money. Ross needed
help with Atari's computer business, and he was prepared to
pay for it. To lure his man from Philip Morris, the show business mogul ended up signing a contract that made Morgan a millionaire. Under the terms of the agreement, Atari will reportedly pay its new chief executive $10 million in salary and
performance bonuses over the next seven years.

One of Morgan's first tasks at Atari was to focus on its advertising—now in the hands of Wells Rich Greene. The executive
realized that in order for the high-tech company to broaden its
consumer appeal, it would have to reach out to the growing Societally Conscious audience. His experience with Merit at Philip
Morris had taught him how crucial this emerging group of citizens could be in determining the success of a product. Morgan
knew that Atari's strength within the shrinking Emulator-

Achiever segment simply could not carry it through the upcoming decade.

Fortunately for the marketer, Wells Rich had assessed the situation in the same way and had created a series of commercials that featured Alan Alda, the star of "M*A*S*H." The agency believed that Alda, who had played the introspective and irreverent Hawkeye on television for so many years, would have tremendous appeal among inner-directed consumers.

The shop's spots show Alda fiddling with one of Atari's computers in his home, demonstrating how simple and easy to use the machines actually are. The friendly, nonthreatening ads are designed to soften the high-tech firm's hard-edged public persona. In one of these half-minutes, Alda is seen in his cluttered den studying Italian on his new Atari computer. The faithful dog at the celebrity's side resents the machinery, which seems to have won over his master's heart. Alda interrupts his language lesson to reassure the insecure hound that even though Atari's computer can perform many useful functions, it still can't bring him his slippers or lick his face. Commercials like this one help position Atari's technology as an essential ingredient in a low-key—but intellectually stimulating—life-style.

It's still unclear at this point whether Wells Rich's fresh advertising approach will help Atari to attract counterculture customers. By the first quarter of 1984, sales had improved slightly, but they still remained weak. It appears that Warner's subsidiary still has a long way to go in order to gain the confidence and patronage of inner-directed consumers in this country. Undoing almost a decade of materialistic salesmanship won't be easy, and Atari will have to demonstrate patience and persistence with its new marketing strategy over the next few years if it wants to remain a significant factor in the microcomputer industry.

9 SOUR GRAPES

Wine Tries to Become Our National Drink

Northern California was the site of another marketing milestone during the 1970s, when America's wine business took off.

Fourteen years ago, a slew of prosperous conglomerates entered the previously private world of viticulture and transformed it into a mass-market enterprise. Joining such large-scale operations as Gallo, Almadén, and Paul Masson, savvy packaged-goods corporations—Pepsi, Nestlé, Standard Brands, and Norton Simon among them—bought large vineyards and began selling wine with the same techniques they had used to move soft drinks, coffee, and frozen foods. For the first time, television advertising became as important an ingredient in the winemaking process as the grapes themselves. Commercials touting a bottle's social cachet as much as its tasty contents helped convince millions of consumers to make wine a central part of their everyday lives. Over the next decade, between 1970 and 1980, wine sales in the United States doubled—to approximately 500 million gallons a year; the industry's annual volume jumped to $4 billion; and yearly per capita wine consumption in this country moved from 1.1 to 2.2 gallons.

To a large extent, this oenological boom reflected changing American life-styles, as a generation of health-conscious young people in the United States started turning from hard liquor—the scotch, bourbon, and gin that their fathers and grandfathers had poured for decades—to lighter, smoother wines. In an effort to learn more about this new drink, hundreds of thousands of neophyte sippers across the nation started informal viticultural educations.

Between 1970 and 1973, wine tastings were held in thirty-five states and were attended by more than 400,000 people. Wine appreciation courses proliferated, and 750,000 students a year learned the difference between Cabernet and Chardonnay. Wine publications and newsletters blossomed into a big business almost overnight, and wine bars, which offered patrons various vintages by the glass, became the latest fad. Even universities went with the flow, with oenological programs launched at over 100 American colleges. By 1973, the country's wine consciousness had been thoroughly awakened, and bottles were being regularly uncorked at home, in restaurants—even in airplanes. Sales for the beverage began growing faster than those for all other libations except mineral water.

Madison Avenue's contribution to the burgeoning grape revolution in America manifested itself in advertising that took one of two distinct approaches to the wine-drinking experience. First, there were spots that underscored the beverage's mystique. These serious, sober-sounding commercials for such vintners as Gallo, Taylor, and Paul Masson extolled wine's elegance and sophistication—that certain *je ne sais quoi.* Endorsements by oenological authorities and award presentations reinforced for consumers the drink's status-enhancing attributes.

Half-minutes from these companies, which ran throughout the 1970s, were directed primarily at the affluent and acquisitive—Emulator-Achievers—who viewed a bottle of Chablis or rosé as yet another outward sign of material prosperity. To reach this upwardly mobile consumer group, each vintner employed the same basic marketing strategy—positioning its wine as a prestigious and priceless vintage gem.

Gallo, for example, compared its $3 Hearty Burgundy with some of the great French reds by showing an elegant tasting session in Paris. According to the 30-second spot, the California winemaker outclassed its European opposition and was awarded a basketful of gold medals for excellence. One of Taylor's campaigns tried to establish an aura of sophistication in another way. Each of the firm's half-minute sales messages featured oenological experts who would present the company's wine and then extol its virtues. By publicly endorsing Taylor California Cellars, such specialists as Steven Spurrier, founder of a wine-tasting school in France, helped to create a rich, refined image for the moderately priced bottles.

Almadén used television to create upscale acceptance for its simple wine, too. Each of the company's commercials took viewers on a guided tour of its beautiful vineyard, hoping to impress them with the rich soil, copious vines, and exquisite vistas. The stately spots made Almadén's winery seem more like a baronial estate in the English countryside than a modern manufacturing operation, and the announcer seemed to be saying that consumers could share in this posh patrician fantasy by merely purchasing one of the company's bottles or jugs.

Paul Masson took the celebrity presenter route in its attempt to win over the snobbish segment of society. For much of the 1970s, the vintner employed Orson Welles as its spokesman. Welles's public persona is synonymous with taste, quality, and attention to detail; his films and theatrical presentations stand out in people's minds as finely crafted works. When the imposing thespian rhapsodized about Paul Masson in his sonorous voice, consumers immediately got the message. They would keep in mind that the vintner would "sell no wine before its time."

Recently, Masson—a subsidiary of Seagram, the liquor conglomerate—replaced Welles with an even more dignified and upper-crust endorser, Sir John Gielgud. The firm's new campaign features the cultivated British actor at a chic cocktail party, where he makes certain that viewers understand Masson's impressive aristocratic lineage.

The wine industry's other strategy promoted its beverage as a "life-style" drink, one that could be imbibed informally anytime and anywhere. Ads for Riunite and Cella—two imported Italian Lambruscos—showed carefree folks cheerfully sipping these sweet-tasting vintages at outdoor cafés, ball games, and beach parties. Aimed primarily at impressionable Emulators, these commercials attempted to wean youngsters from soda and beer by turning them on to the bright, zesty taste of the grape. In one of Riunite's vibrant spots, for example, the wine is brought to a community picnic in an icetub and served with hot dogs and hamburgers. Frosty bottles are drunk with the same gleeful abandon as Coke, Pepsi, or Bud would be.

Whether the message was classy or sassy, jug wine makers spent significant sums marketing their products during the past decade. Together, domestic vintners allocated only $30 million for advertising in 1970—a fraction of the amount spent by advertisers in other product categories, fast foods or automobiles, for example. But as the wine business expanded and became more profitable, aggressive companies, such as Gallo, Taylor, Almadén, Inglenook, and Paul Masson, began to increase their media expenditures. By 1980, American vineyards were channeling nearly $150 million annually into the promotion of their brands.

But despite this major financial commitment, with the onset of the 1980s, the wine business in this country gradually lost steam. After a decade of steady growth, sales have begun to slow; and several major wineries have found themselves in trouble. For example, Almadén's parent, National Distillers & Chemical Corporation, reports that over the past two years the vintner's operating profits have fallen by 50 percent, to $10.5 million. *Business Week* recently noted that Inglenook—a subsidiary of Heublein—ended last year 4 percent off its 1982 pace. And Coca-Cola, owner of Taylor California Cellars, decided to get out of the wine business altogether in 1983 after watching its vintner's profit margin shrink over a two-year period. Coke sold the business late last year to Seagram.

Two important factors are behind the current viticultural slump. With the American dollar holding strong against European currencies, vintners in the United States have had to face an onslaught of relatively inexpensive wines from France, Italy, and Spain. Second, domestic wineries have, to some degree, lost touch with their consuming public. Their continued emphasis on wine as either a status symbol or a fun-and-games drink in their commercials has, for the most part, failed to take into account the values and attitudes of inner-directed citizens.

A confidential 1982 research study, conducted by a large Madison Avenue agency for a major California vintner, reveals that counterculturalists view wine as a personal beverage, one that is relaxing and rewarding to drink. Although they can be devoted oenophiles, they don't uncork a bottle to impress other people, and they rarely gulp a glass down at the seashore or stadium. The Societally Conscious nurse their Riesling, Merlot, or Chenin Blanc in intimate surroundings—savoring the rich bouquet and sharing the pleasure with special friends or family.

Although several major American vineyards have recently begun to produce small batches of classier vintage-dated wines (Gallo's 1978 Cabernet Sauvignon has been much praised by critics, for example), the vast majority of their television spots today ignore the inner-directed wine-drinking experience. The vintners' apparent unwillingness to shift gears in their advertising campaigns and their attachment to Emulator or Emulator-Achiever marketing strategies have left the Societally Conscious segment to European imports and California boutique wineries.

The mass-production of wine in the United States began modestly in California's Central Valley just over fifty years ago, when two brothers named Ernest and Julio Gallo started the E. & J. Gallo winery in 1933. From their humble origins as apprentices in California's pre-Prohibition vineyards, the Gallos have built a viticultural empire worth approximately $700 million and have amassed a combined personal fortune of almost $1 billion. For the last thirty years, the formidable Gallo enterprise has been the American wine industry's undisputed leader. Today, the firm sells nearly 30 percent of all wine purchased in this country.

The fiercely ambitious brothers have been willing to take major risks throughout their long careers in order to achieve success in the winemaking business. In the early 1930s, the Gallos, sons of Italian immigrants, plunked down $5,900 for a parcel of deteriorating property near Modesto. Operating out of a small shed, they slowly improved their newly purchased land, which had been neglected for many years. Once the soil was repaired, they planted grapes and began to produce wine.

At first the Gallos sold mostly "fortified" wines—sherry, port, and muscatel. These sweet but strong beverages were extremely popular among many of the nation's poor, largely because they were high in alcohol content but low in price. To retain this consumer base, Ernest and Julio employed an effective sales slogan: "Fewer pennies per proof." The shrewd marketers also made sure their products retailed for 50 percent less than the competition's. This "bigger buzz for a buck" strategy helped launch the winery on its profitable course. Throughout the late 1930s and 1940s, the Gallos made millions of dollars, which they methodically plowed back into their rapidly expanding business.

The company became so big and prosperous after World War II that the brothers were forced to divide their management responsibilities. Julio worked exclusively in the vineyards—supervising the planting, picking, squeezing, and fermenting of the grapes—while Ernest crisscrossed the country, handling wholesale distributors, who sold Gallo's wines to liquor stores. In the days before television advertising, distributors held an enormous amount of power in the wine industry—they could easily make or break a vintner. These salesmen visited liquor merchants on a regular basis to ensure that local dealers stocked their firms' products in abundance. Without television commercials to influence them, people bought whatever bottle was most prominently displayed in a store.

Ernest Gallo, perhaps more than any wine executive of the late 1940s and early 1950s, recognized the direct correlation between shelf space and profits, and he channeled most of his energy into building a loyal, disciplined army of distributors that extended from coast to coast.

The Gallo brothers increased their dominance over the American wine industry during the 1960s, thanks, in large part, to a fortuitous experiment conducted in the vineyards. Julio had noticed that many of the nation's inner-city blacks were imbibing an odd mixture of white port and lemon juice. Sensing an opportunity for profit, the winemaker concocted his own version of the beverage. After several months, when the grapes were finally blended perfectly, he discovered that his liquid creation had a much greater potential than he had expected; young people—members of the Pepsi Generation, not just blacks—loved the drink's fruity, fizzy taste.

The Gallos named their new "lollipop wine" Thunderbird, and they began offering it all over the country for just 60 cents a pint. Even though Thunderbird had minimal advertising support, it still sold 2.5 million cases in less than a year, setting an American viticultural sales record.

Seeking to capitalize on Thunderbird's success, Gallo next came out with an entire line of "training wines" for postadolescents. First, there was Boone's Farm, a sweet, carbonated, apple-based beverage; then came Ripple, which tasted more like soda than wine; and last there was Madria Madria Sangria, a cold drink that could be chug-a-lugged like lemonade. Despite limited advertising, these sugary refreshments became instant winners in the youthful marketplace of the 1960s, and by the end of the decade, Ernest and Julio (whose last name means "rooster" in Italian) really had something to crow about. The pop wine boom, which they had launched just several years earlier, had earned them over $500 million.

The Gallos took this windfall and embarked on a major expansion program that radically altered the dynamics of the old-fashioned American wine business. Using General Motors as their model, the brothers slowly transformed their growing company into a massive, high-volume, vertically integrated operation in which technology controlled the winemaking process. Mechanized mass production ensured that each of Gallo's jugs was filled with a standardized, sanitary, scientifically blended wine; consumers did not have to worry about getting a "bad" bottle. More important, as Ray Kroc had demonstrated at McDonald's, automation fattened up the bottom line.

Ernest and Julio spent close to $300 million to fulfill their grand vision. Much of this money was invested in a gigantic space-age winery the size of five football fields, located just outside Modesto. This awesome and sterile building, which many oenologists considered the eighth wonder of the world, bore no sign of corporate identification anywhere, and it was totally surrounded by barbed wire. Within its vast confines was a completely computerized and self-sufficient wine-producing complex.

The Gallos erected their huge monument to viticulture at a perfect time. Soon after construction was completed on the gargantuan building, the American wine boom of the 1970s took hold, and, unlike other more traditional California vintners, the brothers were able to cash in on the growing consumer demand for grape-based drinks quickly. The company's annual sales surged ahead during this great national oenological awakening, and it became obvious to many savvy marketing analysts that Ernest and Julio would remain atop the American wine industry for decades to come.

Throughout this period of rapid growth, the Gallos continued to resist making any substantial commitment to advertising, placing greater faith in their aggressive, tight-knit distribution network. The few campaigns the company did run were basic and fairly uninspired. In one early television commercial, for example, Ernest's daughter-in-law pitched the firm's products, portraying the winery as a small, homey place and implying that Gallo wines were still made the old-fashioned way. In another ad, Peter Ustinov acted as a spokesman for the company's higher-priced wines. In his endorsement, the actor came off as one of Ernest and Julio's intimate friends. The gist of these advertisements was that Gallo was just a simple family operation that made quality wine—not the high-tech mass producer it really was.

Suddenly, in the mid-1970s, the powerful brothers ran into a streak of bad luck that threatened to destroy the big business they had ferociously built over the past four decades. First they had to deal with a takeover proposal made by the affluent Seagram Company. Then they became involved in a bitter and protracted labor dispute with Cesar Chavez, head of the United Farm Workers, who represented the company's grape pickers. Things went from bad to worse for Ernest and Julio when the Federal Trade Commission launched an investigation into the company's marketing tactics. The inquiry was prompted by the testimony of Gallo's former Miami distributor, who alleged that the firm had driven him out of business after he refused to stop handling a competing wine brand.

Although Gallo never lost its leadership position in the American wine business, Ernest and Julio's huge enterprise was reeling from the body blows that Seagram, Chavez, and the federal government had landed. And Gallo also had to contend with several well-heeled corporate competitors who had recently invaded its turf. Although they were new to California's vineyards, such powerful companies as Coca-Cola had already made their mark in other areas—soft drinks and packaged goods, for example—and were now eager to repeat these successes in the oenological world. Evidence of their commitment to grape growing could easily be seen in the large sums of money these firms were spending on television commercials. If Gallo was to rebound from its current crisis, the company would clearly have to match the newcomers' big media expenditures.

Ernest and Julio Gallo had always disliked Madison Avenue's slick executives, and they continued to doubt the efficacy of consumer advertising. But they were also realistic. Toward the end of the 1970s, they realized that their many years of hard work would go down the drain unless they made a major commitment to television commercials. A call went out to Young & Rubicam, Gallo's longtime agency, which had been largely confined to the dreary task of preparing liquor store fliers and unimaginative ads over the past years. The shop was told to come up with a fresh and effective television campaign.

After a prolonged period of creative stagnation on the wine account, the executives at Y&R were surprised and pleased by this new assignment. A major research study was undertaken to find out about wine-drinking attitudes in the United States. The analysis provided the agency with an understanding of the beverage's recent popularity. Perhaps the most important finding in the report, which was based on extensive consumer interviews, was that large numbers of inner-directed citizens were drawn to the drink because of its intimate qualities. They believed that wine's mellow taste stimulated good times with friends and families and helped create a soothing sense of peace and harmony in their lives. Y&R's copywriters and art directors incorporated this information into a series of commercials for Gallo.

One of the proposed spots focused on several couples sipping the company's wine as they prepared a big bowl of pasta together in the kitchen; another spot featured two female friends sharing a bottle of Gallo Hearty Burgundy while engrossed in a conversation about life, love, careers, and happiness; and a third zoomed in on a husband and wife who were quietly reflecting over a glass of Chablis after having put their newborn baby to bed.

When Ernest saw these new commercials for the first time, according to one of the meeting's participants, the winemaker had an icy look on his face. After several uncomfortable minutes of silence, one of Y&R's more courageous copywriters asked the executive what he thought about the ads he had just seen. Gallo slowly rose from behind his desk and then reportedly said: "I don't want any hippies in my commercials. Give me beautiful people." There was no further discussion, and the meeting ended just like that.

Y&R's executives returned to their office to regroup. It was obvious to them that Ernest, who handled all the company's advertising matters, had very different ideas about marketing than they did. Y&R's suggested strategy of reaching an inner-directed target audience was foreign to him. Despite the fact that Societally Conscious households had been shown by the agency's research to be enthusiastic about wine drinking, Gallo still wanted to position his product as a prestigious status symbol.

Y&R eventually went back to the "Monster of Modesto"—as Ernest was now being called by the shop's copywriters—and presented a slightly different set of commercials. The new spots retained much of their counterculture feeling, but they also had a touch more sophistication. The cantankerous winemaker vetoed this effort, too. For much of the next year, the persistent agency tried to come up with a campaign that would meet with Ernest's approval yet also appeal to inner-directed sippers in American society. Time after time, Gallo's president rejected the shop's ideas.

After a certain point, Y&R's quest for success became ridiculous, and news of Gallo's intransigence reached the agency's top management. The shop finally decided to resign the difficult and nonproductive account. Angered by this sudden defection, Ernest hired Ogilvy & Mather—Young & Rubicam's archrival. Without much prodding, Ogilvy gave the grape grower exactly what he wanted.

O&M's $25 million campaign for Gallo, targeted at upscale Emulator-Achievers, sold wine as a precious and prestigious asset, not as a warm social tonic. Many of the spots emphasized the vintner's successes at elegant wine tastings and featured a slew of gold medals that it had won against an impressive array of competitors.

A recent commercial features a wine-savvy Frenchman returning to his country château, a bottle of Gallo Hearty Burgundy in hand. Later, the landowner asks a sophisticated group of dinner guests to estimate the price of the wine he is serving. As the easy banter continues in French, viewers are informed that the diners' guesses range from $12 to $20. Smiling knowingly, the host reveals that the delicious wine costs a mere $4 a bottle. *"Ce n'est pas possible!"* the guests protest. O&M's worldly commercials have pleased Ernest and have also helped his company to retain the loyalty of status-conscious Emulator-Achiever consumers over the past few years.

Today, Gallo remains the United States' viticultural leader, selling roughly 150 million gallons of wine annually. Its sales are more than double those of Seagram, its nearest competitor. With an airtight distribution system that ensures the company prominent displays in supermarkets and liquor stores across the country, Gallo has proved to be one of the few firms in corporate America that can ignore the nation's changing psychographic profile and still prosper. Industry analysts believe that the business empire that Ernest and Julio have built—because of its vast financial resources and aggressive retailing—is essentially impervious to current societal trends. The strong-willed brothers probably won't be remembered for their insightful marketing or their high-quality grapes, but they will most certainly go down in the annals of oenological history as the first mass producers of wine in America.

Gallo may have achieved the initial technological breakthrough in the American wine industry, but it took a small, relatively unknown import from Italy to make the first giant strides in television advertising. Riunite (pronounced *ree-you-nee-tee*), an inexpensive wine with a fruity carbonated taste, capitalized on an imaginative electronic marketing strategy during the late 1970s to become one of the most powerful vintners in America. Without its clever television commercials, which positioned it directly against beer and soda as an "anytime" refreshment, the beverage would never have found its way into the refrigerators of millions of consumers in this country. Unlike Gallo, whose success was based on a domineering distribution network, Riunite sold well (11 million cases in 1983) because of the power of the tube. It was the original media wine.

Often described as fizzy Kool-Aid with alcohol or an Italian Coca-Cola, Riunite has been a major hit among postadolescents. The brand's youthful, enthusiastic advertising invites fun-seeking Emulators to enjoy life with a bottle of Riunite. The company's half-minute spots show young people ebulliently passing around the wine at barbecues and beach parties. It could be Coke or Pepsi.

Imported by Villa Banfi, the spirited Riunite first acquired its reputation in the late 1960s, when Ripple, Thunderbird, Boone's Farm, and other pop wines were busy turning young viticultural virgins on to the pleasure of the grape. It was at this time that John Mariani, who ran the small import house, decided to compete with Gallo by coming out with his own alcoholic Pepsi Generation drink. In an effort to cash in on the training wine boom, Mariani worked long and hard to find a fruity, grape-based liquid that kids would enjoy.

The vintner kept searching for the right taste, but he never quite found it. Finally, on a trip to Italy, the executive sought out several oenologists for advice. One of the experts suggested that Mariani visit a small town named Reggio Emilia, near the Po Valley, in the northern part of the country.

When he arrived in the charming and verdant village, the American was introduced to a fascinating fellow named Walter Sacchetti, who represented the agricultural workers of the nearby Cantine Cooperative Riunite (United Cooperative Winery). Sacchetti was a loyal Communist Party member, but he also had a shrewd business sense. He immediately grasped the nature of Mariani's problem and took the executive out to the vineyards.

There he acquainted his visitor with the Lambrusco grape. The wine tasted sweet, fruity, and slightly *frizzante* (carbonated). The Banfi executive was dazzled by what he swallowed—bubbly, thirst-quenching Lambrusco was just what he was looking for, and he believed it would be an extremely popular beverage in America. Mariani signed an agreement with Sacchetti that guaranteed him the exclusive rights to Riunite's crop each year.

Instead of pursuing the traditional distribution methods that had worked so well for Gallo, Mariani eventually decided to take his product directly to the public through advertising. His scheme was a bold one; no vintner—not even the gargantuan E. & J. Winery—had ever before been willing to spend enormous sums of money promoting its bottles or jugs on the tube. Even the use of radio was considered extravagant by most wine executives, although it had proved to be a successful marketing tool. Jerry Della Femina, the brash New York ad man, for example, had put the ethnic comedy team of Stiller and Meara on the air during rush-hour drive time and sold over a million cases of Blue Nun, a sweet white Rhine wine imported by Schieffelin. Mariani was willing to go further than this, however. He believed that the power of television could generate big consumer sales.

The vintner's initial ads—in which several Banfi employees formed a bargain-basement chorus and sang "It's Riunite Time" to the tune of the old Howdy Doody theme song—did not succeed. Consumers tuned this effort out, and the wine's sales floundered. But Mariani was undeterred by this disaster, and he came up with a new television approach, which was intended to appeal to the romantic instincts of postadolescents. In each of these 30-second spots, a young man who was madly in love warmed the heart of his standoffish girlfriend by bringing her Riunite—instead of roses, candy, or perfume. This advertising wasn't especially memorable either, and Riunite's great potential remained largely unfulfilled.

Refusing to give up his fight, the tenacious executive turned for marketing assistance to a small New York–based shop named Hicks & Greist. The agency soon began working on a new psychographic campaign for Riunite. Charles Skoog, Hicks & Greist's chairman, understood how the drink had to be positioned if it was to succeed. The longtime Madison Avenue veteran had watched the soft-drink industry grow during the 1960s and early 1970s, and he believed that many of the same advertising techniques that had helped Coke and Pepsi could now be used to sell Banfi's wine. Life-style commercials, according to the venerable ad man, were the only thing that could fulfill Mariani's ambition for Riunite.

While a creative team from Hicks & Greist was laboring on Banfi's new campaign, it came across a line from one of the vintner's earlier unused efforts that captured its imagination: "Riunite on Ice, Tastes So Nice." The agency executives decided to put the phrase to bouncy disco music and then use the song as a sound track for the life-style spots that were in the process of being created. The shop eventually completed its 30-second commercials for Riunite, and the resulting picnic spots were unlike anything the wine business had ever seen before.

These joyous televised celebrations were an instant hit with Emulators from coast to coast, and Riunite's sales immediately began to climb. Throughout the late 1970s, liquor stores and supermarkets across the country were jammed with postadolescents clamoring for Banfi's libation. By 1981, the vintner had become tremendously prosperous, with sales approaching $225 million a year. To sustain this momentum, Mariani spent freely on advertising—allocating at least $20 million annually for Riunite's media budget.

Recently, Riunite's advertising has begun to focus less on frivolity and more on the wine's adaptability to more subdued everyday occasions. Current commercials show a tempting array of casual meals—from pizza to salads—that the bubbly beverage complements perfectly. The product appears to have outgrown its early adolescence, and is now attempting to reach a more mature, wine-attuned audience. The move is a shrewd one, especially since the brand's original Emulator base will offer little in the way of growth opportunities.

Riunite's unexpected rise into the major leagues of American winemaking during the late 1970s stunned marketers across the nation and proved that the tube could sell grapes as well as it moved soda, beer, fast food, or automobiles. No corporation was as surprised by Banfi's rapid ascent to the top of the oenological world, however, as the $6.8 billion Coca-Cola Company of Atlanta.

For almost a hundred years, Coke had earned the bulk of its revenues from the sales of soft drinks; but in the early 1970s, when the wine boom began, the firm's marketing chief, Albert Killeen, saw a profitable opportunity for diversification and recommended that the company leap into the vineyards. Unfortunately, Killeen's viticultural zeal was snuffed out by Coke's board of directors. These conservative men didn't believe that there was money to be made in the wine industry, even though many other Fortune 500 enterprises were entering it at the time.

The corporate elders had their reasons for holding back. First, they were reluctant to venture onto Gallo's turf—they believed it would be extremely difficult to win a wine war against the powerful vintner. Second, they saw grape growing as a risky, unpredictable, agriculturally intensive business—one bad harvest and you were out millions of dollars. Third, they thought the sale of alcoholic beverages might tarnish Coke's all-American image in the heartland; booze still wasn't acceptable in the Bible belts of this country. And last—but most important—they didn't understand how to sell grapes effectively without a crackerjack distribution system like Gallo's. Wine wasn't like cola, they said. You couldn't just get on television and advertise a product until people eventually got the message and headed out to purchase your brand.

For the next few years, Coca-Cola watched passively from the sidelines as its corporate brethren invaded California's lush vineyards and pushed wine sales in this country through the roof. But it wasn't until Riunite demonstrated how to use television to sell even more bottles and jugs to the American public that Killeen was able to get Coke's senior management seriously interested in a wine acquisition. After reviewing the Italian importer's successful media campaign, the board agreed with the marketer that there was money to be made in the grape trade; the multibillion-dollar soft-drink firm soon began to map out its plan of attack. Coca-Cola was about to become a winemaker, too.

Killeen and his staff spent almost a year scouting around for a winery that Coke could buy. After crisscrossing the country, however, they still hadn't found an acceptable vineyard. Most of the available wine-producing facilities were too small, and many were growing inferior grapes on depleted soil. Killeen realized that in order to compete with Gallo, Almadén, Inglenook, and Paul Masson, Coca-Cola would have to start off with a big-volume operation right away; the vintner that Coke bought would also have to have a publicly recognizable brand name. To satisfy these dual requirements, Killeen came up with a creative acquisition strategy.

In January 1977, he paid $100 million for the Taylor Winery in upstate New York. Wine industry analysts sneered at Coke's initial foray into the viticultural world. Taylor, which primarily produced port, sherry, and champagne, was practically bankrupt, the experts said. It had a declining consumer base, a rickety, broken-down fermentation plant, and deficient soil and vines. Even worse, the vintner was some $25 million in debt.

The cynics were right—Taylor was in desperate shape. But despite this hearty criticism, Killeen stuck to his guns; he knew exactly what he was doing. A research study that Coke had recently commissioned revealed that for all its problems, Taylor was still the second-best-known winery in America, just several percentage points behind Gallo. The soft-drink company wasn't interested in Taylor's grapes. It wanted its good name.

The full scope of the cola manufacturer's shrewd game plan became obvious to interested observers in the summer of 1977, when it laid out $75 million for two high-quality California vineyards—Sterling and Monterey. These classy western vintners would produce the fruit for Coca-Cola's new winemaking endeavor, and their eastern cousin would provide the all-important label. This bicoastal marriage was an oenological match made in heaven: Taylor's strong identity hitched to Sterling's and Monterey's grape-growing expertise. Satisfied that he had created a product that brought together the best of all viticultural worlds, Killeen christened Coke's line of "hybrid" wines Taylor California Cellars.

Once the marketer had put all the complicated pieces of the acquisition puzzle together, Coke began building a $50 million state-of-the-art winery near Gonzales, California. This plant was smaller than Gallo's awesome facility, but it was just as technologically advanced. The entire winemaking process was expedited by computers and industrial robot machines, and the finished product took just weeks to turn out. Bottles and jugs were then quickly transferred to railroad cars and shipped across the country to waiting distributors.

After Killeen had worked the kinks out of the new factory, he turned his attention to Taylor California Cellars' introductory television campaign. Coke had spent relatively little to gain a foothold in the booming wine business—approximately $225 million—so it had plenty of money left over for advertising. This was encouraging, because, in the long run, 30-second commercials would make or break the fledgling enterprise. The importance of media salesmanship was reinforced when execu-

tives from the Atlanta-based company began reviewing Philip
Morris's successful entry into the beer business in the early
1970s. George Weissman's dynamic firm had successfully challenged Anheuser-Busch, the powerful industry leader—the way
newcomer Coca-Cola hoped to compete with Gallo—by pump-
ing more money into half-minute television spots than its rival
had. Philip Morris had also flourished because its ads were psy-
chographically on target.

To uncork Taylor California Cellars (TCC), Killeen allocated
almost $40 million for advertising—twice the amount that
Gallo, Almadén, Inglenook, or Masson was spending. The marketer then assigned the lucrative TCC account to Kenyon &
Eckhardt. After compiling an enormous research study on the
wine market of the late 1970s, K&E concluded that in order to
take upscale Emulator-Achiever customers away from the established competition, TCC's advertising would have to be
very combative, clearly pointing out the differences between itself and the other jugs on the supermarket or liquor store shelf.
If Coke's new wine brand failed to present a distinct image, it
would get lost in the crowd.

To separate TCC from all other grape-based beverages, the
shop devised an aggressive comparative taste campaign that
would leave little doubt in the public's mind as to who made
the best popularly priced domestic wine in America. In the
summer of 1978, it hired twenty-seven members of the San
Francisco Vintners Club to sample and rate several unidentified
bottles and jugs in front of television cameras. Each person in
the group was shown reflectively sniffing and studying wines.
When the competition was over, the tasters declared their preference, and almost all of them chose Brand A. Brand A, of
course, was Taylor California Cellars.

After praising TCC, the "experts" panned Brands B, C, and D
(Almadén, Inglenook, and Sebastiani). An announcer then came
on the air and said in a deep voice: "The great California wine
tasting, San Francisco, July 22, 1978—twenty-seven wine authorities judge new Taylor California Cellars to be better than
Almadén; better than Inglenook; and better than Sebastiani."

When they aired in the fall of 1978, K&E's hard-hitting commercials for TCC caused an immediate firestorm of opposition and outrage. Even though the spots had been monitored by the National Consumer Testing Institute, the wine industry was stunned. Almadén threatened Coke with a multibillion-dollar lawsuit; Inglenook decried the 30-second sales pitches as "laundry detergent advertising"; and Sebastiani claimed that Taylor had destroyed the last remaining shred of camaraderie left in the grape business.

While the rest of California's major vineyards carped and complained, Gallo, which wasn't included in TCC's campaign, sat back and smiled. The winemaker from Modesto was one of the few relaxed parties in this controversy. Even the Vintners Club of San Francisco was angry, asserting that K&E had violated a written agreement that prohibited the use of its name on television.

The U. S. government eventually got into the act, too. Several weeks after Taylor's commercials began running, the Bureau of Alcohol, Tobacco and Firearms, the federal agency that regulates wine advertising, found the comparative spots objectionable and threatened legal action if they remained on the air. The governmental watchdog expressed serious doubts about the credentials of the "authorities" who endorsed TCC and disparaged the competition on the air. These people were merely wine drinkers, not wine experts, said the public agency, and they shouldn't be allowed to masquerade as knowledgeable specialists on television. K&E's advertising was criticized by the bureau because it misled viewers into believing that an average citizen's personal preference was the gospel.

Coca-Cola kept K&E's comparative spots on the tube while industry criticism and the threat of criminal prosecution mounted. Finally, however, the pressure became too much, and the company discontinued its controversial campaign. Although they were despised by other vintners and censured by the government, the withdrawn commercials had remained in the public's eye long enough to achieve their primary purpose—boosting TCC's sales.

In just a matter of months, Taylor, the newest brand on the market, became the fifth-largest-selling jug wine in America, surpassing Seagram's popular Paul Masson label. Coke's viticultural success extended over the next three years, thanks to its strong Emulator-Achiever advertising—which, this time, featured real wine authorities who endorsed TCC without knocking the competition. By 1981, Taylor had become the third-ranked vintner in the United States, with annual sales of $100 million.

Unfortunately, however, Coca-Cola's string of good luck began to run out in early 1983. The company's profit margin in the wine business was declining. Signs of trouble first became apparent to industry analysts when Taylor slashed its advertising budget to a mere $5 million and began laying off some of its employees. It was ultimately decided by Coke's management that Taylor's slumping fortunes did not justify the cola giant's continued involvement in the wine business. Finally, in September 1983, the soft-drink firm sold its vineyard to Seagram for $200 million and left the wine world with its initial investment intact.

Coca-Cola may have exited from California's vineyards, but the soft-drink conglomerate has left an indelible impression on the American wine industry. During its five-year viticultural experiment, the soda king demonstrated—as Riunite had on a much smaller scale—that advertising can sell almost any product, even an esoteric beverage like wine.

In the same way that computer makers have used television commercials to help Americans get over their high-tech anxiety, wine marketers have been able to convince insecure consumers that their drink doesn't require a degree in oenology in order to be enjoyed. They have taken wine's once intimidating snob appeal and turned it into one of the beverage's most attractive assets. For striving upwardly mobile citizens, wine advertising today demystifies the product's complex properties and ancient lineage, while stressing its all-important and now accessible social cachet. The underlying message in current television spots for such brands as Gallo and Paul Masson is that serving a bottle of Chenin Blanc is an easy way for status-conscious purchasers to attain instant class and sophistication.

   This materialistic approach has won American vintners a loyal Emulator-Achiever following, but it hasn't taken into account the country's burgeoning inner-directed populace. Thus far, there has been little effort made on the part of established vineyards to capture the Societally-Conscious segment of the population. Counterculture campaigns could open up new vistas for wine producers in the United States, and several foresighted Madison Avenue executives have even speculated that with a bold new advertising approach, the beverage could someday become a truly national drink.

10 CABLE CLOUT
America Gets Wired

Today's fragmented marketplace represents a tough challenge for most advertisers. Selling products in the 1980s demands the creation of sophisticated targeted appeals based on the new psychographic profiles of America's consumers. Reaching this country's diverse audience has been especially difficult for Madison Avenue in recent years, however, because of television's mass orientation. Fortunately, a new form of electronic technology, which can easily deliver sales messages to specific consumer segments, has recently come into its own and may ultimately save the day for the marketing community.

Unlike traditional broadcasting, the powerful medium that created a national audience in the years following World War II, cable television (also known as narrowcasting) recognizes and responds to the splintered psychographics of contemporary America. Each of its thirty-seven national channels provides individualized programming designed to appeal to the special interests and unique tastes of small groups of citizens. There's something for everyone on this diverse tube of plenty.

People who want to keep abreast of world affairs, for example, can switch on the Cable News Network any time of the day or night and catch a live report direct from the Middle East or an interview with a high-ranking State Department official. For those interested in meteorological happenings, there's the Weather Channel, which provides viewers with a complete forecast of climatic conditions in the United States twelve times daily. MTV offers rock-music aficionados the latest video performances around the clock. Sports fans can take in six consecutive pro basketball games or an entire evening of stock-car racing on ESPN.

Cable presents plenty of highbrow entertainment, too; the Arts & Entertainment network—focusing on theater, dance, opera, and classical music—recently put together a twenty-four-hour cultural smorgasbord, consisting of Ravel's *La Valse,* Verdi's *Ernani,* and Shakespeare's *Macbeth.* Kids also benefit from narrowcasting; Nickelodeon, for instance, which is devoted exclusively to children's education, helps elementary school students improve their reading skills by airing a series of video comic books. And the new television technology teaches adults as well as youngsters; Ted Turner's WTBS, in its "Woman Watch" show, for example, supplies women with career counseling and support. Fitness fanatics who want to improve their bodies can tune in the Health network and participate in a rigorous aerobic dance regimen or an hour of plain old calisthenics. And busy executives on the move can pick up the current Federal Reserve statistics before they leave for the office each morning by watching ESPN's Business Times.

In sharp contrast to the corporate leaders at ABC, CBS, and NBC—who have tranquilized much of the public with a steady diet of soaps, sit-coms, and shoot-'em-ups for the past thirty years—cable executives are currently stimulating once passive viewers and transforming television into an exhilarating instrument of personal choice. This video liberation is one of the primary reasons that the narrowcasting revolution—for so long a mere figment of the Future Shock crowd's imagination—has finally taken hold in this nation.

America is rapidly becoming a wired society. Cable's copper strands are blanketing the continent in much the same way that railroad tracks first covered the country a century ago. Almost 60,000 miles of circuitry were laid in 1982, at a cost of over $100,000 per mile, and two-thirds of all television households in the United States are now able to plug into the wide range of new programming. The latest research reports from the media departments of several large Madison Avenue agencies reveal that 34 million families, or 40 percent of the total number of television homes in this country, are currently subscribing to cable—paying an average fee of $12.50 each month for its varied services. These impressive statistics help to illustrate just how fast the concept of narrowcasting has caught on among television viewers from coast to coast. A decade ago, cable watchers could be found in only 8 million living rooms in this nation. The new electronic medium's dynamic growth, its tremendous popularity, will continue through the 1980s and on into the 1990s, according to most broadcast analysts. Over the next six years, it's expected that the vibrant video technology's usage will spread to approximately 60 million households. Nearly 60 percent of all American television homes will be happily hooked up.

The narrowcasting movement has been loyally supported by members of every consumer segment in our society—Belongers, Emulators, Emulator-Achievers, and Societally Conscious Achievers—but, not surprisingly, it's the inner-directed who are leading the rapidly expanding cable crusade in this country. Madison Avenue researchers generally agree that baby-boomers are largely responsible for the increase in narrowcasting subscriptions. The driving force behind this counterculture rush to plug in, they say, is the Woodstock Generation's dissatisfaction with traditional network television.

Extensive consumer interviews conducted by several major Ad Alley agencies indicate that inner-directed viewers don't watch such mass audience shows as "Dallas," "Three's Company," and "Magnum P.I.," which have been created with the least-common-denominator principle in mind. These Societally Conscious citizens want their television sets to nourish—rather than neglect—their intellectual and informational needs. Their criticism of the networks extends far beyond disillusionment

with prime-time programming, however. Counterculture consumers believe that the three big broadcasters are negatively
influencing our society—poisoning the national consciousness—by presenting entertainment that distorts the roles of
women, minorities, and the elderly and promotes sexism, vio-
lence, and bigotry.

The Societally Conscious rejection of conventional television
has recently taken a significant toll on the large networks. In
1976, for example, ABC, CBS, and NBC combined for a 91 percent share of the American television audience; but over the
past eight years, this figure has steadily diminished. Today, the
once formidable broadcast trio find themselves reaching just 78
percent of all viewers in this country, and analysts believe that
by 1990 only 59 percent of viewers will be watching their
programming. Additional research from the A. C. Nielsen Company, which monitors the nation's television-viewing habits,
indicates that the networks could someday become extinct, following such mass circulation magazine counterparts as *Life,
Look,* and *The Saturday Evening Post* to the media graveyard.

According to these studies, the three electronic outlets could
eventually be replaced by a host of special-interest cable channels, which cater to the specific psychographic demands of
each segment of society. The Nielsen data relate the decline of
broadcasting in the United States to the rise of narrowcasting,
pointing out that viewers in cable-equipped homes are less
likely to watch traditional network television.

In Omaha, Nebraska, for example, where cable television's
penetration is only 12 percent, the networks' share of audience
is still a strong 93 percent. In San Francisco, on the other hand,
where 40 percent of all homes subscribe to cable, the networks'
share has dropped sharply, to 70 percent.

Nielsen's survey of Tulsa, Oklahoma, reveals the growing
power of narrowcasting even more graphically. In noncable
households there, the networks have a 90 percent share of audience; yet, in homes equipped with thirty-six or more cable
channels, this number slides to 56 percent.

Despite the networks' shrinking number of viewers and the
future trends, which favor cable and its expanding Societally

Conscious audience, Madison Avenue has thus far refused to endorse fully the new segmented television technology. Most American marketers work hard to create commercials that are targeted at specific groups of consumers today, but when it comes time to make media selections, they somehow seem to abandon their psychographic sales strategy. The majority of advertising executives in the United States are obsessed by *how many* people see their television spots, not *who* sees them.

The three major broadcasters, which received approximately $16 billion from Ad Alley last year, prey on the average marketer's numbers-oriented anxiety by hammering home the fact that even though cable is flourishing, none of its channels can provide as large an audience as conventional television. This bigger-is-better argument, as opposed to the concept of less-is-more targeting, seems to have intimidated agency media executives and has allowed the networks—even with declining shares of market—to raise their prices by 15 to 20 percent annually.

A number of major companies are currently running ads on cable, but in comparison to their huge network commitments, the firms' involvement with the new electronic medium is minuscule. In fact, cable's $383 million advertising income last year represents just 2.5 percent of the total amount that ABC, CBS, and NBC made from selling commercial time during the same period. Until the vast majority of marketers in the United States are able to shift their frame of reference from quantity to quality of audience, cable television will continue to limp along in the shadow of the networks.

According to cable executives, one of narrowcasting's major advantages over broadcasting as a commercial medium is that it provides advertisers with a more active and responsive audience. People who pay a monthly fee for cable service and who want to get their money's worth are more apt to watch the programs and products on the screen closely.

Buying advertising time on the new television channels is also more efficient for marketers than running spots on network shows. By its very definition, broadcasting is a mass communications system; a sales message carried by the networks reaches a vast number of consumers. But many of the people who are exposed to that commercial aren't interested in the product being promoted, so they tune out the pitch and go about their business. Most clients who advertise on traditional television are wasting a part of their media budget, because they get a lot of chaff along with the wheat. Cable, on the other hand, appears to be a sound investment—it offers Madison Avenue targeted audiences, not the entire sociological spectrum. When a marketer uses narrowcasting, he can pinpoint the segment of society he wants and then channel all his energy and resources into winning it over. Cable attracts fewer people than network television, but it provides more value: In addition to furnishing a focused clientele, many of the new television channels also charge Ad Alley agencies 25 to 40 percent less on a cost-per-1,000-viewer basis than ABC, CBS, or NBC.

Cable television also offers Madison Avenue greater flexibility than the rigid networks. Unlike their broadcast competitors, who rarely accept commercials that are more than one minute long, narrowcasters allow marketers to run spots of almost any length. This luxury of time enables companies to describe and demonstrate their goods and services in great detail. Several cable sponsors are also using these extended promotional periods to create new forms of advertising. One fresh approach, called the Infomercial, blends both hard and soft sell by combining a product message with an interesting or instructive consumer feature. Mazda, for example, touts its automobile and then often gives viewers several minutes of easy car care lessons.

Ad Alley's refusal to recognize cable television as a dynamic marketing asset is strangling the new electronic medium in its infancy—before it has had an opportunity to prove what it can do for clients. Fifteen cable networks are currently losing money; over the last two years, they have collectively accumulated losses estimated at more than $375 million.

Keeping the narrowcast revolution alive is in the best interest of American marketers, who need all the help they can get in this perplexing society. Pulling the plug on the cable cause would be foolish and self-destructive; it would deprive ad people of the most potent sales tool since network television.

Ironically, when cable television was first invented, in the late 1940s, nobody realized its enormous commercial potential or understood its far-reaching social implications. In fact, very few people noticed its arrival at all. Perhaps that was because over-the-air broadcasting—with Uncle Miltie, Sid Caesar, and Imogene Coca leading the way—was a technological novelty at the time.

But while most of the nation ignored narrowcasting's humble birth, the citizens of Lansford, a small rural hamlet located in the rugged hills of northeastern Pennsylvania, paid close attention, and even rejoiced at the new medium's discovery. Tucked away in the Appalachian Mountains and cut off from such large metropolitan centers as Philadelphia and New York, Lansford was plagued with fuzzy or nonexistent television reception—a problem that greatly disturbed the tiny town's residents. Fortunately for the village's inhabitants, however, a local merchant, Robert J. Tarlton, came to the rescue.

Tarlton, who owned a small television repair store, realized that his customers were unable to enjoy the new entertainment medium fully, so he began searching for a way to remove the snow from their television screens. The shopkeeper tried everything, from customized rabbit ears to specially built roof antennas; he even constructed a weird contraption that looked like a metal windmill to help his neighbors' television sets work better. But despite his tremendous effort and the many long hours he spent wrestling with this technical dilemma, the repairman couldn't improve the situation. Lansford's families were still greeted by waves of static whenever they flicked on the tube.

Finally, however, after much frustration and thought, Tarlton solved the reception riddle. One day, while hiking in the hills surrounding Lansford, he realized that if an antenna tower was erected on top of the Appalachians, a strong television signal could be picked up from Philadelphia, some seventy miles to the south. Once the transmission was received, cables running down into the small town and into individual homes could carry the picture.

Tarlton's idea was brilliant, but he discovered that it would be enormously expensive to implement. Lansford's small tax base was unable to support a project of such magnitude, so the resourceful merchant began raising money for the antenna and cable system. He formed a cooperative enterprise called the Panther Valley TV Company and persuaded each resident of the village to chip in for the new reception equipment. Work was begun on the mountaintop tower, and strands of coaxial cable were strung from telephone poles. By 1950, Lansford was a completely wired community. Television watching was no longer a technical impossibility, and Bob Tarlton was suddenly the toast of northeastern Pennsylvania.

During the 1950s and 1960s, the cable concept spread to several other small American towns with reception problems, but for the most part, the new technology remained a simple backwoods utility until the mid-1970s. Part of the reason that Tarlton's electronic invention made its way into the world so slowly had to do with the Federal Communications Commission, which created a tangle of legal restrictions that prevented cable systems from entering large, populated urban areas. Even if the government had been supportive of the new television, however, the cost of wiring millions of homes in a given city was prohibitive at the time. More important, nobody understood back then that cable could provide a variety of new programs for viewers—fresh alternatives to "I Dream of Jeannie," "The Beverly Hillbillies," and "The Flying Nun."

In 1975 a confluence of three factors finally helped launch the cable industry as we know it today. The big breakthrough came when the FCC backed off its previous position and deregulated the television business to a considerable degree; Washington said that major metropolitan centers in the United States could now be plugged into the new television technology. At the same time, RCA launched Satcom, a sophisticated communications satellite that orbited 22,300 miles above the earth and could inexpensively beam a host of cable programs throughout the nation. This space-age development made it possible for a narrowcasting company to send a show's signal from a studio in, say, New York up to the big bird in the sky; the satellite would, in turn, relay the program down to small dish-shaped antennas located in neighborhoods all over the country; the signal would then be transmitted through thick coaxial cables into people's living rooms, with the entire 45,000-mile trip taking just one-fifth of a second and costing only pennies.

The green light from the government, the newfound ability to distribute a plethora of programs cheaply via satellite, and the growing demand for a new electronic order all combined to create a mad rush into cable a little less than a decade ago—despite the fact that wiring the nation's cities and suburbs cost billions and billions of dollars. For the first time in this country, narrowcasting was perceived as a commercial, moneymaking enterprise—not just a master antenna service to keep television screens in Dogpatch U.S.A. clean. To cash in on this unique communications opportunity, cable executives spent a fortune building dish antennas here on earth and leasing satellite transponders up in space. They also recruited some of the best and brightest programmers in the television business—people whose creative instincts had often been stifled at the networks—to develop new shows that would appeal to various targeted audiences, including the alienated inner-directed segment.

But amid all this feverish activity, the real action during the mid-1970s was taking place at the municipal level, where individual companies were frantically bidding against one another for the rights to wire various cities. Every firm, in its desperation to lay cable through a particular town, ran a slick public relations campaign designed to curry the favor of important local citizens and politicians. To win over the general populace, the hungry corporations usually placed ads in community newspapers to promote their services; one concern even donated money to an influential St. Louis charity and promised to build a new library if it was allowed to hook up that metropolis.

Several fascinating success stories emerged from the near-carnival atmosphere that surrounded narrowcasting in its formative years. One of the pioneers, a shy, diminutive wirer in his early fifties named Chuck Dolan, landed the cable rights for part of Long Island in the 1970s. At first Dolan was hampered by a lack of funds, so he was able to hook up only a small area. But adversity was nothing new to the fledgling television entrepreneur. Operating out of a cramped Cleveland apartment, he and his wife had struggled to build a small newsreel business during the 1950s; and in the 1960s, he had tried—without much luck—to install a cable TV system in New York City hotel rooms.

Despite his undercapitalization, Dolan managed to hang on to his Long Island franchise. Working day and night, he gradually built up a large subscriber base of suburbanites, and soon he was able to lay more cable and expand his domain. By the early 1980s, the tenacious television executive had struck it rich. In less than a decade, he had amassed enough capital to purchase cable systems in Westchester, New Jersey, and Chicago, and his company—Cablevision—had moved to the top of the narrowcasting industry, stringing thousands of miles of coaxial copper strands each year. Cablevision, which was launched with such modest hope in the 1970s, has mushroomed into a booming enterprise whose estimated worth of $200 million makes it one of the most important privately held cable firms in America today.

Irving Kahn also made a fortune by hooking America up to the new segmented television technology, but he achieved his success by using much more aggressive business tactics than Dolan. Kahn first learned how to wheel and deal in Hollywood after World War II, when he served as director of publicity for Twentieth Century–Fox. During his tenure at the studio, the gruff, cigar-smoking publicist gained a reputation as a master of Lotusland flim-flam. According to a *Fortune* magazine profile, for example, Kahn never watched a movie before he wrote a press release for it—because, he said, "It never could be as good on the screen as it was in my mind."

When he left Fox, in the early 1950s, the former press agent began dabbling in a series of video-related projects over the next few years. First he bought a company that manufactured a contraption that displayed a readable script in front of an actor, but off-camera. The Teleprompter, as the invention was called, eventually became a staple in the burgeoning network television industry.

Next Kahn launched a firm that produced fancy audiovisual equipment for hotel conference rooms. A contract with Holiday Inns made this venture successful, too. With money in his pocket, Kahn could now afford a failure or two. Always a gambler, he took a chance in 1960 on something called Key TV, a sophisticated electronic system that allowed consumers to shop for merchandise at home using their television sets, but the scheme never took off. Kahn rebounded from this fiasco by getting involved in closed-circuit boxing production during the mid-1960s, when Muhammad Ali first burst onto the scene. And ten years later, this led him to the doorstep of cable television.

Kahn was one of the first people in this country to grasp fully the nature of narrowcasting's potential. Sensing a fiscal bonanza, he spent much of his time in the early 1970s cultivating political heavyweights across the nation—with the hope that his goodwill would someday be translated into lucrative cable franchises. This ingratiating strategy paid off in a big way. The fast-talking operator was eventually awarded the wiring rights to several major cities as well as a portion of New York's borough of Manhattan. Kahn helped to hook up millions of homes to the new television programming a decade ago, adding millions of dollars to his already impressive bank account in the process.

But then Irving Kahn's bubble burst. The state of New Jersey revealed that he had agreed to pay $50,000 to several Trenton officials in order to secure the cable franchise there, and a court in Pennsylvania found him guilty of making unlawful payments to city officials and their relatives in Johnstown, where he was attempting to solidify his wired kingdom. Over the next twenty months, Kahn was forced to run his electronic empire from jail. When he returned to civilian life, he continued to acquire the cable rights in communities all over the country, concentrating his efforts in the area surrounding Philadelphia—not far from Lansford, narrowcasting's birthplace.

While cable was being laid from coast to coast during the

1970s, programmers were creating shows that were different from the run-of-the-mill network fare and beaming them up to satellites for national distribution. The first company to jump aboard Satcom—at a cost of $7 million—was Time Inc.'s HBO (Home Box Office). In its first year of existence, HBO presented narrowcast viewers with a lineup of rather pedestrian shows, including many B-movies. But after Time decided to stop publication of *Life* magazine, the fledgling video subsidiary received a major injection of capital, which enabled it to buy first-run films from Hollywood and create its own series of show business specials.

HBO's subscribers were able to watch such movies as *The Sting, Butch Cassidy and the Sundance Kid,* and *The Way We Were* in the comfort of their living rooms, just months after they had played in theaters. Before the cable service came into being, people usually waited years until ABC, CBS, or NBC got around to airing such popular pictures on conventional television, and even then they had to watch the "edited for television" version. Seeing the Beach Boys, Bette Midler, Diana Ross, or Frank Sinatra in concert was an exciting treat for the narrowcast channel's clientele, too. Normally, music fans paid $20 or more to catch these superstars live and in person. Time Inc.'s cable network took all the hassle out of going to concerts and movies, and it was much cheaper as well. For a mere $15 each month, HBO transformed the traditional tube into an entertainment center.

Time has become one of the most powerful players in the cable television arena today. In just twelve years, HBO has increased its subscriber base from 2 million people to almost 20 million. These consumers are so pleased with the programs the show business channel presents that they don't mind paying an extra monthly fee for them on top of a basic cable service charge. As a result of this incremental customer revenue, HBO—unlike the vast majority of other narrowcasting networks—doesn't depend on advertising for its survival; it operates independently of Madison Avenue and the marketing community. The fast-growing $450 million cable enterprise is also starting to operate independently of Hollywood—its major video supplier.

Under the aggressive leadership of thirty-seven-year-old Michael Fuchs, a former lawyer at The William Morris Agency, HBO is now financing and producing its own movies as well as purchasing them from the film studios. Recently HBO helped support *On Golden Pond* in return for the rights to show this film before the networks. Over the next few years, the company is expected to channel $750 million into new movie production. Someday, say entertainment industry analysts, HBO may even eclipse Hollywood in terms of overall media clout.

HBO's only real rival for narrowcasting supremacy in this country is a fearless, flamboyant, combative, and charismatic forty-five-year-old cable programmer named Ted Turner. The owner of Atlanta-based superstation WTBS and Cable News Network, Turner has done more to promote the new television technology in the United States over the past decade than anyone else. For years he has bucked incredible odds and taken on impossible challenges—but he has always emerged unscathed.

A large part of Turner's grit, determination, and ambition comes from his rugged father, Ed, who grew up on a hardscrabble farm in Mississippi. Discipline and success were the watchwords of Ed Turner's life, and he imbued his only son with these simple values early on. When the elder Turner entered the billboard business, for example, he worked around the clock to support his small family, sometimes traveling as many as 300 miles a day on bumpy, rutted back roads to check his properties.

While Ed was busy building his fledgling highway advertising company, young Ted was studying at a spartan military academy in Georgia. At first, the cadet had difficulty getting along with his classmates. He refused to play team sports, preferring to read Greek mythology or military history in the library by himself. Fortunately, however, Turner discovered sailing—a solitary pursuit that required plenty of brains and nerve. His daring boating exploits eventually helped to make him a hero at school, where he led the sailing squad to many victories.

His love of the sea prompted Turner to apply to the United States Naval Academy after completing military school, but his father insisted that he go to Brown University, in the Ivy League, instead. During his rebellious years at Brown, he was twice suspended from classes for carousing with women after curfew, and he was reprimanded by university officials for burning down a fraternity's homecoming display. Turner dropped out and headed for the beaches of Florida, where he spent the next year and a half living the good life. Eventually, however, he ran out of money and was forced to return to Atlanta, the headquarters for his father's billboard business.

Once he was back in Georgia, Turner was drafted into the family company and required to take an informal crash course in business administration from his father. Each morning as the pair drove to work, Ed would hammer away about tax law, depreciation, amortization, sales strategy, management techniques, and construction. Soon Ted was given an office and responsibility of his own. He developed a good feel for outdoor advertising strategy and, at times, even appeared to enjoy his work.

The calm in Ted Turner's life was temporary, however. Just when he was beginning to feel comfortable as a billboard executive, his father's business—faced with a sudden onslaught of competitors—started to unravel. This unexpected setback dismayed the young man, but it absolutely crushed his father. Ed Turner couldn't handle failure. He sold his firm quietly— behind Ted's back—and then retreated to the family plantation, where he committed suicide in 1963, at the age of fifty-three.

For the twenty-four-year-old Turner, this combination of death and betrayal was almost too much to cope with. The stunned executive spent several weeks in a virtual state of shock, barely able to comprehend what had happened to him. Overnight, it seemed, he had lost everything. When he finally gained some perspective on the situation, however, Ted became determined to win back his father's billboard enterprise— despite the fact that it was saddled with debt. Unfortunately, when he made the company's new owners an offer for the business, they turned him down. Undeterred by this rejection, Turner resorted to a form of corporate guerrilla warfare to achieve his goal. As reported in *Time* magazine, over the next few months, the young rebel lured away many of his father's former employees, threatened to destroy financial records still remaining in his possession, and warned that he would build billboards in front of those put up by the rival company. Finally, the firm's newly installed management relented—it would return Ed Turner's outdoor advertising business to his son for a mere $200,000.

The terms of this deal suited Ted perfectly. He borrowed the money he needed and began to resuscitate the commercial enterprise. Young Turner worked like a demon over the next few years, trying to convince Madison Avenue to place its ads on his billboards. He charmed and cajoled marketers in New York, Chicago, and Los Angeles, and eventually he restored the company to financial health. By 1969, he had amassed a personal fortune in excess of $25 million.

Always eager to explore new horizons Turner began looking in 1970 for ways to invest his newly acquired wealth. A team of financial advisers suggested that he start dabbling in real estate or municipal bonds, but Ted rejected this conventional and conservative advice—he didn't want to do things the easy way. Instead, the young dynamo chose to sink his dollars into the broadcasting business, because, he said, it sounded like an exciting and challenging place to be.

Turner bought a run-down independent television station in Atlanta. When word of his purchase leaked out, television industry analysts across the country couldn't understand what the brash thirty-one-year-old billboard executive saw in Channel 17. After all, the station was running last in a market dominated by the three big national networks; it had a weak, distorted signal that made it difficult for Georgians to pick up; its video equipment was antiquated; its cramped studios were housed in a dilapidated building that looked like an abandoned Civil War supply depot; and on top of all this, Channel 17 was losing money—about $500,000 a year.

While broadcast insiders chuckled, the indefatigable Turner—a man with a plan—began to transform the station. The first order of business—changing the channel's call letters to WTCG (for Turner Communications Group)—was strictly cosmetic. For the next few months, the supersalesman pounded the pavement along Madison Avenue in an effort to drum up advertising revenue for his new video acquisition. Convincing skeptical agency media directors to run their commercials on Channel 17 wasn't easy—even for a glib, persuasive chap like Turner. The Atlanta station's poor ratings were common knowledge throughout the marketing community, and most executives on Ad Alley wanted nothing to do with the faltering enterprise.

Unfazed by this negative reaction to his product, Turner came up with a unique sales pitch that impressed even the most reluctant advertisers. The majority of Channel 17's programs were old favorites from television's golden age during the 1950s and 1960s—"Leave It to Beaver," "I Love Lucy," "Gilligan's Island," and "Star Trek." Since these shows were aired—for the most part—in black and white, claimed Turner, a sponsor's color commercial on WTCG would stand out and gain greater viewer attention than it would on other, more modern stations that presented all-color lineups. This original reasoning struck a responsive chord among agency people, who are always looking to avoid clutter on the tube, and as a result, many shops began including Channel 17 on their media schedules.

Turner funneled this newfound advertising income back into his business, hoping that major capital expenditures would improve WTCG's poor ratings. Initially, he spent several million dollars strengthening and refurbishing the station's fading signal. Then he purchased a handful of prime-time shows that NBC's Atlanta affiliate wasn't interested in airing. Viewers flocked to WTCG when the brazen entrepreneur started running billboard messages announcing "The NBC Network Moves to Channel 17" all over the state of Georgia. Turner's most dazzling maneuver came next, however, when he bought the Atlanta Braves baseball franchise and then began showing its games on WTCG. Two years after the Braves hooked up with Channel 17, the station recorded its first profit in history, and by the mid-1970s, it had become one of the most popular television outlets in the entire southeastern section of the United States.

Regional broadcasting excellence was nice, but it wasn't nearly enough for the ambitious and aggressive Turner, who wanted desperately to run a national television network. In an effort to fulfill this fantasy, the executive tried to piece together a syndicate of 300 stations, stretching from New York to California but, unfortunately, he was forced to drop this idea when it became too impractical and expensive to implement. Then WTCG's owner heard about Satcom and realized that cable's advanced technology could help make his big dream come true—by cheaply beaming Channel 17's programs all over the country. Suddenly the new television medium had become Ted Turner's future.

The former billboard salesman moved into the cable revolution with typical enthusiasm. Soon after deciding to plug into narrowcasting's rapidly expanding world, he had blueprints on his desk for a new studio complex. Construction on the building in Atlanta commenced quickly. Meanwhile, Turner spent his free time renting satellite space, touting WTCG's upcoming programming (including the Braves games) in wired communities, and convincing advertisers to run their commercials on the forty-eight-state electronic hookup.

Everything came together by early 1977, and WTBS (the cable network's new call letters)—dubbed "the superstation that serves the nation"—began sending its shows up into the heavens. With the mere flick of a switch, Turner had converted Channel 17, once a weak over-the-air outlet in Atlanta, into a sleek cable operation that could respond to a much larger American audience.

After WTBS was set up and running smoothly, Turner took a deep breath and began focusing his attention on less serious matters. He had made his mark in the cable industry, and now it was time to relax a little. He started spending many of his leisure hours at the stadium watching his baseball team play. Unfortunately, however, the Braves were a ragtag bunch of journeymen in the mid-1970s, and their inept performance on the field frequently consigned them to the cellar of the National League's Western Division. The team's lackluster record, its inability to give Atlanta something to cheer about, concerned Turner greatly, so in an effort to boost attendance—and distract fans from the club's poor play—the franchise owner turned showman. One night during the seventh-inning stretch, he entertained the ballpark crowd by riding an ostrich around the infield; on another occasion, he pushed a baseball across the outfield with his nose; and when things became really dull, he got into uniform and managed the Braves himself.

Turner returned to narrowcasting in the late 1970s, determined to play an even more important role in the new electronic medium's growth. Several research surveys commissioned by the innovative television man revealed that even though the three broadcasting networks were spending bundles of money trying to improve their newscasts, they were still alienating people. The studies showed that many viewers felt uneasy watching the slick, polished anchormen on ABC, CBS, and NBC—they didn't fully trust the information they were receiving each night from these so-called voices of authority.

More important, serious-minded citizens were disturbed by the ratings-oriented local news focus on disaster, gossip, and sensationalism. Turner believed that a no-frills narrowcasting channel—devoted to reporting the events of the day in a simple, straightforward manner—would be enormously popular, so in early 1980 he decided to launch CNN (Cable News Network).

The cable entrepreneur invested almost every penny he had or could borrow—approximately $150 million—in his new narrowcasting operation. Seven domestic bureaus were set up across the United States, and five foreign bureaus were established around the globe, primarily in Europe and Asia. An antebellum mansion situated on twenty-two acres of prime Atlanta property was acquired and renovated for $10 million and then transformed into the station's headquarters. And finally, $25 million worth of space-age cable equipment was purchased to transmit newscasts throughout the country on a twenty-four-hour basis.

In an effort to make CNN different from the trio of broadcast news packagers, the narrowcasting executive recruited a group of provocative commentators, including such outspoken politicians as Barry Goldwater, Bella Abzug, and William Simon. Against-the-grain media figures—such as Daniel Schorr, a former CBS reporter with a flair for controversy, and Evans and Novak, hard-nosed investigative columnists—were also brought aboard and given plenty of exposure.

According to a *Time* magazine cover story, in its first two years of operation, CNN's no-nonsense news service captured the attention of viewers in some 14 million households. At the same time, the station also received a vote of confidence—in the form of advertising revenue—from the American marketing community. Madison Avenue had watched WTBS grow into a surprisingly strong and profitable cable enterprise in just a few years, and as a result of this success story, it believed that Turner's new narrowcasting venture would also be an audience hit. Despite good consumer response across the country and Ad Alley's financial backing, the information channel lost $60 million between 1980 and 1983, largely because of huge start-up costs. In 1984, however, television industry analysts predict that CNN will begin to make its owner some money.

Unfortunately, most of the narrowcasting channels on the dial today haven't been as lucky as WTBS, CNN, or HBO. Without the charismatic salesmanship of a Ted Turner or the tremendous financial commitment of a Time Inc., the majority of the new television stations in this country have had to struggle to carve out a niche for themselves. Viewer enthusiasm for cable continues to grow—especially among the influential inner-directed segment—but Madison Avenue has, for the most part, failed to recognize the targeted electronic medium's potential as an effective marketing tool. Almost every major agency on Ad Alley continues to place great fiscal faith in broadcasting while giving minimal dollar support to narrowcasting.

This neglect of narrowcasting is already having serious repercussions. For example, nearly 40 percent of all cable networks in the United States are currently losing money. The Weather Station, as a case in point, lost close to $10 million last year; and ESPN, a large sports-oriented channel, has been unprofitable since it began operating full time in late 1979.

Madison Avenue's unwillingness to run more of its commercials on cable has also led to a series of cost-cutting mergers and consolidations in the narrowcasting industry. Viacom International's Health Network, for instance, recently allied itself with the Daytime Station, jointly owned by ABC and the Hearst Corporation.

In addition to its many wounded players, the new medium has had its share of fatalities as well. After dropping $40 million in a little over a year, Westinghouse's Satellite News Network was forced to shut down; and with losses approaching $35 million after only nine months in operation, the Entertainment Channel—an importer of British programs backed by Rockefeller Center—was required to do the same.

Narrowcasting's biggest and most painful loss took place in late 1982, when the CBS Cable Channel, devoted to cultural programming, folded. The arts-oriented station, which presented everything from Beethoven to Sophocles, had attracted an audience of 5 million subscribers during its one year in operation, but the marketers on Madison Avenue weren't impressed. As a result of Ad Alley's lack of support, the sophisticated cable outlet accumulated losses in excess of $30 million and was forced out of business.

In addition to depriving viewers of satisfying television, the death of CBS Cable also prevented the network's founder and chairman, eighty-three-year-old William S. Paley, from realizing a long-held dream. For several decades—from the time the tube first appeared in American living rooms after World War II—the broadcast baron had provided this country with a steady diet of easygoing programs, including "Lassie" and "Mr. Ed." These shows had been extremely popular in their day, and they had helped the television titan to amass a personal fortune of over $200 million. But despite his enormous wealth and great fame, in the 1970s Bill Paley was becoming a troubled and unfulfilled man.

According to a lengthy profile in *New York* magazine, the network chairman felt that broadcasting had alienated a large number of educated Americans, who were tired of the usual sitcoms. He believed that for a growing percentage of the country's viewing public, traditional television fare was often insipid and unwatchable. The time was ripe, Paley sensed, for bringing these citizens quality programming.

Paley's first attempt to improve American television had actually taken place in the late 1960s, when he brought his counterparts from ABC and NBC together in one room to discuss the issue. During the meeting, CBS's chief proposed that each of the networks set aside two hours of prime time every week for "educational programming." Each broadcast company, suggested Paley, would have its own high-quality evening so that all three enterprises could equally absorb the losses in ratings that could be expected from such a venture. But the leaders of ABC and NBC rejected this idea out of hand; they were unable—or unwilling—to recognize the merits of narrowcasting, preferring to continue with their mass entertainment schedules instead.

Despite the lack of interest in his segmented programming plan, Paley refused to give up. In the 1970s, he was responsible for "Beacon Hill," an American version of the much-praised British drama "Upstairs, Downstairs." Unfortunately, the show had trouble attracting advertisers and a significant audience. After just several months, the executive was forced to admit failure, and he pulled the plug on his series.

The cablecasting revolution of the early 1980s provided Paley with one more opportunity—perhaps his last—to bring America what he considered intelligent and introspective television. After reviewing CBS's carefully compiled research several years ago, the broadcast pioneer realized that many enlightened consumers were spending much of their free time involved in the world of the arts. According to the statistics, attendance at theater, dance, and music events was up by over 50 percent since 1970, and enrollment in adult education humanities courses had jumped 35 percent during the same period. Why not keep these civilized people at home, thought Paley, by providing them with a cable channel all their own, one that would produce and run fine cultural programs?

To help implement his new narrowcasting scheme, Paley hired a man named Dick Cox, a former Madison Avenue media executive who could talk to potential advertisers in a language they'd understand. During the 1950s and 1960s, when he worked in Young & Rubicam's large television buying department, Cox, like everyone else on Ad Alley in those days, had been enamored of big electronic audiences; he believed in the selling power of broadcasting. The executive had come a great distance since then, and along the way he had changed his opinion of the three major networks. In 1981, as president of CBS Cable, he knew that narrowcasting made great marketing sense. Now his problem was convincing the agencies.

Despite Madison Avenue's skepticism, Dick Cox was optimistic about his new cultural channel's prospects. A sign on his desk read: "The future can't be predicted, but it can be invented." As the narrowcasting executive prepared his salesmen for their assault on Ad Alley, he reminded them of this inspiring bit of philosophy and reinforced the advantages of cable television. The sales force hit the streets in late 1981—at about the same time that Paley's lavish arts programming was first beamed into highbrow households.

While viewers were treated to films by Fellini and Fassbinder, dance by Balanchine and Tharp, music by Bernstein and Mehta, and theater by Stoppard and Pinter, Cox's people struggled to convince agency media directors to run their commercials on CBS Cable. Even though the cultural network was generally praised by both consumers and critics, Madison Avenue wasn't interested in supporting it. One cynical marketer summed up the advertising community's antipathy toward the cultural channel by saying: "Smaller is not better; CBS's elitist approach to television goes against every merchandising theory I've been taught."

Obviously, Cox's crusaders were unable to generate much advertising revenue in this negative environment, and soon they were forced to reduce the rates for commercials aired during CBS's arts programs. This bargain-basement discounting in effect spelled the end for Bill Paley's stylish and elegant dream. Several months later, with losses in the $30 million range, CBS's cultural experiment on cable was over.

Despite the death of CBS Cable and the troubles facing most other narrowcasting services today, there is still a small glimmer of hope for the new segmented television medium. Recently, a group of large Madison Avenue advertisers, such as Anheuser-Busch, Bristol-Myers, and General Foods, began to reconsider their noninvolvement in the wired world.

As part of this reassessment, the marketers undertook individual studies in an effort to find out who was watching cable and whether these targeted audiences were the right ones for their various products. What they discovered was that they would indeed be able to reach concentrated consumer constituencies that would be favorably disposed to their sales pitches. For example, a beer advertiser could buy time on a cable sports network to reach its male blue-collar target group. And a packaged-goods company could similarly benefit by running its commercials on narrowcasting shows geared toward homemakers or working women.

While it was impossible for these studies to predetermine whether this advertising strategy would lead to increased sales, the focused marketing approach would help ensure interested audiences. As a result of the research, a handful of heavy-spending blue-chip advertisers decided to commit a portion of their financial resources to the alternative electronic medium. This fiscal support of narrowcasting was really small potatoes in comparison to the huge amounts of money the companies allocated for conventional television, but it was a start—a meaningful endorsement of the struggling new technology.

The largest investor in cable television's future is the Anheuser-Busch Brewing Company of St. Louis, which is spending approximately $10 million a year. Although this sum works out to only 5 percent of the big beer producer's total annual advertising and promotion budget, it nonetheless represents a sizable chunk of income for the narrowcasting industry. ESPN, in particular, is benefiting from Busch's participation in the wired revolution. Not long ago, the brewer—which bottles Budweiser, among other brands—signed a five-year $25 million agreement with the sports channel that guarantees the fledgling station commercial backing through 1988. Under the terms of the contract, Busch will receive a large amount of sponsor time on ESPN in return for its willingness to make a long-range financial commitment to the cable outlet. The brewer has already begun to saturate the sports network—which is watched primarily by young working-class men—with its advertising.

Several adventurous packaged-goods companies—in search of a more inner-directed female audience—have also joined the cable crusade recently. Campbell's Soup, for instance, now sponsors a program called "Woman Watch," which deals with such important topics as career advancement, sexism in the office, and the proper balance between job and family. General Foods has pooled its resources with *Woman's Day* magazine to create "Woman's Day Today," a cable show that provides females with all sorts of helpful advice—such as how to cope with stress or how to stir-fry vegetables in a hurry. The response to this service program has been so positive that GF will continue to support it for the next ten years. American Express, stepping up its effort to attract female cardholders, is backing a narrowcast series entitled "Women the Achievers," which presents an inspiring look at successful ladies who have accomplished great things. And Bristol-Myers—the maker of such analgesics as Bufferin, Excedrin, and Comtrex—is spending over $3 million a year to ensure that "Alive and Well," an exercise and health show, remains wired.

In addition to packaged-goods advertisers, a variety of marketers from other product categories are now reaching specific, targeted audiences on cable television, too. Hallmark, for example, sponsors a program called "Kaleidoscope"—narrowcasting's answer to "Sesame Street"—which is directed at young children. Kimberly-Clark, the Wisconsin-based company that produces Huggies disposable diapers, is responsible for "The American Baby" show. Mazda, the Japanese car importer, backs "Sports Look," an athletic series. And Chevrolet is promoting its supercharged youthmobiles—Camaros and Corvettes—with sassy and surreal commercials on MTV.

Aside from the fact that it zeroes in on a clearly defined group of consumers in a cost-effective way—something that the mass-audience broadcast networks fail to do—cable's additional advantage for advertisers is its rapport with the inner-directed segment. Unlike conventional television, narrowcasting appeals to Societally Conscious Achievers by catering to their individualistic tastes—by transforming the "idiot box" into more of an "intellectual box." You'll seldom find a villainous character like J. R. Ewing on cable, the usual car chase scenes are few and far between, and there's rarely a *femme fatale* vamping her way into someone's bedroom either. Instead, for the most part, the new wired medium offers members of the Woodstock Generation informative and educational shows.

Narrowcasting has the potential to become an even richer and more stimulating technology. In the not too distant future, cable will have the capacity to turn the television set—traditionally an impersonal electronic device—into an interactive one. Someday soon, citizens throughout the country will be able to participate in community-oriented cable programs themselves, by talking back to the screen and expressing their opinions, attitudes, and beliefs from the comfort of their living rooms. This form of electronic democracy, developed by Warner-Amex and still in the experimental stage, is known as Qube. In the past six years it has been tested in a variety of cities, including Pittsburgh, Cincinnati, Dallas, Houston, St. Louis, and Columbus, Ohio.

The focus of Qube's technology, which will eventually allow us to have dialogues with our Sonys and Zeniths, is a hand-held, book-sized console that contains five response buttons. When a television announcer calls for an audience decision, viewers push the appropriate signal on their command pad. This message is then relayed to the cable channel's computer in the studio, which instantly tabulates the consumer input and flashes the results of the query onscreen in just six seconds. One of the advantages of this system is that it enables the concerned and involved citizen to have his say, to contribute to the shaping policies of his city or town. Not long ago in Columbus, for example, Qube subscribers voted down a developer's huge shopping mall project, passed an ordinance banning the consumption of alcoholic beverages in local parks, and upheld the enforcement of strict building maintenance codes.

There are also tremendous business possibilities for advertisers on Qube. The interactive cable medium provides marketers with an opportunity to get in touch with their target audiences, actually to talk *with*—not *at*—the people they want to impress. This commercial dialogue, which gives the buyer as well as the seller a chance to express himself, could become an excellent vehicle for helping Ad Alley to reach consumers who don't respond to traditional advertising.

Recently, Ralph Lauren Cosmetics, working in conjunction with the Lazarus department store in Columbus, was able to harness Qube's commercial potential successfully. The firm ran a series of 30-minute demonstrations on the two-way television system showing women getting made up. Each half-hour spot concluded by offering viewers a free beauty consultation. Qube subscribers interested in making an appointment at one of Lazarus's in-store salons were asked to push a specific button on their console. Over 2,000 women responded to the ad, and about 800 actually booked a makeup session. More important, Lauren Cosmetics sold approximately $50 worth of its products to each of the female Qube viewers who attended its retail clinics.

Despite its great promise as a sales tool, Qube has thus far been a costly disappointment for Warner-Amex. Viewer involvement with the interactive television service has been much lower than anticipated, and the company has lost more than $30 million trying to perfect it. Even with its inauspicious beginnings, however, media experts still believe that Qube has a bright future as an advertising medium because it enables citizens to participate in the marketing process.

During the 1980s and 1990s, advertising on cable television may prove to be the only way for Madison Avenue to communicate effectively with American consumers. The three blind broadcasting networks show no sign of improving their programs, so the exodus to narrowcasting will almost certainly continue in the coming years. As a result, involvement with the new individualistic wired medium will eventually become a psychographic—and financial—necessity for marketers.

But in supporting cable's responsive and segmented technology, Ad Alley has an opportunity to gain more than just profits. By helping the alternative television system to grow, the advertising industry—so often maligned for its greedy and manipulative ways—can finally contribute to the quality of life in this country and give something back to the consumers from whom it has always taken.

11 ON TARGET
Psycho-Sell Looks to the Future

What will the American consumer culture be like ten years from now, in the mid-1990s?

For one thing, it will be even more inner-directed than it is today. Societally Conscious Achievers, who now constitute about 20 percent of the United States population, will represent almost one-third of the nation by then, accounting for approximately half of our country's purchasing power.

The counterculture movement will continue to gain strength over the next decade from both Belonger and Emulator-Achiever converts. Many former stay-at-home housewives will discover a stimulating new world outside the kitchen. Their working experiences will have a liberating effect on them and will broaden their once conventional views. And many materialists, frustrated in their quest for extra rewards and riches, will hop off the emotionally draining commercial treadmill, reorder their priorities, and adopt a new, more humanistic perspective.

This life-style transformation has already begun in many parts of the nation. For example, a recent defector from the Emulator-Achiever ranks who has chosen a Societally Conscious path might be someone like Charles. A high-powered Wall Street lawyer making close to a quarter of a million dollars, this forty-eight-year-old attorney left his lucrative practice not long ago to teach legal ethics at a local community college in upstate New York. Although his new salary will barely reach $40,000, this financial loss doesn't bother Charles, because instead of working eighty-hour weeks, he is now able to spend more time with his wife and two teenage daughters. He also tends to his vegetable garden and volunteers his services as a counselor at the state prison located near his small farm.

Susan, who once spent her days cleaning, cooking, and car-pooling in Minneapolis, has undergone a similar change in her life. After years as a home-bound wife, she got a job as a secretary at a data processing company in 1976 to help supplement her husband's income from the factory. Encouraged by her boss, she attended night school and eventually became a computer programmer. With increased confidence and skill, Susan recently decided to start her own small high-tech consulting business. But rather than taking on corporate clients, she specializes in retraining blue-collar workers so they can become computer-literate and find employment in the new postindustrial marketplace.

The growing number of Societally Conscious consumers in this country will retain their values and ethics through the late 1980s and on into the 1990s—they won't relax their high standards or become any less demanding of marketers, even as they settle into middle age.

Health and fitness will remain essential to the graying counterculturalists, and they'll refuse to purchase any product that doesn't contribute to their physical well-being. In addition to decaffeinated sodas, coffees, and teas, there will be a variety of low-alcohol beers and wines. Salt-free dishes will become the rule rather than the exception. Meat, especially beef, will be shunned. Fish, pasta, and vegetables will increase in popularity. Soybean-based foods will become more commonplace—and more palatable. Exercise gear will continue to sell with gusto.

But the cigarette industry will become even more troubled—regardless of how low-tar its smokes become.

Environmental concerns will grow in importance, too. The company that perfects and markets a small, sporty nonpolluting electric or battery-powered car, for example, is bound to make a fortune.

Simplicity, integrity, and *practicality* will continue as buzzwords. More firms will attempt to sell their goods using unpretentious, low-key advertising. A company such as Clinique cosmetics, with its quiet, understated image, will see its profits soar.

High-tech hardware—as long as it's sold with a smile and a soft touch—will also become an integral part of the inner-directed life-style. Silicon Valley manufacturers who extol the space-age innovation of their products without humor or warmth will have trouble finding a receptive audience.

Individual expression will remain a critical counterculture need over the next decade. Baby-boomers, who grew up in a liberated era of protest and free speech, refuse to allow advertisers to dictate the terms of a sale. Inner-directed consumers want Madison Avenue to listen to what *they* have to say. During the 1980s and 1990s, the superclass will demand an increasingly active role in the advertising arena.

The commercial dialogue between Ad Alley and Societally Conscious Achievers will deepen and grow in the coming years. The direct marketing systems pioneered by Lester Wunderman in the 1970s, which personalize the selling proposition and give consumers a sense of participation in the marketing process, will become widely accepted. Toll-free numbers will be set up by most large companies so that people can merely pick up the phone and dial corporate America. And two-way television, despite its shaky start, will emerge as the most significant marketing breakthrough since psychographics was developed. Interactive services such as Qube will give baby-boomers a chance to talk back to Madison Avenue, while better acquainting advertisers with their most important audience.

Subtle New-Age marketing techniques, first discovered and employed by advertising executives in the early 1970s, will be refined even further in the coming years. Ad Alley's leaders will have to hone their persuasive strategies and get to know the prickly Societally Conscious customer better if they want to continue moving their clients' products out of the store. Given their successful track record over the past decade, however, these image technicians should have no problem meeting this challenge, because in their business, consumer insights mean big profits. As always, the image-makers will continue to dig and probe until they find the right buttons to push. Then they'll sit back and watch the sales pour in.

SELECTED
BIBLIOGRAPHY

Chapter 1. Psychographics: Advertising Discovers the World According to VALS

Bernstein, Peter W. "Psychographics Still an Issue on Madison Avenue." *Fortune,* January 16, 1978.

Drucker, Peter. "Why Consumers Aren't Behaving." *The Wall Street Journal,* January 13, 1976.

Hacker, Andrew. *U/S—A Statistical Portrait of the American People.* New York: Penguin Books, 1983.

Harris, Lou. "A New Breed of Buyers." *Adweek,* August 1981.

Jones, Landon Y. *Great Expectations: America and the Baby Boom Generation.* New York: Ballantine Books, 1981.

Meyers, William. "Of Belongers, Emulators, Achievers, etc." *The New York Times,* December 5, 1982.

Packard, Vance. *The Hidden Persuaders.* Rev. ed. New York: Pocket Books, 1981.

Pierce, Kenneth M. "America the Multiple: Marketing Tasks of the 1980's." *Adweek,* August 1981.

Rosenshine, Allen. "The Image of Imagery." Speech given at *Ad Age* Creative Workshop, 1982.

Schumer, Fran R. "Downward Mobility." *New York,* August 16, 1982.

Span, Paula. "Madison Avenue Chases the Baby Boom." *The New York Times Magazine,* May 31, 1981.

Yankelovich, Daniel. *New Rules: Searching for Self-Fulfillment in a World Turned Upside Down.* New York: Bantam Books, 1982.

Ziff, Ruth. "What Does the Future Hold and Who's Worried About It? A Study of Americans' Personal Hopes, Fears and Expectations in the Decade of the 1980's." Doyle Dane Bernbach Research Study, 1982.

Chapter 2: Pioneers of Persuasion: The Wheel Is Invented

Alden, Robert. "Bernbach's Advertising: A Formula or Delicate Art?" *The New York Times,* May 7, 1961.

Bernbach, William. "Facts Aren't Enough." Speech given at meeting of American Association of Advertising Agencies, 1980.

Carlson, Walter. "Rosser Reeves and the Reality Concept in Advertising." *The New York Times,* January 24, 1965.

Cone, Fairfax M. *With All Its Faults: A Candid Account of Forty Years in Advertising.* Boston: Little, Brown, 1969.

Della Femina, Jerry. *From Those Wonderful Folks Who Gave You Pearl Harbor.* New York: Simon & Schuster, 1970.

Elsner, David M. "Leo Burnett: The Solid Sell." *The Wall Street Journal,* January 12, 1977.

Gunther, John. *Taken at the Flood: The Story of Albert D. Lasker.* New York: Harper and Brothers, 1960.

Hixon, Carl. "Leo." *Advertising Age,* February 8, 1982.

Hopkins, Claude. *Scientific Advertising.* Rev. ed. New York: Chelsea House, 1980.

Klaw, Spencer. "Is Ogilvy a Genius?" *Fortune*, April 1965.

Lloyd, Kate. "Mary Wells: The Best-Paid Woman in America." *Vogue*, February 15, 1972.

MacDougall, A. Kent. "Doyle Dane Bernbach: Ad Alley Upstart." *The Wall Street Journal*, August 12, 1965.

Meyers, William. "Mary Wells: Dedicated Pro or Gifted Opportunist?" *Adweek*, January 25, 1982.

Ogilvy, David. *Confessions of an Advertising Man*. New York: Atheneum, 1963.

Prial, Frank J. "Wells Rich Greene: The Hot Agency." *The Wall Street Journal*, May 6, 1968.

Rubicam, Raymond. "Memoirs." *Advertising Age*, February 9, 1970.

Spielvogel, Carl. "The Ogilvy of the Offbeat Ideas." *The New York Times*, September 7, 1958.

Whiteside, Thomas. "Rosser Reeves: The Man From Iron City." *The New Yorker*, September 27, 1969.

Chapter 3. Image Technicians: Ad Alley Discovers Freud

Abrams, Bill. "Y & R's Whole Egg." *The Wall Street Journal*, March 2, 1982.

Cummings, Bart. "An Interview With Ed Ney." *Advertising Age*, January 3, 1983.

Dougherty, Philip. "Steve Frankfurt: The Creative Man at Y & R." *The New York Times*, March 17, 1968.

———. "Ed Ney: Ad Man on the Go." *The New York Times*, December 20, 1970.

"Dr. Pepper: The Out-of-Towner." *Newsweek*, September 28, 1970.

"Edward Ney: The Reorganization Man." *Time*, December 3, 1973.

Fannin, Rebecca. "Behind Merrill-Lynch's Success: The Bull Who Walks by Himself." *Marketing and Media Decisions*, Spring 1982.

Frazier, Steve. "Dr. Pepper: Selling a Soda." *The Wall Street Journal*, June 5, 1980.

Kanner, Bernice. "Alex Kroll Plays to Win." *New York,* November 8, 1982.

_____ . "At Y & R, Ed Ney Does It Differently." *Advertising Age,* July 28, 1980.

_____ . "The Surreal Thing." *New York,* April 12, 1982.

Levy, Steven. "John Ferrell: Making It on 16 Hours a Day." *Esquire,* July 1982.

McDowell, Edwin. "Number One Madison Avenue." *The New York Times,* July 8, 1979.

Meyers, William. "Lincoln-Mercury's School of Surrealism." *The New York Times,* August 29, 1982.

_____ , and Morgan, Richard. "Turnaround at Y & R: How Ney Did It." *Adweek,* November 9, 1981.

Sammons, Donna. "Kentucky Fried Chicken Can Cackle Again." *The New York Times,* March 2, 1980.

Sloane, Leonard. "Selling Kentucky Fried Chicken." *The New York Times,* March 27, 1978.

White, Hooper. "A New Wave Has Landed." *Advertising Age,* November 2, 1981.
"Young & Rubicam: Showing Agencies How To Grow." *Business Week,* June 1, 1974.

Chapter 4. Giant-Killer: Philip Morris Takes On the Marketing Establishment

Astor, David. "Pepsi's Power Play." *Marketing Communications,* July 1980.

Chavez, Lydia. "A Small Agency That's No Small Beer." *The New York Times,* June 21, 1981.

Dougherty, Philip. "Backer & Spielvogel Sets the Standard for Growth." *The New York Times,* June 1, 1980.

Flanagan, William. "Charge of the Lite Brigade." *Esquire,* July 18, 1978.

Forkan, James P. "Pepsi Generation Bridges Two Generations." *Advertising Age,* May 5, 1980.

Free, Valerie. "Philip Morris: Imagery and Positioning Spur Dynamic Growth." *Marketing Communications,* December 1979.

Garino, David, and Abrams, Bill. "The War Between Miller and Anheuser-Busch." *The Wall Street Journal,* March 14, 1979.

Guyon, Janet. "It's Miller Time." *The Wall Street Journal,* February 10, 1983.

———. "Philip Morris: Tough Competitor." *The Wall Street Journal,* June 30, 1982.

Kanner, Bernice. "Tobacco Road." *New York,* January 17, 1983.

———. "The Hottest Agency in Town." *New York,* January 18, 1982.

———. "Coke versus Pepsi: The Battle of the Bubbles." *New York,* October 5, 1981.

Kleinfield, N. R. "Diet Coke Reflects Changes in the Industry and Market." *The New York Times,* August 23, 1982.

———. "Philip Morris: Closing in on R. J. Reynolds." *The New York Times,* January 17, 1983.

Koten, John. "Coke's Challenge." *The Wall Street Journal,* March 5 and 6, 1980.

Lohr, Steve. "The Cigarette Wars Intensify." *The New York Times,* January 16, 1981.

Metz, Robert. "Analysts Favor Philip Morris." *The New York Times,* May 22, 1980.

"Miller's Fast Growth Upsets the Beer Industry." *Business Week,* November 8, 1976.

Morgan, Richard, "Seven-Up and the Great Caffeine War." *Adweek,* August 1982.

———. "Seven-Up Effort to Aim Beyond Consumers." *Adweek,* March 1, 1982.

Schmidt, William E. "Putting the Daring Back in Coke." *The New York Times,* March 4, 1984.

"Seven-Up Uncaps an Industry Feud." *Business Week,* March 22, 1982.

Taubman, Philip. "The Great Soft-Drink Shoot-Out." *Esquire,* March 27, 1979.

Chapter 5. Patriots on Wheels: Detroit Starts to Fight Back

"Detroit's New Sales Pitch." *Business Week,* September 22, 1980.

Holusha, John. "Japanese Put Dazzle in Car Ads." *The New York Times,* June 24, 1981.

―――― . "Iacocca Rides High in Detroit." *The New York Times,* August 29, 1982.

"Lee Iacocca: In the Driver's Seat." *The Wall Street Journal,* November 2, 1978.

McDowell, Edwin. "Behind Chrysler's Long Decline." *The New York Times,* August 17, 1979.

Miller, Judith. "Detroit's Battle for Survival." *The New York Times Magazine,* January 6, 1980.

Schnapp, John. "America Breaks Off Its Romance With the Car." *The Wall Street Journal,* February 28, 1983.

Sease, Douglas R. "With Topaz, Ford Treats Far West as Separate Market." *The Wall Street Journal,* May 31, 1983.

―――― . "Ford Awaits Payoff on Its New Topaz." *The Wall Street Journal,* May 4, 1983.

―――― , and Simison, Robert L. "Stripped Down Chrysler." *The Wall Street Journal,* July 15, 1983.

"Why Detroit Is Not Selling Cars." *Business Week,* August 30, 1982.

Wunderman, Lester. "Frontiers of Direct Marketing." Speech given at Twelfth International Direct Marketing Symposium, 1980.

Chapter 6. Falling Arches: America Gets Burger Fatigue

Dougherty, Philip. "Hard Sell at Burger King." *The New York Times,* November 25, 1981.

Friedman, Mel. "The Battle for Hamburger Hill." *Madison Avenue,* January 1983.

Giges, Nancy. "Comparative Advertising." *Advertising Age,* September 22 and 29, and October 6, 1980.

Ingrassia, Paul. "Whopper War." *The Wall Street Journal,* April 5, 1978.

"McDonald's: The Burger That Conquered the Country." *Time,* September 17, 1973.

McDowell, Edwin. "The Fast-Food Chains Get Indigestion." *The New York Times,* July 15, 1979.

Metz, Robert. "The Future Growth of McDonald's." *The New York Times,* October 15, 1981.

Meyers, William. "Is Music Drowning Out the Pitch?" *Adweek,* September 14, 1981.

Millman, Nancy. "The Reinhard Touch." *Advertising Age,* July 18, 1983.

Raddock, Steve. "The Mammoth, Marvelous McDonald's Money Machine." *Marketing and Media Decisions,* Spring 1982.

Reinhard, Keith. "I Believe in Music." Needham Harper & Steers in-house publication, 1981.

_____ . "Emotion in Advertising: The Pulse Beneath the Message." Speech given at *Ad Age* Creative Workshop, 1978.

Smith, Lee. "Burger King Puts Down Its Dukes." *Fortune,* June 16, 1980.

"Success and Failure in the Fast-Food Business." *Business Week,* January 18, 1982.

Chapter 7. Gender Gap: Mrs. Olsen Gets an American Express Card

Bartos, Rena. *The Moving Target: What Every Marketer Should Know About Women.* New York: The Free Press, 1982.

Engelmayer, Paul A. "Food Concerns Rush to Serve More Quality Frozen Dinners." *The Wall Street Journal,* October 20, 1983.

Fannin, Rebecca. "Kellogg's: Daring to Be Different." *Marketing and Media Decisions,* May 1982.

"Female Executives Become a Target for Ads." *Business Week,* August 22, 1977.

"Gordon McGovern of Campbell's: A Profile of the Marketer of the Year." *Advertising Age,* January 3, 1983.

Kanner, Bernice. "Coffee Nerves." *New York,* September 13, 1982.

"Lauder's Success Formula." *Business Week,* September 26, 1983.

Meyers, William. "Maxwell House Moves Out of the Kitchen." *The New York Times,* August 29, 1982.

Reinhard, Keith. "We've Come a Short Way, Baby." Speech given at The Women's Advertising Club of Chicago, June 1983.

Salmans, Sandra. "Big Hopes for Pudding Pops." *The New York Times,* July 14, 1981.

Chapter 8. Gold Mine: Computers Get Personal

Bernstein, Peter W. "Atari and the Video Game Explosion." *Fortune,* July 27, 1981.

"The Coming Shakeout in Personal Computers." *Business Week,* November 22, 1982.

"The Computer Blitz on Television." *Business Week,* March 14, 1983.

Dougherty, Philip. "Parental Guilt and Computers." *The New York Times,* September 16, 1983.

Guyon, Janet. "How Apple Lured President From Pepsi." *The Wall Street Journal,* April 15, 1983.

"Hawking Hardware." *The Wall Street Journal,* September 12, 1983.

Hayes, Thomas C. "New Marketers for Computers." *The New York Times,* July 27, 1983.

"IBM: A Colossus That Works." *Time,* July 11, 1983.

"IBM: D-Day for the Home Computer." *Time,* November 7, 1983.

"IBM: Softening a Starchy Image." *Time,* July 11, 1983.

Kanner, Bernice. "Can Atari Stay Ahead of the Game?" *New York,* August 16, 1982.

Larson, Erik, and Dolan, Carrie. "Growing Pains at Apple." *The Wall Street Journal,* October 4, 1983.

"A New World Dawns." *Time,* January 3, 1983.

"Now No. 2, Apple Tries Harder." *Time,* September 26, 1983.

Paul, Gary S. "Selling Sci/Tech." *Adweek,* August 1981.

Petre, Peter D. "Marketing the Computer." *Fortune,* October 31, 1983.

Pollack, Andrew. "The Game Turns Serious at Atari." *The New York Times,* December 26, 1982.

"Zapped: Losses and Layoffs at Atari." *Time,* June 13, 1983.

Chapter 9. Sour Grapes: Wine Tries to Become Our National Drink

"Alors! American Wines Come of Age." *Newsweek,* September 1, 1980.

"Coca-Cola's Full-Court Press." *Time,* October 23, 1978.

"Coca-Cola's Spurt Into Wine." *Business Week,* October 15, 1979.

"Creating a Mass-Market for Wine." *Business Week,* March 15, 1982.

"The Gallos Showed How." *Business Week,* February 23, 1974.

"The Gallos: Their Cup Runneth Over." *Forbes,* October 1, 1975.

Kanner, Bernice. "Riunite: It Sells So Nice." *New York,* April 19, 1982.

Meyers, William. "The Wine Boom Yields Rosy Ad Outlook." *Adweek,* July 13, 1981.

"Now It's Coke The Winemaker." *Dun's Review,* April 1979.

Sewall, Gilbert T. "Trouble for California's Winemakers." *Fortune,* April 18, 1983.

"Uncorking a Legal Tangle." *Business Week,* October 23, 1978.

"Young Bacchus Comes of Age." *Time,* January 14, 1980.

Chapter 10. Cable Clout: America Gets Wired

Abrams, Bill, and Landro, Laura. "Cable's Ad Sales Fall Below Expectations." *The Wall Street Journal,* November 11, 1982.

"Cable T.V.: The Lure of Diversity." *Time,* May 7, 1979.

"Cable T.V.: The Race to Plug In." *Business Week,* December 8, 1980.

Coombs, Orde. "Bill Paley's Big Gamble on CBS Cable." *New York,* May 24, 1982.

"Culture Shock on Cable." *Newsweek,* March 15, 1982.

Egan, Jack. "HBO Takes on Hollywood." *New York,* June 13, 1983.

Holsendolph, Ernest. "Tougher Times for Cable Television." *The New York Times,* July 11, 1982.

Levy, Steven. "Speak Up, Columbus." *Panorama,* February 1981.

Mink, Eric. "Why the Networks Will Survive Cable." *The Atlantic,* December 1983.

Rudnitsky, Howard. "Don't Count Ted Turner Out." *Forbes,* August 31, 1981.

"The Rush Into Cable Is Turning Into a Retreat." *Business Week,* October 17, 1983.

Smith, Sally Bedell. "Specialized Choices in Cable T.V. Dwindling." *The New York Times,* November 24, 1983.

"Ted Turner Tackles T.V. News." *Newsweek,* June 16, 1980.

"Ted Turner: Shaking Up the Networks." *Time,* August 9, 1982.

Vaughan, Roger. "Ted Turner's True Talent." *Esquire,* October 10, 1978.

INDEX